Warm Welcomes

River Road Recipes IV

JUNIOR LEAGUE OF BATON ROUGE, LOUISIANA

Warm Welcomes

ENTERTAINING
MENUS FROM OUR
HOMES TO YOURS

*Photography by
David Humphreys*

MISSION

The Junior League of Baton Rouge, Inc., is an organization of women committed to promoting voluntarism, developing the potential of women, and improving communities through the effective action and leadership of trained volunteers. Its purpose is exclusively educational and charitable.

VISION

The Junior League of Baton Rouge, Inc., will enhance the quality of life in the Baton Rouge community in the areas of physical health, education, and cultural development.

RIVER ROAD RECIPES IV: *Warm Welcomes*
ENTERTAINING MENUS FROM OUR HOMES TO YOURS

Copyright © 2004
Junior League of Baton Rouge, Inc.
9523 Fenway Avenue
Baton Rouge, Louisiana 70809
800-204-1726

www.juniorleaguebr.com

Library of Congress Catalog Number: 2004102576

ISBN: 0-9613026-7-4

Edited, Designed, and Manufactured by
Favorite Recipes® Press
An imprint of

FRP™

P. O. Box 305142
Nashville, Tennessee 37230
800-358-0560

Art Director: Steve Newman
Book Design: Starletta Polster
Project Editor: Debbie Van Mol
Photography: © David Humphreys

Manufactured in the United States of America

First Printing: 2004 50,000

FOREWORD

You may wonder why Baton Rouge's River Road cuisine is universally respected. It's because of our melting pot, or as we prefer to think, "gumbo-like," culinary history.

The people who make Louisiana home, the French, Spanish, English, Native American, African, and of late, Vietnamese, Mexican, and Indian, bring with them rich culinary traditions. Once here, residing in a semi-tropical climate atop a ridge overlooking the Mississippi River flood plain, their cooking adapts to the fertile land and the bounty of Louisiana foods. Ingredients are substituted, dishes changed, recipes swapped with neighbors—everyone's cooking evolves.

Today, our capital city's cuisine, the sum of its ethnic influences, is wonderfully diverse. How could it not be since the essence of nearly every great cuisine is stirred into our gumbos, jambalayas, salsas, and étouffés.

Come to the dinner table. Savor the aroma, behold the presentation of food, listen to the lively conversations…life is good along the River Road.

Tommy C. Simmons

Tommy C. Simmons
Food Editor, *The Advocate*

PREFACE

In 1959, the Junior League of Baton Rouge held a contest to name its new cookbook.
Mrs. Sidney V. Arbour, Jr., submitted the winning title, *River Road Recipes*. When asked how she
arrived at this particular name, she responded that many of the contributors lived along the Mississippi
River Road and good cuisine was a vital part of their lives. She considered various titles and finally one
night dreamed of the title *Good Cooking Along the River Road*. When daylight arrived, however, she
thought that was too long and decided upon *River Road Recipes*. She also liked the title because she felt
that the name offered both a local and national connotation; anywhere in America where you have a river,
you usually have a river road. The title fit perfectly, and forty-five years later, with four titles in print, the
River Road Recipes series has sold over 1.8 million books, making it the all-time best-selling community
cookbook series in the nation.

To those league members all those years ago who dared to dream that they could create and sell a
few cookbooks, simply saying, "Well done!" would be an understatement. To those who have been buying
and cooking from our cookbooks for decades, we thank you for your loyalty and continued support.
To our new *River Road Recipes* fans, we welcome you into our homes, our community, and our culture.
We hope you will fall in love with its traditions and cuisine.

• denotes comments about previous cookbooks

INTRODUCTION

Most people who have never been to Louisiana picture in their minds the revelry of Mardi Gras parades or endless waterways and bayous. It is true that the state has bayous aplenty, and parade-going has evolved into an official state pastime. However, driving over the Mississippi River bridge into Baton Rouge for the first time and catching a glimpse of our modern skyline leaves no doubt that this is a sophisticated city that just happens to also be blessed with a rich culture that is centered around a passion for food, family, friends, and tradition.

A Louisiana celebration takes place wherever friends and family gather, including the sidewalk or the street. This can mean anything from a Good Friday fish fry in the driveway to a tailgate party on campus. Nowhere but in Louisiana is one just as likely to be invited to dine in a friend's or relative's carport as in their dining room. If a special event takes place away from the house, everything is packed up, including food, tents, furniture, even music and flowers…whatever is needed to make a party come alive, no matter how modest the surroundings.

Louisianians are known the world over for their easy view of life and reverent view of cooking. But, while they take their food very seriously, they never stress over the details. The only rule that needs to be followed is that guests are made to feel comfortable and welcome and that everyone has a good time.

The Junior League of Baton Rouge created *River Road Recipes IV: Warm Welcomes* as the natural next step in our long history of successful cookbooks. This book illustrates the way we cook and entertain today in Baton Rouge and also reflects how our past and our present influence our cuisine.

River Road Recipes IV: Warm Welcomes offers a peek into our homes and lifestyles. It has been arranged into chapters that represent entertaining in different areas of the home and at sites throughout the community. Each chapter is divided into menus for specific occasions. Some are unique to our area while others are celebrated around the country. Alternative suggestions are presented in every menu along with inspiring ideas and useful information. Full-color pictures throughout the book suggest the types of table settings, decorations, and floral arrangements that would enhance the featured menus and recipes.

River Road Recipes IV: Warm Welcomes is an attempt to paint a picture of our town, our food, and the joie de vivre, or joy of life, we have inherited from our ancestors. As you read and cook from our book, may you experience the spicy warmth of our cuisine, dream of the tropical warmth of our climate, and recreate the generous warmth of our hospitality. We hope that it transports you to Baton Rouge and the way we celebrate life through cooking.

CONTENTS

WHAT IS THE RIVER ROAD?

First of all, to dispel a common notion, the River Road is not a single road at all. It is actually two distinct roads—one along the east bank and one along the west bank of the Mississippi River between Baton Rouge and New Orleans. They are, for the most part, narrow, potholed, winding, and whimsically numbered as they trace the running, green levees that protect the flat, delta land of South Louisiana from the vagaries of the mighty Mississippi.

But the real River Road is much more than roadways. It is the landscape through which these two strips of asphalt run—created over more than three hundred years, a blend of history, culture, and local lore by the people who settled here...Native Americans, French, Germans, Spanish, Acadians (know locally as Cajuns), African slaves, black slaves, and white from the West Indies, free people of color, Anglo-Americans, Italians, and others. Their traditions and influences—from food to architecture, names of people and places to customs and lifestyles—have evolved as a distinctive and unusual place, with the Mississippi River as its centerpiece. Its importance was heralded when the National Trust for Historic Preservation included the area on its 1991 list of endangered places, a call to action that has been actively heeded.

The River Road is one of those places people love to visit, especially the wonderful antebellum mansions open to the public. But this often creates the mistaken impression that the River Road is merely another southern plantation parade—white pillars, magnolias, and mint juleps, flavored with South Louisiana's reputation for charming decadence. Or sometimes, the River Road is viewed as a petrochemical corridor where there's nothing else to see between industrial sites and a few mansions but derelict buildings and endless sugar cane fields.

Fortunately, nothing could be further from the truth. The real River Road offers much more—in addition to the well-known attractions for natives, visitors, and lovers of spirit of place. Examples of Creole architecture (also called Louisiana Colonial, the only vernacular colonial building style in the new America), century-old "company towns," old plantation stores, small local museums, atmospheric churches, cemeteries with headstones in French, Civil War sites, and prehistoric Indian sites are all found here. All along the way, fields, mills, and refineries mark the importance of the sugar industry in this area. These are our first planned communities, river towns that evoke life along the Mississippi when the river was central to daily existence, and a variety of river attractions, both historical and contemporary, all of which define the real River Road.

New Orleans, on the downriver end, was, and in many ways still is, the cultural, social, and commercial hub for the River Road, with Baton Rouge being the upriver anchor. (Along the Mississippi River in South Louisiana, directions are given as "upriver" and "downriver" since the Big Muddy's perpetual meanders make north, south, east, and west impossible.)

Family names along the River Road are as varied as its cultures. Examples of old family names abound and reflect Frenchmen from France, French Creoles from the West Indies, Spaniards from Spain and the Canary Islands, Germans, many of whose names were gallicized during the eighteenth century, Italians, Anglo-Americans who moved in after the Louisiana Purchase, and more.

The centerpiece of the River Road is, of course, the Mississippi River, although today it is completely invisible from the roadway because of the protective levees and is primarily an artery of commerce. But for two hundred years, the river was the lifeblood of the settlers, not only as an artery of commerce but also as the most dependable means of transportation, a reliable source of fuel and food, even a site for baptisms and recreation.

So the River Road is much more than it appears at first glance, which is the best reason I know to not only taste its offerings, but also to visit its diverse sites and attractions, to soak up the local color by exploring a place as unique and delightful as any in the United States.

Mary Ann Sternberg

Mary Ann Sternberg is author of Along the River Road *(LSU Press), a guide and history to Louisiana's most historic byway.*

Creole Country Brunch

Stuffed Eggs
Basil Chiffonade

Mixed Berries
crème Anglaise

Sautéed Shrimp and Peppers
cheese Grits

Pecan Praline Bacon

Whole Wheat Pancakes

Café au lait Punch

From the Kitchen

The closed-off, strictly utilitarian kitchen is out. Kitchens these days are designed for entertaining, with fireplaces and comfortable furniture in addition to top-of-the-line equipment. An island often serves as the focal point, especially if it includes seating for guests.

Entertaining in the kitchen is relaxed, with the focus on friends and food, not on creating the perfect party. Letting guests help with the preparations puts everyone at ease. A kitchen gathering is smaller, more intimate, and definitely cozier. By the end of the meal, even people who've just met feel like old friends.

Menus

Creole Country Brunch

Soup's On!

Cozy Weekend Family Dinner

Breakfast for Supper

Wednesday Night at Home

Cravin' Asian

Late-Night Fiesta

After-School Snack

CREOLE COUNTRY BRUNCH

*Pamper out-of-town guests with a brunch the morning after a big event,
such as a wedding or big game. You'll feed them a
proper meal before they leave and give them a gracious send-off.*

6 to 8 Guests

Café au Lait Punch

Pecan Praline Bacon

Deviled Eggs
(RRRIV page 191)

Sautéed Shrimp and Peppers over Cheese Grits

Whole Wheat Pancakes

Crème Anglaise over Mixed Berries

Optional Menu Item
Blueberry Pancakes

Café au Lait Punch

A favorite for ladies' luncheons. Coffee extract may be substituted for the strong coffee when making this a mid-morning treat.

> 1 cup sugar
> 1 cup dark roast coffee or coffee extract, at room temperature
> 1 liter ginger ale, at room temperature
> 1 liter club soda, at room temperature
> 2 cups half-and-half
> 1/2 gallon vanilla ice cream

Combine the sugar, coffee, ginger ale, club soda and half-and-half in a large punch bowl and mix well. Fold in the ice cream and ladle into punch bowls.

Makes 12 to 14 (2-cup) servings

In a world of lattes and mochas at every corner coffeehouse, Louisianians still prefer their **Café au Lait,** or coffee with milk. Coffee is brewed strong in Louisiana, and coffee with chicory (a dried, roasted, and ground root with a strong, deep flavor) has been a local preference since the Civil War. Even those who find the basic local brew too strong will enjoy a cup of rich, creamy café au lait. The steaming, foamy milk gives a velvety touch to the bracing coffee. When making café au lait, be sure to heat the milk. Otherwise, the cold milk will chill the coffee. Try this quick and easy recipe for the preferred drink of Louisianians. Heat 4 1/2 cups milk in a saucepan over low heat just until barely boiling and whisk until foamy. Pour the warm milk and 4 1/2 cups freshly brewed coffee or espresso into a heated carafe.

Pecan Praline Bacon

This is nice to make for company since it's fancier than plain bacon and can be made ahead of time.

1 pound thick-slice bacon
1/4 cup sugar
1 1/2 teaspoons chili powder
1/4 cup pecans, finely chopped

Arrange the bacon slices in a single layer in a shallow microwave-safe dish. Microwave on High for 5 minutes; drain. Transfer the slices to a rack in a large baking pan. Bake at 425 degrees for 10 minutes.

Mix the sugar and chili powder in a bowl and sprinkle over the bacon. Top with the pecans. Bake for 5 minutes longer or until brown and crisp. Drain the bacon praline side up on paper towels.

Serves 6

Sautéed Shrimp and Peppers over Cheese Grits

The red and green peppers and the Canadian bacon make this casserole pretty and satisfying.

1/2 cup chopped Canadian bacon
1 cup red bell pepper strips
1 cup green bell pepper strips
1 (10-ounce) can diced tomatoes with green chiles, drained
1 1/2 pounds shrimp, peeled and deveined
1/2 cup chopped green onions
1 2/3 cups milk
1 (16-ounce) can chicken broth
1 cup quick-cooking golden grits
1 cup (4 ounces) shredded sharp Cheddar cheese

Brown the bacon in a skillet. Stir in the bell peppers and cook for 10 minutes, stirring frequently. Add the tomatoes and mix well. Cook for 5 minutes, stirring occasionally. Stir in the shrimp and cook for 3 minutes longer or until the shrimp turn pink, stirring occasionally. Mix in the green onions. Remove from the heat and cover to keep warm.

Bring the milk and broth to a boil in a saucepan and stir in the grits. Return the grits mixture to a boil; reduce the heat. Cook for 5 minutes, stirring occasionally. Add the cheese to the grits and stir until melted. Spoon the shrimp mixture over the grits on a serving platter.

Serves 6 to 8

WHOLE WHEAT PANCAKES

A healthy touch of wheat germ provides a wholesome, nutritious start to the day.

1¹/2 cups all-purpose flour
1 cup wheat germ
¹/2 cup whole wheat flour
2 tablespoons sugar
2 teaspoons baking powder
1 teaspoon baking soda

1 teaspoon salt
2 cups buttermilk
1 cup milk
4 egg yolks, lightly beaten
3 tablespoons butter, melted
4 egg whites

Mix the all-purpose flour, wheat germ, whole wheat flour, sugar, baking powder, baking soda and salt in a bowl. Whisk the buttermilk, milk, egg yolks and butter in a bowl until blended. Beat the egg whites in a mixer bowl until stiff peaks form.

Add the milk mixture to the flour mixture and mix well. Fold in the egg whites. Pour approximately ¹/4 cup of the batter per pancake onto a hot lightly greased griddle. Cook until bubbles appear on the surface and the underside is golden brown; turn. Cook until brown on the remaining side. The flour mixture may be prepared in advance and stored, covered, in the refrigerator.

Makes approximately 2 dozen small pancakes

BLUEBERRY PANCAKES

Use fresh or frozen blueberries to make these extra-special homemade pancakes.

1¹/3 cups flour
¹/3 cup sugar
1¹/2 teaspoons baking powder
¹/2 teaspoon baking soda
¹/2 teaspoon salt
1 cup low-fat cottage cheese

3/4 cup skim milk
2 eggs, lightly beaten
2 teaspoons freshly grated lemon zest
1 teaspoon vanilla extract
2 cups fresh or frozen blueberries

Mix the flour, sugar, baking powder, baking soda and salt in a bowl. Make a well in the center of the dry ingredients. Whisk the cottage cheese, skim milk, eggs, lemon zest and vanilla in a bowl until combined. Add the cottage cheese mixture to the well and stir just until moistened. Fold in the blueberries.

Heat a large nonstick skillet over medium heat or an electric pancake griddle to 375 degrees. Moisten a crumbled paper towel with vegetable oil and use to coat the skillet or griddle. Pour approximately ¹/4 cup of the batter per pancake into the hot skillet.

Cook for 3 minutes or until bubbles appear on the surface and the underside is brown; turn. Cook for 1 minute longer or until the remaining side is brown. Spray the skillet with nonstick cooking spray or coat with additional oil between batches. Serve hot with maple syrup. Double the recipe and freeze the leftovers between sheets of waxed paper for future use.

Makes 18 pancakes

Crème Anglaise over Mixed Berries

Crème Anglaise is the French term for a rich custard sauce that can be served hot or cold. This delicious cream is good over any type of fruit, pound cake, or cobbler.

> 2 cups heavy cream
> 1/2 cup sugar
> 3 egg yolks, beaten
> 2 tablespoons Grand Marnier (optional)
> 1 teaspoon vanilla extract
> Assorted fresh berries

Heat the heavy cream in a saucepan just until bubbles form around the edge. Remove from the heat. Add the sugar and stir until dissolved. Stir a small amount of the hot cream mixture into the egg yolks. Stir the egg yolks into the hot cream mixture.

Cook until slightly thickened, whisking constantly. Stir in the liqueur and vanilla. Chill, covered, in the refrigerator until serving time. Spoon the crème anglaise over a mixture of sliced strawberries, raspberries and/or blackberries in dessert bowls or stemmed goblets. Add sliced or chopped fresh fruit to the berry mixture for variety.

Serves 6 to 8

SOUP'S ON!

*Hot or cold, soup is so versatile. On a cold afternoon, a pot of simmering
soup makes the whole house smell warm and wonderful.
Prepare several different soups and let guests try them all, serving themselves
from the stove. Serve soup in tiny demitasse cups as a
pre-theater appetizer, or pack it into a thermos and take along to the game.*

8 Guests

CRAB AND CORN SOUP

SOUTHERN GREENS AND ANDOUILLE SOUP

CREOLE TOMATO SOUP
(RRRIII page 52)

CRAWFISH CORN BREAD

MONKEY'S SALAD DRESSING
(RRRI page 23)

NO-KNEAD BREAD

COCONUT POUND CAKE
(RRRII page 201)

CRAB AND CORN SOUP

A rich and creamy soup recipe that is simplified by the use of frozen corn. Fold in the crab meat at the last minute to prevent it from breaking apart.

1/2 cup chopped onion
1/2 cup chopped celery
1/2 cup (1 stick) butter
1/4 cup flour
1 cup low-sodium chicken broth
2 cups half-and-half
1 (15-ounce) can cream-style corn
1 cup frozen corn
1 pound lump crab meat, shells removed
1/4 cup chopped green onion tops
1/4 cup sherry
1 1/2 teaspoons salt
1/4 teaspoon cayenne pepper

Sauté the onion and celery in the butter in a saucepan for 3 minutes or until tender. Add the flour and mix well. Cook for 3 to 5 minutes, stirring constantly. Add the broth gradually, stirring constantly. Cook until thickened, stirring constantly. Stir in the half-and-half, and corn.

Cook over medium-low heat for 10 minutes, stirring occasionally. Fold in the crab meat and green onion tops. Stir in the sherry, salt and cayenne pepper. Simmer just until heated through and ladle into soup bowls.

Serves 8

Southern Greens and Andouille Soup

This hearty, broth-based soup gets its beautiful green color from mustard greens, but other greens will do as well. Choose from turnip greens or milder kale or Swiss chard. Cut the greens into pieces before adding, and remember that even though the volume of them appears enormous, they will soften and wilt as they cook.

1 1/2 cups sliced spicy andouille, cut into halves
1 cup chopped onion
2 tablespoons chopped garlic
1/2 cup chopped carrot
1/2 cup chopped green bell pepper
1 (16-ounce) can diced tomatoes
1 cup red wine (merlot or cabernet)
1 quart low-sodium beef broth
1 bunch mustard greens, turnip greens, kale or Swiss chard,
   trimmed and chopped (about 3 to 4 cups)
2 teaspoons Tabasco sauce
Salt and pepper to taste

Sauté the sausage in a stockpot for 5 to 7 minutes. Remove the sausage to a bowl using a slotted spoon, reserving the pan drippings. Sauté the onion and garlic in the reserved pan drippings until light brown. Add the carrot and bell pepper and mix well.

Cook for 2 minutes, stirring frequently. Return the sausage to the stockpot. Stir in the undrained tomatoes and wine. Bring to a boil; reduce the heat.

Simmer for 5 minutes, stirring occasionally. Stir in the broth and mustard greens and cook for 20 to 30 minutes or until the greens are tender, stirring occasionally. Mix in the Tabasco sauce, salt and pepper and ladle into soup bowls.

Serves 8 to 12

To clean greens, fill a sink or large bowl with cool water. Discard the stems or any large ribs from the greens. Immerse the greens in the water and swirl to allow the grit to fall to the bottom of the sink. Repeat this process two or three times or until the greens are free of any dirt or sand, changing the water as needed.

Follow these steps to season and care for your new cast-iron skillet.

Wash and rinse thoroughly to remove the protective wax coating. Heat on the stovetop over low heat for several minutes or until completely dry.

Pour two tablespoons of vegetable oil into the skillet. Using a paper towel, coat the entire surface of the pan inside and outside with the oil, including the handle. Do not use any kind of saturated fat, which could cause the skillet to become rancid during storage.

Preheat the oven to 500 degrees for thirty minutes. Arrange the skillet upside down on a baking sheet.

Bake for one hour. Turn off the oven. Let stand in the oven with the door closed for four to six hours or until completely cool. Remove the skillet from the oven and wipe with a paper towel.

Clean the skillet with a plastic scrub brush or stiff brush in hot soapy water. Immediately place the skillet on the stovetop over low heat until completely dry. Coat the entire surface of the pan with a thin layer of vegetable oil.

Repeat the seasoning process as needed.

CRAWFISH CORN BREAD

Instead of serving the usual French bread or crackers with soup, purchase a bag of frozen crawfish tails and bake this corn bread in a cast-iron skillet.

1 yellow onion, chopped
1/2 cup chopped bell pepper
1/4 cup chopped green onions
1/4 cup (1/2 stick) butter
2 jalapeño chiles, chopped
2 cups yellow cornmeal
1 tablespoon baking powder
1 teaspoon salt
1/2 teaspoon baking soda

1 1/2 cups (6 ounces) shredded
   Cheddar cheese
1 (15-ounce) can cream-style corn
1 cup milk
1/2 cup vegetable oil
3 eggs, lightly beaten
1 pound frozen crawfish tails,
   thawed

Sauté the yellow onion, bell pepper and green onions in the butter in a skillet until tender. Stir in the jalapeño chiles. Combine the cornmeal, baking powder, salt and baking soda in a bowl and mix well. Stir the cheese, corn, milk, oil and eggs into the cornmeal mixture. Add the onion mixture and mix well. Stir in the crawfish tails.

Spoon the batter into a greased 9-inch cast-iron skillet. Bake at 400 degrees for 35 to 45 minutes or until light brown. Serve with a bowl of soup and/or a mixed green salad. You may bake the corn bread in a greased 9×13-inch baking pan.

Serves 8 to 10

No-Knead Bread

Even those who may be intimidated by the thought of making fresh bread can master this easy recipe because the process has been streamlined with no yeast proofing or rising involved.

3 envelopes dry yeast
3³/4 cups warm (105 to 115 degrees) water
10 cups flour
2¹/2 cups egg substitute
6 tablespoons sugar
6 tablespoons margarine, melted
1 tablespoon salt

Dissolve the yeast in the warm water in a 7-quart Tupperware container with lid. Let stand for 5 minutes. Add the flour, egg substitute, sugar, margarine and salt and stir until blended. Cover with the lid and seal. Let stand at room temperature for 1 hour or until the lid pops off.

Spoon the dough evenly into three 5×9-inch loaf pans sprayed with nonstick cooking spray. Let rise, covered, in a warm place free from drafts for 30 minutes or until doubled in bulk. Bake at 350 degrees for 40 minutes or until the loaves sound hollow when lightly tapped. Cool in the pans for 10 minutes. Remove the loaves to a wire rack to cool completely.

Makes 3 loaves

Really, this is absurd how I (and everybody else) sell these cookbooks! Why don't you consider putting out Volume II? Then everybody who has River Road Recipes I *will buy Volume II, and we'll all be rich! That is, until Volume III comes out, and we'll be richer yet! Whoopee! On the profits from Volume IV, I'll go to Europe, I think! Please consider!*

—Carol, Carol's Corner Bookshop, 1961, Covington, Louisiana

COZY WEEKEND FAMILY DINNER

*Dining at home is an especially welcome idea after the
hectic holidays. Gray skies and cold weather afford the perfect
excuse to stay inside and cook something wonderful.*

12 Guests

WILD MUSHROOM TORTE

MIXED GREENS WITH WARM GOAT CHEESE
(RRRIII page 67)

FRENCH-STYLE POT ROAST

TRI-COLOR ROASTED POTATOES

ZUCCHINI PEPPER SAUTÉ

APPLE PIE

Optional Menu Items
PAN-ROASTED VEAL CHOPS

GLAZED CHICKEN AND PEARS

WILD MUSHROOM TORTE

This is a fuss-free phyllo recipe. Spray each sheet of phyllo with nonstick cooking spray, then layer. Brushing the sheets with butter or covering with a damp cloth is not required.

6 pints assorted mushrooms	1 tablespoon coarsely ground pepper
1/4 cup minced shallots	Salt to taste
1 1/2 teaspoons minced garlic	10 phyllo pastry sheets, thawed
8 ounces cream cheese, softened	Rye melba toast rounds
2 tablespoons chopped fresh basil	

Process the mushrooms in a food processor until chopped. Sauté the mushrooms, shallots and garlic in a large nonstick sauté pan until the mushrooms and shallots are tender and the juices have evaporated. This is called a duxelle. Let stand until cool. Mix the cream cheese, basil, pepper and salt in a bowl and stir in the mushroom mixture.

Fit 1 of the pastry sheets over the bottom of a 6-inch springform pan and fold the pastry into the edge of the pan. Spray lightly with nonstick olive oil cooking spray. Layer with another pastry sheet and spray with nonstick olive oil cooking spray. Repeat this process 3 more times, resulting in 5 layers.

Spread the mushroom mixture over the prepared layers. Bring the edges of the pastry together in the center to enclose the filling and twist to resemble a flower. Decorate the torte with shapes cut from the remaining pastry sheets. Bake at 375 degrees for 25 minutes. Serve warm with melba rounds.

Serves 12 to 14

A duxelle is a mixture of chopped mushrooms, shallots, and herbs cooked into a paste and used for flavoring sauces or soups or as a spread.

FRENCH-STYLE POT ROAST

This home-style roast makes delicious roast beef po-boys the following day.

1 (7- to 8-pound) rump roast	3/4 cup chopped onion
1 (12-ounce) can tomato juice	1/2 cup brandy
8 ounces fresh mushrooms, sliced	2 garlic cloves, finely chopped
1 cup chopped carrots	2 tablespoons chopped fresh parsley
3/4 cup dry red wine	Salt and pepper to taste
3/4 cup chopped celery	3 tablespoons flour

Brown the roast on all sides in a Dutch oven. Add the tomato juice, mushrooms, carrots, wine, celery, onion, brandy, garlic, parsley, salt and pepper and mix well. Cook, covered, over low heat for 5 hours or until the roast is tender, stirring occasionally. Remove the roast to a serving platter, reserving the pan drippings. Cover to keep warm.

Whisk the flour into the reserved pan drippings. Cook until thickened, stirring constantly. Season with salt and pepper. Slice the roast and serve with the wine gravy.

Serves 12

PAN-ROASTED VEAL CHOPS

6 (1¹/2- to 2-inch) veal chops
Salt and pepper to taste
¹/2 cup chopped fresh rosemary
Olive oil

1 cup merlot
1¹/2 cups demi-glace
2 tablespoons butter, chilled
Juice of ¹/2 lemon

Liberally sprinkle both sides of the chops with salt and pepper and rub with the rosemary. Arrange the chops in a single layer on a platter. Chill, covered, for 1 hour.

Pour enough olive oil into a large sauté pan to measure ¹/4 inch and heat to the smoking point. Brown the chops on both sides in the hot oil. Remove the chops to a baking pan, reserving the pan drippings. Bake at 350 degrees for 15 to 20 minutes or until the chops are firm but springy to the touch.

Bring the wine and reserved pan drippings to a boil. Boil until reduced to 1 cup or less, stirring occasionally. Stir in the demi-glace. Bring to a rapid simmer and simmer for 10 minutes, stirring occasionally. Remove from the heat. Add the butter and lemon juice and stir until blended. Taste and adjust the seasonings. Serve the wine sauce with the veal chops.

Serves 6

GLAZED CHICKEN AND PEARS

2 (16-ounce) cans pear halves in
   heavy syrup
4 teaspoons cornstarch
2 cups water
¹/4 cup fresh lemon juice
4 teaspoons soy sauce

1 teaspoon dry mustard
¹/2 teaspoon salt
¹/2 teaspoon pepper
¹/2 teaspoon grated lemon zest
12 boneless skinless chicken breasts
3 tablespoons vegetable oil

Drain the pears, reserving the syrup. Whisk the reserved pear syrup and cornstarch in a bowl until blended. Stir in the water, lemon juice, soy sauce, dry mustard, salt, pepper and lemon zest.

Brown the chicken on both sides in the oil in a large skillet over medium-high heat. Add the pear syrup mixture to the skillet and bring to a boil; reduce the heat. Simmer, covered, for 45 minutes, stirring occasionally. Remove the chicken to a platter using a slotted spoon and reserving the pan drippings. Cover to keep warm.

Add the pears to the reserved drippings and mix gently. Cook over medium-high heat until the sauce is reduced by ¹/2, stirring occasionally. Spoon the pear sauce over the chicken and serve immediately.

Serves 12

Tri-Color Roasted Potatoes

2 sweet potatoes, peeled and chopped
4 new potatoes, chopped
4 purple or Yukon Gold potatoes, chopped
Salt to taste
1/2 cup olive oil
Pepper to taste

Blanch the potatoes in boiling salted water in a saucepan for 3 minutes; drain. Toss the warm potatoes with the olive oil in a bowl until coated. Season with salt and pepper.

Arrange the potatoes in a single layer on a greased baking sheet. Roast at 400 degrees for 20 to 25 minutes or until golden brown.

Serves 12

Zucchini Pepper Sauté

Using poblano chiles in place of green bell peppers adds an extra peppery flavor without the heat of jalapeño chiles. Serve this stir-fry as a side dish or as a vegetarian entrée.

5 zucchini, cut into spears
1 red bell pepper, julienned
1/2 poblano chile, julienned
Olive oil
1 tablespoon minced garlic
Salt and pepper to taste

Sauté the zucchini, bell pepper and poblano chile in olive oil in a sauté pan over high heat for 4 minutes or until tender-crisp. Stir in the garlic and season with salt and pepper. Serve immediately.

Serves 12

APPLE PIE

This all-time favorite couldn't be easier to make. Simply fill a commercially prepared pastry shell with layers of apple slices, sugar, and spices. Don't fret about the large amount of apples. . .pile them high for a gorgeous, bountiful pie.

2 refrigerator pie pastries
2/3 to 1 cup sugar (determined by the tartness of the apples)
1 tablespoon flour
1 teaspoon lemon juice
1 teaspoon grated lemon zest
1/4 teaspoon nutmeg
1/8 teaspoon salt
5 tart apples (McIntosh or Rome), peeled and sliced
1 1/2 teaspoons butter

Fit 1 of the pastries into a 9-inch pie plate. Mix the sugar, flour, lemon juice, lemon zest, nutmeg and salt in a bowl. Layer the apples and sugar mixture alternately in the prepared pie plate until all of the ingredients are used. Dot with the butter. Top with the remaining pie pastry, fluting the edge and cutting vents.

Bake at 400 degrees for 40 minutes; reduce the heat to 325 degrees. Bake for 20 minutes longer. Tent with foil if the pastry browns too quickly.

Serves 6

You and the Junior League of Baton Rouge were most kind to remember me with the beautifully bound cookbook. I am delighted to have the River Road Recipes. *It is my only one from your section of the country so famous for its many delicious and interesting foods. I shall enjoy it very much and hope to learn some of your culinary secrets.*

With appreciation and best wishes to you and each member of the league.

—Patricia Nixon, 1969

BREAKFAST FOR SUPPER

When the time changes in the autumn, days are shorter and evening comes more quickly. It can be difficult to adjust to eating dinner at an "earlier" time, so pretend it's morning and serve up a hearty breakfast instead.

6 Guests

MAPLE-GLAZED CANADIAN BACON

CHILI CHEESE EGG CUPS

YEAST WAFFLES

BROILED GRAPEFRUIT WITH VANILLA SUGAR

This easy menu can be prepared on Mother's Day and taken to mom on a beautiful tray with the newspaper and a vase of fresh flowers. While mom is enjoying her breakfast in bed, get a hot bubble bath ready to start off a well-deserved day of pampering.

Maple-Glazed Canadian Bacon

Maple syrup and Dijon mustard are combined to give this bacon a sweet-and-sour taste in addition to a smoky ham flavor.

> 1/2 cup maple syrup
> 1/2 teaspoon Dijon mustard
> 1 pound Canadian bacon, sliced

Combine the maple syrup and mustard in a bowl and mix well. Heat a skillet sprayed with nonstick cooking spray over medium heat until hot. Sear the bacon in batches on 1 side in the hot skillet for 3 to 5 minutes. Turn the bacon and brush with the maple glaze. Cook for 2 minutes longer. Turn and brush with the maple glaze. Remove the bacon to a serving platter. Repeat the process with the remaining bacon and remaining maple glaze.

Serves 6

Chili Cheese Egg Cups

Chili powder and Pepper Jack cheese give these fluffy and savory egg custards a little punch. Easy to prepare and fun to serve.

> 5 eggs
> 1/4 cup flour
> 1/2 teaspoon baking powder
> 1/2 teaspoon chili powder
> 1/4 teaspoon salt
> 8 ounces Monterey Pepper Jack cheese, shredded
> 1 (4-ounce) can diced green chiles, drained
> 1 cup cottage cheese
> 1/2 cup sour cream
> 1/4 cup (1/2 stick) butter, melted

Whisk the eggs in a bowl. Add a mixture of the flour, baking powder, chili powder and salt to the eggs and whisk until blended. Add the Pepper Jack cheese, green chiles, cottage cheese, sour cream and butter, mixing well after each addition.

Spoon the egg mixture into 6 buttered ramekins. Bake at 350 degrees for 25 to 30 minutes or until set. Serve immediately.

Serves 6

Yeast Waffles

The yeast in the batter gives off the delicious aroma of freshly baked bread when the waffles are baking.

2¹/2 cups flour
1 envelope dry yeast
1 teaspoon salt
1 teaspoon sugar
2 cups milk
5 tablespoons vegetable oil
2 eggs

Sift the flour, yeast, salt and sugar into a mixing bowl. Add the milk, oil and eggs to the flour mixture and beat until blended. Let rise, covered, in the refrigerator for 8 to 10 hours or until doubled in bulk.

Pour ¹/2 cup of the batter onto a hot waffle iron. Bake until brown using the manufacturer's directions. Repeat the process with the remaining batter. Serve with warm syrup.

Serves 6

Broiled Grapefruit with Vanilla Sugar

The hard caramelized sugar topping is cracked like a crème brûlée when you eat this dessert. These are simple to prepare for a crowd. Just arrange the grapefruit halves on a baking sheet and bake all at once.

1¹/2 cups sugar
¹/2 cup chopped crystallized ginger
1 tablespoon vanilla extract
6 large pink grapefruits

Finely grind the sugar, crystallized ginger and vanilla in an electric coffee or spice grinder. Cut each grapefruit crosswise into halves and run a knife around each section to separate from the tough membranes.

Arrange the grapefruit halves cut side up in a baking pan just large enough to hold in a single layer and sprinkle with the sugar mixture. Broil 1¹/2 inches from the heat source for 10 to 15 minutes or until the sugar melts and the tops begin to brown. Serve at room temperature.

Serves 12

WEDNESDAY NIGHT AT HOME

*Elaborate meals may be memorable, but people have a special
nostalgia for the humble foods they were served as children. Every family has its
own favorite comfort foods, enjoyed by all and remembered fondly.*

8 Guests

SMOTHERED PORK CHOPS
WITH RED WINE

WRAPPED GREEN BEANS
(RRRII page 69)

ROASTED ROOT VEGETABLES IN
GINGER BUTTER

BLUEBERRY CRUNCH

Optional Menu Items
MEAT LOAF

ROAST BEEF PO-BOYS

CHICKEN AND DUMPLINGS

SMOTHERED PORK CHOPS WITH RED WINE

Simple but so satisfying, this dish makes loads of delicious gravy and smells wonderful when cooking.

8 thick center-cut pork chops
Salt and pepper to taste
6 tablespoons olive oil
2 onions, sliced
2 large bell peppers, sliced

2 cups red wine
4 (14-ounce) cans petite-cut diced
   tomatoes
2 teaspoons beef bouillon granules
1 cup chopped fresh parsley

Season the chops with salt and pepper. Heat the olive oil in a large Dutch oven over high heat. Brown the chops on both sides in the hot oil. Remove the chops to a platter using a slotted spoon, reserving the pan drippings. Cook the onions and bell peppers in the reserved pan drippings until they start to caramelize, adding additional oil if needed.

Deglaze the pan with the wine, stirring with a wooden spoon to loosen any browned bits. Stir in the undrained tomatoes and bouillon granules. Return the pork chops to the Dutch oven. Simmer, covered, for 45 minutes, stirring occasionally. Stir in the parsley and cook for 15 minutes longer. Season with salt and pepper.

Serves 8

MEAT LOAF

1 (16- to 17-ounce) can diced tomatoes
2 tablespoons seasoned bread crumbs
2 pounds ground sirloin
1 cup chopped onion
2 eggs, beaten
2 slices bread, torn
2 tablespoons (heaping) chunky salsa

1 tablespoon Worcestershire sauce
2 teaspoons (or more) minced garlic
2 teaspoons (or more) oregano
2 teaspoons (or more) basil
1/2 onion, sliced
4 slices bacon, crisp-cooked and crumbled

Drain the tomatoes, reserving the juice and tomatoes. Mix the reserved juice and bread crumbs in a large bowl. Add the ground sirloin, chopped onion, eggs, bread, salsa, Worcestershire sauce, garlic, oregano and basil to the bread crumb mixture and mix well.

Shape the ground sirloin mixture into a loaf and arrange on a rack in a 9×13-inch baking pan. Bake at 350 degrees for 45 minutes or until the loaf begins to brown. Remove the meat loaf from the baking pan. Discard the pan drippings and remove the rack. Return the meat loaf to the baking pan and top with the reserved tomatoes.

Bake for 15 minutes longer. Sauté the sliced onion in a nonstick skillet until brown. Spoon the sautéed onion over the top of the meat loaf and sprinkle with the bacon. Serve immediately. You may substitute one 10-ounce package frozen chopped onions for 1 cup chopped onion. Thaw the frozen onions in a colander under hot running water before adding to the ground sirloin mixture.

Serves 8

ROAST BEEF PO-BOYS

1 (6-pound) beef rump roast
4 large onions, cut into quarters
Salt and pepper to taste
1/2 cup vegetable oil
1/4 cup flour
2 bunches green onions, chopped
1 bunch celery, trimmed and
 chopped
1/2 cup chopped fresh parsley

3 garlic cloves, crushed or mashed
2 (6-ounce) cans tomato paste
1 (16-ounce) can whole tomatoes
1 tablespoon dark brown sugar
2 tablespoons Tabasco sauce
2 tablespoons Worcestershire sauce
1 teaspoon minced garlic
1 teaspoon minced onion

Combine the roast and onion quarters with enough water to cover in a large stockpot.
Season liberally with salt and pepper. Bring to a boil; reduce the heat. Cook for 1 hour.
Drain, reserving 3 cups of the broth. Cool slightly. Chill the reserved broth and roast in
the refrigerator for 4 hours. Cut the chilled roast into 1-inch-thick slices and skim the fat
from the broth.

Heat the oil in a large heavy saucepan over medium heat and stir in the flour.
Cook for 2 minutes, stirring constantly. Add the green onions, celery, parsley and
crushed garlic. Sauté for 3 minutes. Stir in the reserved broth, tomato paste, undrained
tomatoes and brown sugar; reduce the heat.

Simmer for 10 minutes, stirring frequently. Add the Tabasco sauce, Worcestershire
sauce, minced garlic and minced onion and mix well. Bring to a rapid simmer. Simmer
for 1 hour, stirring occasionally. Add the reserved beef and mix gently. Cook just until
heated through. Serve with New Orleans-style French bread baguettes.

Serves 8

CHICKEN AND DUMPLINGS

Chicken and Dumplings is one of those foods that offers soul-satisfying contentment. This recipe is very easy to make using frozen prepared dumplings or frozen biscuits cut into quarters.

4 chicken breasts	Salt and pepper to taste
4 chicken legs	1 (15-ounce) can chicken broth
1 large white onion, cut into quarters	1 (10-ounce) can cream of chicken soup
3 ribs celery, cut into halves	1 teaspoon poultry seasoning
2 bay leaves	1 (12-ounce) package frozen dumplings

Combine the chicken, onion, celery, bay leaves, salt and pepper with enough water to generously cover in a large stockpot. Bring to a boil. Boil until the chicken is tender. Remove the chicken to a platter using a slotted spoon. Strain the stock and reserve, discarding the solids. Chop the chicken, discarding the skin and bones.

Mix the canned broth, soup and a small amount of the hot reserved stock in a bowl. Stir the soup mixture into the hot stock and bring to a boil. Stir in the poultry seasoning and season with pepper. Drop the dumplings 1 at a time into the boiling stock; the dumplings should barely touch. Stir in the chicken and simmer until the dumplings are tender. Serve immediately.

Serves 8

ROASTED ROOT VEGETABLES IN GINGER BUTTER

A mixture of winter vegetables roasted in the oven with ginger butter. In Louisiana, the most prolific root vegetable is the turnip, which is available in many different varieties.

6 cups water	1 cup (1/2-inch) chunks red potatoes
1 cup (1/2-inch) chunks turnips	1/4 cup (1/2 stick) butter, melted
1 cup (1/2-inch) chunks carrots	1 tablespoon grated fresh gingerroot
1 cup (1/2-inch) chunks parsnips	Salt and pepper to taste

Bring the water to a boil in a large saucepan. Add the turnips, carrots, parsnips and potatoes to the boiling water. Cook for 3 to 5 minutes or until tender-crisp; drain. Toss the turnip mixture with the butter, gingerroot, salt and pepper in a baking pan. Roast at 400 degrees until brown.

Serves 8

Do not rinse blueberries before freezing, as this tends to make the skin tough. Freezing blueberries that are dry also makes it easier to pour out just the specific amount required for a recipe. Discard all stems and pack the berries into resealable plastic freezer bags or containers, leaving a 1/2-inch headspace. As the need arises, simply remove the desired amount of frozen berries from the container, rinse, and use immediately.

BLUEBERRY CRUNCH

Serve topped with ice cream.

> 4 cups fresh or frozen unsweetened blueberries
> 1 cup packed dark brown sugar
> 3/4 cup flour
> 3/4 cup old-fashioned oats
> 1/2 cup (1 stick) butter, melted

Spread the blueberries in a 9×9-inch baking pan. Combine the brown sugar, flour and oats in a bowl and mix well. Stir in the butter. Spoon the crumb mixture over the blueberries. Bake at 350 degrees for 45 minutes. Serve warm in dessert bowls or goblets.

Serves 8

I was very excited to attend a cookbook seminar in Tennessee with my promotions chairman, Colette Dean. Everyone at the seminar kept referring to RRR as the ULTIMATE in the industry. "If only we all could enjoy such accolades as RRR has received!" they would say. "Not everyone can get a quote from Craig Claiborne!" Finally, I leaned over to Colette and said, "Who is this Craig Claiborne guy anyway?" With sheer shock and disbelief on her face, she shamefully bowed her head and said under her breath, "Oh my gosh! You're our fearless leader."

—*Barbara Schwartzenburg, Chairman 1994-1995*

CRAVIN' ASIAN

*Asian food is a culinary adventure and a playful way to gather
close friends for a fun learning opportunity. Get the whole supper club involved
in prepping ingredients for this tropical, Asian-influenced meal.*

12 Guests

ACADIAN SUSHI ROLLS

BLUE CRAB POT STICKERS

SUGAR SNAPS WITH SESAME OIL
(RRRIV page 41 sidebar)

CHICKEN TERIYAKI
(RRRIII page 192)

COCONUT-CRUSTED FRIED SHRIMP

AVOCADO PEACH RELISH

ACADIAN SUSHI ROLLS

Sushi rolls made with crawfish are a staple in Louisiana sushi houses.

3 cups sushi rice or short grain rice
6 cups water
2 (12-ounce) packages crawfish tails
$1^1/2$ tablespoons Creole seasoning
2 teaspoons onion flakes
2 packages sushi seaweed (Nori)
Pickled ginger
Wasabi
Soy sauce

Do not rinse the rice. Bring the water and rice to a boil in a saucepan over high heat; reduce the heat to medium-low. Cook, covered, for 25 minutes. Spread the rice evenly on a baking sheet. Chill in the refrigerator.

Rinse the crawfish in a colander and finely chop. Combine the crawfish, Creole seasoning and onion flakes in a bowl and mix well.

Place a sushi mat on a tea towel on a hard work surface. Layer with 1 sheet of the seaweed shiny side down. Cut a rectangular portion of the rice and arrange on the seaweed. Spread the rice evenly over the seaweed with wet fingers, leaving the top inch of the seaweed uncovered. Spoon $2/3$ cup of the crawfish mixture down the center. Starting at the bottom, roll as for a jelly roll, using the mat or towel to roll and press together. Moisten the uncovered edge of the seawood to seal. Wrap in plastic wrap and store in the refrigerator. Repeat the process with the remaining seaweed, remaining rice and remaining crawfish mixture.

To serve, cut the rolls into 1-inch slices and arrange cut side down on individual plates. Serve with pickled ginger, wasabi and soy sauce.

Serves 12

BLUE CRAB POT STICKERS

These pot stickers are very mild in flavor, a perfect yin to balance the yang in the rest of this Asian-inspired menu.

Pot Stickers
1 pound jumbo lump crab meat, drained and shells removed
1/2 cup finely chopped green onions
1 tablespoon chopped garlic
1 tablespoon chopped fresh gingerroot
1 egg white, lightly beaten
Salt and pepper to taste
1 package won ton wrappers

Ginger Soy Sauce
1/2 cup rice wine vinegar
1 tablespoon finely chopped gingerroot
1 tablespoon soy sauce
1 teaspoon sugar

For the pot stickers, combine the crab meat, green onions, garlic, gingerroot, egg white, salt and pepper in a bowl and mix well. Spoon 1 heaping tablespoon of the crab mixture in the center of each wrapper. Moisten the edges of the wrappers with water and fold the edges up to resemble a star.

Arrange the pot stickers in batches in a steamer or layer in a stackable bamboo steamer. Steam for 12 minutes after the water comes to a boil.

For the sauce, combine the vinegar, gingerroot, soy sauce and sugar in a bowl and mix well. Serve with the pot stickers.

Serves 12 to 15

Sugar snaps go perfectly with Asian cuisine and are so simple to prepare. To prepare **Sugar Snaps with Sesame Oil,** toss drained blanched sugar snap peas with sesame oil in a bowl and serve as a side dish. For tips on blanching vegetables, see page 193.

The city of Baton Rouge has an established Asian community, which means the ingredients needed to prepare Asian fare are easy to obtain. Asian markets and Asian sections in grocery stores are now familiar to the general public. This type of meal, with its intriguing aromas and tastes, is a link to their heritage.

COCONUT-CRUSTED FRIED SHRIMP

Pepper jelly adds Louisiana flair to the traditional Thai coconut-crusted fried shrimp.

24 jumbo shrimp (about 1¹/₂ pounds)
¹/₃ cup cornstarch
³/₄ teaspoon salt
¹/₂ teaspoon cayenne pepper

2 cups sweetened shredded coconut
3 egg whites
Peanut oil for frying
Pepper jelly

Using a small sharp knife and starting on the inside curve just below the tail, cut the shrimp down the center to but not through so the shrimp may be opened flat to resemble a book. Press lightly to flatten.

Mix the cornstarch, salt and cayenne pepper in a bowl. Place the coconut in a shallow dish. Beat the egg whites in a mixing bowl until frothy. Coat the shrimp with the cornstarch mixture, shaking off the excess. Dip in the egg whites and coat with the coconut.

Add enough peanut oil to a deep-fat fryer to measure 3 to 4 inches and heat to 375 degrees. Thread the shrimp individually on bamboo skewers. Holding 1 end of each skewer, drop into the hot oil. Fry for 3 minutes or until the shrimp are brown and crisp. Drain on paper towels.

Microwave a mixture of pepper jelly and a splash of water in a microwave-safe bowl until heated through. Serve with the shrimp on skewers.

Serves 6

AVOCADO PEACH RELISH

Jicama is a wonderful root vegetable with a fresh, crisp texture.

2 small ripe peaches, peeled and chopped (1 cup)
1 large tomato, chopped
1 small avocado, chopped (¹/₂ cup)
¹/₄ cup chopped jicama (optional)
1 tablespoon minced red onion

1 tablespoon fresh lime juice
1 teaspoon olive oil
¹/₄ teaspoon salt
¹/₄ teaspoon red pepper
¹/₄ teaspoon black pepper

Combine the peaches, tomato, avocado, jicama and onion in a bowl and mix gently. Add the lime juice, olive oil, salt, red pepper and black pepper and toss until coated. Chill, covered, until serving time. Serve as an accompaniment to grilled fish, especially salmon, or pork tenderloin.

Makes 2¹/₂ cups

LATE-NIGHT FIESTA

*Colorful and inexpensive, informal but festive, Mexican food is ideal party food.
With a Mexican theme, the decorating possibilities are endless. After the prom
or homecoming dance, invite a group of hungry teens over for a Mexican feast.*

6 Guests

AUTHENTIC SALSA

TACO SOUP

CHICKEN BURRITOS

SOPAIPILLAS WITH HONEY ICE CREAM

AUTHENTIC SALSA

Made with fresh ingredients, this flavorful salsa is quick and easy to prepare. The abundance of cilantro gives it a true authentic flavor. The salsa may become spicier if allowed to stand overnight or longer. Add a taste of lemon juice to lessen the heat.

2 or 3 serrano chiles, or 1 jalapeño chile
1 to 2 cups fresh cilantro leaves
1/2 onion, coarsely chopped
1 (16-ounce) can diced tomatoes
2 garlic cloves
1 teaspoon cumin

1/2 onion, cut into wedges
1/2 to 1 cup fresh cilantro leaves
1 fresh tomato, coarsely chopped
1 tablespoon salt
Lemon juice to taste

Combine the serrano chiles, 1 to 2 cups cilantro, coarsely chopped onion, undrained tomatoes, garlic and cumin in a blender. Pulse until blended and pour into a bowl.

Combine the onion wedges, 1/2 to 1 cup cilantro, fresh tomato, salt and lemon juice in the blender. Pulse until chunky; the mixture should be of a coarser consistency than the serrano chile mixture. Stir into the serrano chile mixture and serve with tortilla chips.

Serves 4 to 6

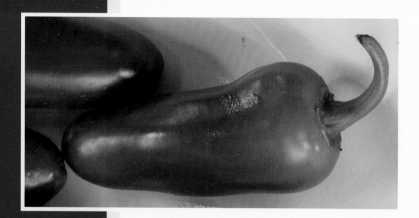

Taco Soup

Part of the fun of serving this simple soup is seeing how many different versions your guests can create when choosing their own toppings. Set out bowls containing creative possibilities such as chopped avocados, chopped green onions, sour cream, and shredded cheeses. Everyone will end up with something different.

2 pounds ground beef
1 onion, chopped
1 (16-ounce) can tomatoes with green chiles, Italian-style tomatoes or
    Mexican-style tomatoes
1 (16-ounce) can whole kernel corn, drained
1 (16-ounce) can Ranch-style beans or pinto beans with jalapeño chiles
1 envelope taco seasoning mix
1 envelope ranch salad dressing mix
1 tablespoon chili powder
Garlic powder to taste
Tabasco sauce to taste
1 cup sour cream
1 cup (4 ounces) shredded Cheddar cheese
1/2 cup chopped green onions
1/2 cup sliced jalapeño chiles
1/2 cup sliced black olives
1 avocado, chopped

Brown the ground beef with the onion in a large saucepan, stirring until the ground beef is crumbly; drain. Stir in the undrained tomatoes, corn, undrained beans, seasoning mix, dressing mix, chili powder, garlic powder and Tabasco sauce. Bring to a boil; reduce the heat.

Cook over low heat for 1 hour, stirring occasionally. Ladle the soup into bowls. Serve with the sour cream, cheese, green onions, jalapeño chiles, olives and avocado.

Serves 6

Give soup bowls a festive look by spraying the rims with nonstick cooking spray and sprinkling with paprika before ladling the soup into the bowls.

CHICKEN BURRITOS

Green Chile Salsa
4 (4-ounce) cans chopped green chiles
1/3 to 1/2 cup olive oil
1/3 cup chopped onion
1 garlic clove, minced
1 1/2 to 2 teaspoons cumin
1 teaspoon salt
1/2 teaspoon pepper
2 cups water

Burritos
10 large flour tortillas
2 cups sour cream
20 ounces Monterey Jack cheese, shredded
5 cups finely chopped cooked chicken breast
Alfalfa sprouts
Chopped fresh tomatoes
Chopped black olives
Guacamole
Toasted pine nuts

For the salsa, process the undrained green chiles, olive oil, onion, garlic, cumin, salt and pepper in a food processor until puréed. Pour the purée into a saucepan and add the water. Bring to a boil; reduce the heat. Simmer for 30 minutes, stirring occasionally. Let stand until cool. Chill, covered, until serving time.

For the burritos, spread 1 side of each tortilla with some of the sour cream. Layer each with some of the salsa, some of the cheese and 1/2 cup of the chicken. Roll burrito-style and arrange seam side down in two 9×13-inch baking dishes. You may prepare to this point up to 24 hours in advance and store, covered, in the refrigerator.

Top the burritos with 1/2 of the remaining salsa and remaining cheese. Bake at 350 degrees for 25 minutes or until bubbly. Serve with the remaining salsa, alfalfa sprouts, chopped tomatoes, olives, guacamole and pine nuts.

Makes 10 burritos

Sopaipillas with Honey Ice Cream

This is an easy version of a Mexican doughnut made with flour tortillas, similar to a Louisiana beignet.

> 6 small flour tortillas
> Peanut oil for frying
> 1/2 cup sugar
> 1 tablespoon cinnamon
> 1 quart vanilla ice cream
> 1/2 cup honey
> 1 tablespoon grated lemon zest

Cut the flour tortillas into quarters or sixths. Heat the peanut oil in a deep-fat fryer to 370 to 400 degrees. Fry the tortilla quarters in batches in the hot oil until brown and crisp. Remove with a slotted spoon to a paper towel to drain.

Mix the sugar and cinnamon in a bowl. Sprinkle the tortilla quarters with the cinnamon mixture. Combine the ice cream, honey and lemon zest in a chilled mixing bowl and beat until blended. Return the honey ice cream to the freezer if desired for a firmer consistency. Serve the sopaipillas with the ice cream.

Serves 6

When cooking and serving from a small kitchen, it is smart to prepare as much as possible ahead of time. That way, you won't have to juggle hot pans around guests who may have nowhere else to stand.

RIVER ROAD RECIPES

The highlight of my tenure as RRR chair 2003-2004 was the taping of RRR on the series "Plantation Nation with Bobby Flay." Kristen Landry, special events chairman, prepared a menu that showcased recipes indigenous to South Louisiana. Mount Hope Plantation was the site of the taping. We started with Louisiana Martinis to begin the show with a bang! I prepared the Shrimp-Stuffed Mirlitons from RRRII. Bobby was impressed with the taste. Kristen began preparing the Spinach Madeleine, a RRRI signature dish. The recipe calls for diced processed cheese. She had Bobby doing the prep work, while she started the roux. As a NY chef extraordinaire, we were pretty sure he was not used to using processed cheese! Bobby was congenial and witty all the way through and made us feel very comfortable in front of the camera. We then moved inside to the extravagant display of food prepared from all four of the River Road Recipes cookbooks. Members of the RRR committee were on hand to present the dishes they prepared for Bobby to taste.

—Mary F. Rothermel, RRR Chairman 2003-2004

AFTER-SCHOOL SNACK

*Kids love to cook, and they love little snacks. Pick a Friday afternoon to
abandon neatness, make something scrumptiously messy, and celebrate the end of
another school week. Get a video and stay up late eating and watching movies.
Go on—you have all weekend to clean up!*

Banana Berry Smoothie

Homemade Granola

Miniature Pizzas

Chocolate Chip Peanut Butter Cookies
(RRRIV page 236)

Optional Menu Item
Blender Drinks for Kids

Banana Berry Smoothie

This basic recipe can be adapted to include yogurt, orange juice, ice cream, and any variety of frozen fruit. The type of fruit you choose will determine the color of the smoothie. The addition of the banana gives it a rich and creamy consistency.

1 banana, chopped
1 cup frozen strawberries
1 cup frozen blueberries
1 cup frozen raspberries
1 cup skim milk
Honey, sugar or sugar substitute

Combine the banana, strawberries, blueberries and raspberries in a blender. Add just enough skim milk to make smooth and creamy, processing constantly. Sweeten with honey. Pour into glasses and serve immediately with straws. Store leftovers in the freezer.

Serves 4 to 5

Kids love to play with **Bubbles,** and it is so easy to make them yourself. Purchase bubble wands at toy and discount stores, or design your own from a wire coat hanger. Mix two cups Joy detergent, three-fourths cup corn syrup and six cups water in a large bowl and chill for four hours. Pour the soap mixture into a flat pan large enough to accommodate the bubble wand.

Blender Drinks for Kids

Here are some great smoothie options.

Grape Ape
1 (12-ounce) can ginger ale or club soda, chilled
1/2 (6-ounce) can frozen grape juice concentrate
6 ice cubes

Perfectly Peachy
1 cup low-fat peach yogurt
1 (8-ounce) can juice-pack peaches, drained
6 to 8 ice cubes

Strawberry Smoothie
1 (10-ounce) package frozen strawberries
1 (6-ounce) can apricot nectar, chilled
2 to 3 tablespoons cold water

Count Choc-Ula
1 cup low-fat frozen chocolate yogurt
1/2 cup low-fat milk
1 chocolate sandwich cookie

Pineapple Freeze
1 cup low-fat frozen vanilla yogurt
1/2 (6-ounce) can frozen pineapple juice concentrate
2 to 4 tablespoons low-fat milk

For the Grape Ape, process the ginger ale and grape juice concentrate in a blender until smooth. Add the ice cubes 1 at a time, processing constantly until of a slushy consistency. Pour into 2 to 3 glasses and serve immediately.

For the Perfectly Peachy, process the yogurt and peaches in a blender until smooth. Add the ice cubes 1 at a time, processing constantly until of a slushy consistency. Pour into 3 glasses and serve immediately.

For the Strawberry Smoothie, process the strawberries, apricot nectar and cold water in a blender until smooth. Pour into 2 to 3 glasses and serve immediately.

For the Count Choc-Ula, process the yogurt and low-fat milk in a blender until smooth. Add the cookie and process until the cookie is coarsely crushed. Pour into a glass and serve immediately.

For the Pineapple Freeze, process the yogurt, pineapple juice concentrate and low-fat milk in a blender until smooth. Pour into 2 glasses and serve immediately.

Serves 1 to 3

Homemade Granola

Granola makes a delicious topping for yogurt, fresh fruit, oatmeal, or ice cream, or it may be eaten by the handful for a quick snack. Commercially prepared granola usually contains a high percentage of sugar. Control the amount of sugar added by preparing the following recipe.

4 cups rolled oats	1 cup wheat germ
1 (12-ounce) package frozen coconut	1/2 cup packed brown sugar
1 1/2 cups chopped pecans	1/3 cup honey
1 cup sunflower seeds	1/4 cup vegetable oil
1 cup pumpkin seeds	3 tablespoons butter
1 cup sesame seeds	3 tablespoons water
	1 1/2 teaspoons vanilla extract

Combine the oats, coconut, pecans, sunflower seeds, pumpkin seeds, sesame seeds and wheat germ in a 9×13-inch baking pan and mix well. Bake at 300 degrees for 30 minutes, stirring several times.

Combine the brown sugar, honey, oil, butter and water in a saucepan. Bring to a simmer over medium heat, stirring frequently. Remove from the heat. Stir in the vanilla. Combine the oats mixture and brown sugar mixture in a bowl and toss to coat. Return the mixture to the baking pan.

Bake at 300 degrees for 1 hour, stirring every 15 minutes. Let stand until cool. Store in an airtight container. Serve as a cereal with milk or with dried fruit.

Makes 10 cups

Miniature Pizzas

4 miniature bagels, cut into halves
1 cup spaghetti sauce
1 cup (4 ounces) shredded mozzarella cheese
8 slices pepperoni (optional)
Sliced green or black olives (optional)

Arrange the bagel halves cut side up on a baking sheet. Spread each half with some of the spaghetti sauce. Layer with the cheese, pepperoni and olives.

Bake at 400 degrees for 7 to 10 minutes or until the cheese melts. Cool slightly before serving.

Makes 8 pizzas

Create nutritious granola-topped parfaits to keep in the refrigerator for a quick grab-and-go treat. Layer one-half cup of your favorite fresh or canned fruit in the bottom of a large disposable plastic cup. Top with one-half cup yogurt or cottage cheese and finish with one-half cup Homemade Granola. Cover with plastic wrap and store in the refrigerator for a fast breakfast or quick snack on the go, or bring one to enjoy at work instead of visiting the vending machine.

About the Home

*S*ince colonial times, Louisiana has been known for the bounty and excellence of its home cooking and its warm hospitality. During the Spanish occupation of Louisiana in the late 1700s, Governor Miro spent 8,000 pesos a year feeding houseguests, though he earned only 4,000 pesos a year. Hospitality was paramount to the governor, and the tradition of offering fine food to guests remains a part of Louisiana's heritage.

Southerners are especially fond of entertaining at home and the gathering around of dear friends and family for life's important milestones. From baptisms to graduations, an invitation to share a meal in a Louisiana home means the fondest greeting, the best cooking, and the most hospitable treatment. Along with these goes the best-dressed table. Fine china, silver, and linens are likely to appear on any occasion, often the legacy of generations past.

Fine food, beautifully set and decorated tables, dear friends and family, special treatment—no wonder Louisiana hostesses' invitations are so highly prized.

Menus

Cocktail Meet and Greet

Afternoon Tea

Mediterranean Mixed Grill

A Southern Tree Trimming

'Round Midnight

Super Bowl Get-Together

Bridge Lunch

Cinco de Mayo

Wedding Day Jazz Brunch

54

COCKTAIL MEET AND GREET

*When you want to invite absolutely everyone you know to meet
the new neighbors or a favorite political candidate,
a fabulous array of creative finger foods is the best way to entertain.
Make the party as lavish or modest as your budget allows.*

12 Guests

SOUTHERN ANTIPASTO

BLUE CHEESE TRUFFLES

TOASTED CANAPÉS

CRAB MEAT GREEN GODDESS

CITRUS-GLAZED SMOKED SAUSAGE

MICROWAVE PRALINES

BOURBON PECAN TARTLETS

Optional Menu Item
CRAWFISH SUPREME

Southern Antipasto

Pickled okra adds a southern touch to this traditional Italian starter.

1 (12-ounce) jar pickled okra,
    drained and rinsed
1 cup fresh green beans, blanched
    and drained
1/4 cup pitted kalamata olive halves
1/4 cup pitted green olive halves
1/4 cup pimento-stuffed olives
1/2 cup fresh lemon juice
1/2 cup extra-virgin olive oil
3 tablespoons fresh thyme leaves
2 garlic cloves, thinly sliced
1/2 teaspoon kosher salt
1/2 teaspoon crushed dried red
    pepper

Combine the okra, green beans and olives in a 1-quart resealable plastic bag. Whisk the lemon juice, olive oil, thyme, garlic, salt and red pepper in a bowl. Pour the lemon juice mixture over the okra mixture and seal tightly. Turn to coat.

Marinate in the refrigerator for up to 1 hour, turning every 15 minutes. Drain before serving.

Serves 12

Blue Cheese Truffles

These bite-size truffles are an elegant new twist on an old favorite and are easier to eat and serve than one large cheese ball. Just about any cheese ball recipe can be utilized. Roll the cheese truffles in chopped nuts and/or fresh herbs.

3 cups pecan halves or pieces, finely chopped
8 ounces blue cheese, softened
8 ounces cream cheese, softened

Spread the pecans in a single layer on a baking sheet. Toast at 300 degrees for 15 minutes or until light brown, stirring occasionally. Let stand until cool and finely chop.

Combine the blue cheese and cream cheese in a mixing bowl and beat until blended. Shape the cheese mixture into balls using a small melon baller and coat with the pecans. Arrange the balls on a baking sheet lined with waxed paper. Chill, covered, until serving time. Serve with sliced apples and/or grapes.

Makes 3 1/2 dozen truffles

Elegant and fun, a rose-color **Kir Royale Cocktail** is a mix of Champagne and crème de cassis, a red currant liqueur. To create this cocktail, soak a sugar cube in a shot glass of crème de cassis for several minutes. When the sugar cube turns red, place it in an empty Champagne flute. Pour Champagne into the flute and watch the red color from the sugar stream up, turning the Champagne a beautiful rose color.

TOASTED CANAPÉS

These delicious appetizers are a nice hot pick-up and are an excellent use for leftover Thanksgiving turkey.

24 slices pumpernickel party rye bread,
    cut into triangles
3 tablespoons butter
3 tablespoons flour
1 cup milk
1/2 cup (2 ounces) shredded sharp
    Cheddar cheese

1 cup chopped cooked turkey
1/2 cup chopped fresh mushrooms
1/4 teaspoon salt
1/2 teaspoon red pepper
1/2 cup (2 ounces) freshly grated
    Parmesan cheese
6 slices bacon, crisp-cooked and crumbled

Arrange the bread slices in a single layer on a lightly greased baking sheet. Bake at 500 degrees for 3 to 4 minutes or until crisp. Heat the butter in a saucepan over low heat. Stir in the flour.

Cook until smooth and bubbly, stirring constantly. Add the milk gradually, stirring constantly. Cook until thickened, stirring constantly. Add the Cheddar cheese and cook until blended, stirring constantly. Stir in the turkey, mushrooms, salt and red pepper.

Spoon some of the turkey mixture onto each toasted bread slice. Sprinkle with the Parmesan cheese and bacon. Bake at 500 degrees for 2 to 3 minutes or until the cheese melts. Garnish with grape tomato slices and fresh chives.

Makes 2 dozen canapés

CRAWFISH SUPREME

Layer this delicious appetizer on a beautiful serving tray and serve with a basket of melba toast rounds or thin baguette slices that have been brushed with olive oil and toasted. Shrimp is a great substitute if crawfish is not available.

1 baguette French bread, thinly sliced
Olive oil to taste
1 pound crawfish tails
1 bunch green onions, chopped
1 teaspoon white Worcestershire sauce

1/2 cup rémoulade sauce
1/2 cup reduced-calorie Italian salad
    dressing
12 ounces cream cheese

Arrange the bread slices in a single layer on a baking sheet and brush with olive oil. Toast at 500 degrees until light brown.

Sauté the crawfish tails and green onions in a skillet sprayed with nonstick cooking spray. Stir in the Worcestershire sauce. Remove from the heat and cool slightly. Stir in the rémoulade sauce and salad dressing.

Microwave the cream cheese until slightly softened. Place the cream cheese on a serving platter and top with waxed paper or plastic wrap. Roll or pat the cream cheese to cover the platter. Discard the waxed paper and spread with the crawfish mixture. Serve with the toasted bread slices.

Serves 10 to 12

CRAB MEAT GREEN GODDESS

A dish containing lump crab meat is usually reserved for special occasions, and there are few dishes better than this rich and luxurious appetizer.

16 ounces cream cheese, softened
1/4 cup (1/2 stick) butter, softened
1 tablespoon mayonnaise or cream
2 tablespoons finely chopped green onions
2 garlic cloves, crushed
Salt and black pepper to taste
Red pepper to taste
Tabasco sauce to taste
Lemon juice to taste
1 cup mayonnaise
1/2 cup sour cream
1/3 cup finely chopped parsley
2 tablespoons lemon juice
1 garlic clove, crushed
1 pound lump crab meat, drained and shells removed

Beat the cream cheese and butter in a mixing bowl until blended, scraping the bowl occasionally. Stir in 1 tablespoon mayonnaise, green onions, 2 crushed garlic cloves, salt, black pepper, red pepper, Tabasco sauce and lemon juice to taste. Spread the cream cheese mixture 1/2 inch thick on a serving tray. Chill, covered, in the refrigerator.

Combine 1 cup mayonnaise, sour cream, parsley, 2 tablespoons lemon juice and 1 crushed garlic clove in a bowl and mix well. Season with salt, black pepper, red pepper and Tabasco sauce. Fold in the crab meat. Spread the crab meat mixture over the cream cheese mixture just before serving. Garnish as desired and serve with assorted party crackers.

Serves 12

Since lump crab meat is so precious, extra precautions should be taken when purchasing and storing. Only purchase crab meat at a reputable market, and save that purchase for the end of the shopping trip. Fresh crab meat should smell slightly sweet with no fishy aroma. Have the fishmonger pack the crab meat in ice for the trip home. If not going straight home, consider bringing along an ice chest in your car. Once home, quickly transfer the crab meat to the refrigerator.

Combine glass, silver, and geometric-shaped vases and serving pieces to create a swanky, southern, avant-garde atmosphere in the dining room. Tall and regal amaryllis make a big impact arranged in square glass vases and look sophisticated next to simple vases of orchids and miniature calla lilies. Long green banana stalks, commonly found in most Baton Rouge yards, are laid across the table and pick up the green colors in the serving pieces.

CITRUS-GLAZED SMOKED SAUSAGE

1 pound smoked sausage, thinly sliced
1/2 cup chopped green onions
6 to 8 tablespoons vegetable oil
1/4 cup lemon juice
3/4 teaspoon dry mustard
1/2 teaspoon salt
1/2 teaspoon pepper

Combine the sausage and green onions in a microwave-safe bowl. Microwave, covered, on High for 2 minutes; stir. Microwave for 1 minute longer.

Whisk the oil, lemon juice, dry mustard, salt and pepper in a bowl until blended. Add the oil mixture to the sausage mixture and mix well. Microwave just until heated through. Serve with wooden picks. You may prepare in advance and reheat just before serving.

Serves 12

MICROWAVE PRALINES

Pralines are a chewy sweet confection made from a mixture of pecans, cream, and brown sugar. Many Louisiana cooks make them from old family recipes, as evidenced by the fact that four different praline recipes can be found in River Road Recipes I *and five recipes appear in* River Road Recipes II. *This recipe is unique because even people who swear that they cannot make candy will have success making these super-easy pralines.*

    1 (16-ounce) package light brown sugar
    1 cup heavy cream
    1/4 cup (1/2 stick) butter
    2 cups pecan pieces
    1 tablespoon vanilla extract

Combine the brown sugar and heavy cream in a microwave-safe bowl and mix well. Microwave on High for 7 minutes; stir. Add the butter. Microwave on High for 7 minutes longer and stir vigorously. Stir in the pecans and vanilla. Drop by teaspoonfuls onto a baking sheet lined with waxed paper. Let stand until set.

Serves 12

BOURBON PECAN TARTLETS

This recipe makes a large amount of tartlets, but they can be frozen for up to one month. These tartlets are quick and easy to make using phyllo pastry shells that are simply filled and baked.

    36 frozen miniature phyllo pastry shells
    1/2 cup (3 ounces) miniature semisweet chocolate chips
    1 cup finely chopped pecans, toasted
    3/4 cup packed light brown sugar
    1 tablespoon butter, softened
    1/3 cup bourbon
    1 egg, lightly beaten

Arrange the pastry shells in a single layer on a lightly greased 10×15-inch baking sheet. Spoon the chocolate chips evenly into the shells. Combine the pecans, brown sugar, butter, bourbon and egg in a bowl and mix well. Spoon the pecan mixture into the prepared shells.

Bake at 350 degrees for 20 minutes or until golden brown. Remove to a wire rack to cool. Store in an airtight container for up to 3 days, or freeze for up to 1 month.

Makes 3 dozen tartlets

Saying "PEE-kans" is a sure way to become the center of a joke in Louisiana. The only acceptable pronunciation is "pih-KAWNS." Similarly, the correct pronunciation for our delectable pih-KAWN candy is "PRAW-leens," not "PRAY-leens."

61

AFTERNOON TEA

A tea party is a gracious way to honor someone special, perhaps a bride-to-be or a debutante. This wonderfully old-fashioned occasion evokes images of elegance, luxury, and indulgence. Tea is usually somewhat formal, providing the perfect opportunity to bring out the fine china, silver, crystal, and linens. If children are invited, set up a small table for them, offering lemonade instead of tea.

8 Guests

SMOKED SALMON CANAPÉS

MUSHROOM PARTY SANDWICHES

CUCUMBER SPREAD

ORANGE ROSEMARY SCONES

OLD-FASHIONED TEA CAKES

LEMON SQUARES
(RRRII page 189)

TEA TIME TASSIES
(RRRII page 191)

Smoked Salmon Canapés

These salmon sandwiches are served already assembled on pita bread, making them easier to eat than the traditional self-serve salmon tray. Especially delicious when made with the Cucumber Spread on page 64.

1 (10-ounce) thin Boboli	1/4 cup finely chopped purple onion
8 ounces cream cheese, softened	1/2 (3-ounce) jar capers, drained
1/2 teaspoon lemon and dill seasoning or seasoning of choice	4 ounces smoked salmon, thinly sliced

Bake the crust at 425 degrees for 3 to 5 minutes. Watch carefully to prevent overbrowning. Let stand until cool. Beat the cream cheese and seasoning in a mixing bowl until light and fluffy.

Spread the cream cheese mixture over the baked crust. Sprinkle with 1/2 of the onion and 1/2 of the capers. Layer with the salmon and sprinkle with the remaining onion and remaining capers. Cut into 12 wedges. For variety, substitute pita rounds for the Boboli, or prepare as individual pizzas for a plated appetizer.

Makes 1 dozen canapés

Mushroom Party Sandwiches

For a ribbon effect, make each sandwich using both a dark and white slice of bread and cut into thin strips using an electric knife. This spread can also be served on toast points, assorted party crackers, and/or pita bread.

8 to 16 ounces fresh mushrooms, sliced	Salt and pepper to taste
1 onion, minced	8 ounces cream cheese, softened
Butter	Sherry (optional)
	1 loaf thinly sliced white bread

Sauté the mushrooms and onion in butter in a skillet until the onion is tender. Season with salt and pepper. Let stand until cool. Combine the mushroom mixture, cream cheese and sherry in a bowl and mix well.

Spread the cream cheese mixture on 1 side of half the bread slices. Top with the remaining bread slices. Trim the crusts and cut into quarters.

Makes 40 sandwiches

The idea of a formal tea always evokes images of a complicated ritual, but brewing up a **Perfect Pot of Tea** is not at all complex. First, heat the teapot you intend to use for serving by filling with very hot water. Second, bring fresh, cold water to a full boil in a teakettle. Third, pour the water out of the warm teapot and add the tea to the empty pot. Use about one teaspoon of loose tea or one tea bag for every three-fourths cup of boiling water that will be added. Pour the boiling water over the tea. Steep for three to five minutes to bring out the full flavor; otherwise, the end result will be just hot colored water. Stir the tea, then discard the tea bags, or use a strainer when pouring to remove the loose tea.

A pitcher of iced tea is a nice offering for those who do not care for hot tea. Take it a step further and add a splash of rose water sweetener, available in most culinary shops, to each glass of tea to make a refreshing rose water iced tea.

CUCUMBER SPREAD

The cucumber spread can also be used as a base for other open-faced sandwiches that include fresh vegetables such as tomatoes, sprouts, or spinach.

6 ounces cream cheese, softened	2 tablespoons mayonnaise
1 cucumber, peeled, seeded and grated	1/2 teaspoon hot sauce
	Salt to taste
1/4 cup grated yellow onion	1 drop of green food coloring

Mash the cream cheese in a bowl. Stir in the cucumber and onion. Add the mayonnaise and hot sauce and mix well. Season with salt and stir in the food coloring.

Spread the cucumber mixture on thinly sliced bread and cut into finger sandwiches, use as a base for open-faced cucumber sandwiches, or add mayonnaise or cream cheese to the mixture and serve as a dip.

Makes 1 cup

ORANGE ROSEMARY SCONES

The blend of orange and rosemary is a classic flavor combination. These scones are lighter, fluffier, and moister than most scones.

2 cups flour	1/4 cup fresh orange juice
1/4 cup sugar	1 egg, beaten
1 tablespoon baking powder	2 tablespoons grated orange zest
1/4 teaspoon salt	1 tablespoon half-and-half
2 or 3 sprigs of rosemary, snipped	1 tablespoon fresh orange juice
1/3 cup butter, chilled and cubed	1 tablespoon sugar
1/4 cup half-and-half	

Combine the flour, 1/4 cup sugar, baking powder, salt and rosemary in a bowl and mix well. Cut in the butter with a pastry blender until crumbly. Mix 1/4 cup half-and-half, 1/4 cup orange juice, egg and orange zest in a bowl. Add the orange juice mixture to the crumb mixture and stir with a fork just until moistened.

Shape the dough into a ball. Pat into an 8-inch circle on an ungreased baking sheet. Score into 8 wedges using a sharp knife. Brush the top with a mixture of 1 tablespoon half-and-half, 1 tablespoon orange juice and 1 tablespoon sugar. Bake at 350 degrees for 25 minutes. Serve warm.

Makes 8 scones

OLD-FASHIONED TEA CAKES

These simple and sweet little cakes are similar to shortbread cookies.

2 cups self-rising flour
1 cup sugar
1/2 cup (1 stick) butter
2 eggs
11/2 teaspoons milk
1/2 teaspoon vanilla extract
1/2 teaspoon nutmeg

Sift the self-rising flour 3 times. Beat the sugar and butter in a mixing bowl until creamy, scraping the bowl occasionally. Add the eggs 1 at a time, mixing well after each addition. Add the self-rising flour, milk, vanilla and nutmeg and beat until blended.

Place the dough on a sheet of waxed paper lightly dusted with additional flour. Roll to the desired thickness and cut with a cookie cutter.

Arrange on an ungreased cookie sheet. Bake at 325 degrees for 15 minutes or until brown. Cool on the cookie sheet for 2 minutes. Remove to a wire rack to cool completely.

Serves 8 to 12

A large tray of sweeteners and flavorings for tea makes teatime playful and turns a simple beverage into something special. Provide every kind of accompaniment you can think of, including milk and light cream, sugar cubes, mint leaves, orange and lemon zest, crystallized ginger, and lemon slices.

MEDITERRANEAN MIXED GRILL

This menu reflects the growing awareness, appreciation, and availability of Middle Eastern foods in the south. An ethnic menu is casual, interesting, and fun and makes for a nice change from the type of foods we normally serve and consume at parties. Lay a small Oriental or Eastern rug across the table and serve buffet-style, or toss large pillows around a coffee table and let everyone sit on the floor for an ethnic meal, authentically served.

12 Guests

HUMMUS

STUFFED GRAPE LEAVES

SWEET AND SPICY CUCUMBER SALAD

CHICKEN SHWARMA WITH YOGURT DILL SAUCE

BALSAMIC-MARINATED LAMB CHOPS WITH ROASTED RED PEPPER BUTTER

POTATOES FORNO

BAKLAVA

HUMMUS

This very popular and versatile spread, made from chick-peas, or garbanzo beans, is usually served with pita bread or toast points.

1 (15-ounce) can chick-peas, drained
1/4 cup extra-virgin olive oil
3 tablespoons fresh lemon juice
2 garlic cloves, chopped
3/4 teaspoon salt, or to taste
2 to 3 tablespoons warm water (optional)
1 tablespoon olive oil
Paprika or cayenne pepper to taste
1 tablespoon finely chopped fresh parsley and/or
   fresh mint

Combine the chick-peas, 1/4 cup olive oil, lemon juice, garlic and salt in a food processor fitted with a steel blade and process until smooth. Scrape the side of the bowl with a spatula. Add the water 1 tablespoon at a time if desired for a thinner consistency, processing constantly until smooth and fluffy.

Spoon the hummus into a bowl and drizzle with 1 tablespoon olive oil. Sprinkle with paprika and top with the parsley and mint. Serve with pita chips, crostini, or fresh vegetables, or use as a sandwich spread. You may store, covered, in the refrigerator for up to 2 weeks.

Makes 2 cups

STUFFED GRAPE LEAVES

Referred to in Greece as dolmas, the flavor of the pickled grape leaves in these authentic Mediterranean tidbits permeates each bite. The filling should be very smooth, so ask the butcher to grind the lamb twice. Fresh mint may be substituted for the parsley.

1 garlic clove, minced
1 tablespoon olive oil
12 to 16 ounces finely ground lamb
1 cup finely chopped onion
3/4 cup currants
1/4 cup lemon juice

1/4 cup finely chopped fresh parsley
1 cup cooked rice
1 jar grape leaves, drained, rinsed and stemmed
1/2 cup lemon juice
1/2 cup water

Mix the garlic and olive oil in a small bowl. Brown the lamb in a skillet, stirring until crumbly; drain. Combine the lamb, garlic mixture, onion, currants, 1/4 cup lemon juice and parsley in a bowl and mix well. Stir in the rice.

Lay the grape leaves on a hard surface and place approximately 1 to 2 tablespoons of the lamb mixture in the center of each leaf. Bring 2 opposite points of each leaf to the center and fold over the filling. Roll tightly as for a jelly roll into a roll about 3 inches long.

Arrange the stuffed grape leaves seam side down in a single or double layer in a 9×13-inch baking dish. Drizzle with a mixture of 1/2 cup lemon juice and water. Bake, covered, at 350 degrees for 40 minutes. Check periodically to ensure enough moisture is present to steam the grape leaves and add water if necessary.

Serves 12

SWEET AND SPICY CUCUMBER SALAD

The added combination of pineapple, jalapeño chiles, and carrots makes this salad sweet, spicy, and colorful.

3/4 cup sugar
2/3 cup white vinegar
2 tablespoons water
1/2 teaspoon salt
1 cup (1/3-inch) pieces fresh pineapple
2 English cucumbers, or 2 medium cucumbers, cut into 1/3-inch pieces

2 carrots, peeled and julienned
1/2 cup thinly sliced red onion
1 tablespoon minced seeded jalapeño chile
1 head green leaf lettuce, trimmed and separated
1 tablespoon sesame seeds, toasted

Bring the sugar, vinegar, water and salt to a boil in a saucepan. Boil until the sugar dissolves, stirring frequently; reduce the heat. Simmer for 4 minutes or until the syrup is reduced to 2/3 cup, stirring occasionally. Pour the syrup into a heatproof bowl and chill in the refrigerator.

Add the pineapple to the chilled syrup and mix well. Chill, covered, for 1 hour. Add the cucumbers, carrots, onion and jalapeño chile to the pineapple mixture and stir until coated. Chill if desired. Spoon the pineapple mixture onto lettuce-lined salad plates and sprinkle with the sesame seeds.

Serves 6 to 8

CHICKEN SHWARMA

Meringue powder is available in most supermarkets or party supply stores and is used in this recipe to hold the chicken together while cooking.

> 1/4 cup paprika
> 3 tablespoons garlic powder
> 2 tablespoons meringue powder
> 2 tablespoons salt
> 1 tablespoon onion powder
> 1 tablespoon pepper
> 5 pounds boneless skinless chicken breasts, trimmed

Mix the paprika, garlic powder, meringue powder, salt, onion powder and pepper in a shallow dish. Pound the chicken 1/4 inch thick between sheets of waxed paper with a meat mallet. Coat the chicken with the paprika mixture.

Cover a sheet pan with a clean tea towel. Arrange 1/2 of the chicken in a single layer on the tea towel. Layer with the remaining chicken overlapping. Cover the layers with a clean tea towel and top with a sheet pan; press together. Chill for 1 hour.

Remove the top sheet pan and tea towel. Using a wooden dowel or the end of a long wooden spoon, roll the sheet of chicken onto the dowel and secure with kitchen twine. Grill the roll over hot coals for 45 minutes or until the chicken is cooked through, turning occasionally. Slice as desired. Serve with the Yogurt Dill Sauce.

Serves 12

YOGURT DILL SAUCE

This chilled Grecian sauce is used as a dipping sauce for the Chicken Shwarma but is also delicious with other dishes in the Mediterranean Mixed Grill menu. The sauce adds a cool and refreshing taste when combined with the warm flavors of a Mediterranean meal.

> 2 cups whole milk yogurt
> Juice of 1/2 lemon
> 1 1/2 teaspoons dill weed

Combine the yogurt, lemon juice and dill weed in a bowl and mix well. Store, covered, in the refrigerator until serving time.

Makes 2 cups

Chicken Shwarma is not truly Greek or Lebanese. It's actually an American adaptation of a lamb dish, using chicken instead, and is more widely eaten in the United States than elsewhere.

Balsamic-Marinated Lamb Chops with Roasted Red Pepper Butter

Dishes containing lamb are very typical in Mediterranean cuisine. The versatile marinade is also delicious on poultry, pork, or beef.

Balsamic Marinade
3/4 cup balsamic vinegar
1/2 cup coarsely chopped shallots
2 tablespoons coarsely chopped garlic
2 teaspoons chopped fresh thyme
1 teaspoon salt
1 teaspoon freshly ground pepper

Lamb
4 pounds lamb loin chops, 1 1/2 to
   2 inches thick
Vegetable oil

Roasted Red Pepper Butter
1/3 cup roasted red bell peppers, chopped,
   or drained chopped pimentos
1/2 cup (1 stick) butter, softened
1 teaspoon lemon juice

For the marinade, mix the vinegar, shallots, garlic, thyme, salt and pepper in a bowl and pour into a resealable plastic bag.

For the lamb, add the chops to the marinade and seal the bag tightly. Turn to coat. Marinate in the refrigerator for 8 to 10 hours, turning occasionally; drain. Pat the chops dry with paper towels. Let stand until room temperature. Brush both sides of the chops with oil and grill over hot coals for 8 minutes per side for medium-rare or to the desired degree of doneness, turning once. Remove the chops to a heated platter. Let stand for 5 minutes.

For the butter, pat the roasted peppers with a paper towel. Process the roasted peppers, butter and lemon juice in a food processor until blended. Serve at room temperature with the chops.

Serves 12

Potatoes Forno

Forno is an Italian word that refers to an oven-baked dish. Serve this quick and easy recipe as an accompaniment to grilled meats.

2 pounds red potatoes
1/2 cup olive oil
1/3 cup lemon juice

2 garlic cloves, minced
1 teaspoon chopped fresh oregano
Salt and pepper to taste

Parboil the potatoes in boiling water in a large saucepan for 5 minutes; drain. Let stand until cool. Peel the potatoes and cut horizontally into halves. Slice each half into a fan. Arrange the potatoes on a greased baking sheet. Whisk the olive oil, lemon juice, garlic and oregano in a bowl. Brush the olive oil mixture over the potatoes and sprinkle with salt and pepper. Roast at 400 degrees for 35 to 40 minutes or until tender and brown.

Serves 12

BAKLAVA

Although it appears complicated, making baklava is really quite easy. The entire process consists of layering phyllo pastry that has been sprinkled with nuts. The trick is to cut it into squares before baking.

Baklava
1/4 cup sugar
1 teaspoon grated lemon zest
1/2 teaspoon cinnamon
1 pound phyllo pastry
1 cup (2 sticks) unsalted butter, melted
3 cups finely chopped toasted nuts
    (walnuts, pistachios, almonds or pecans)

Syrup
1 1/3 cups sugar
1 1/3 cups water
1/3 cup honey
1 tablespoon lemon juice
1 strip orange zest

For the baklava, mix the sugar, lemon zest and cinnamon in a bowl. Coat the bottom and sides of a 9×13-inch baking dish with butter. Trim the pastry into 9×13-inch sheets. Cover the pastry with damp paper towels.

Remove 2 sheets of the pastry and arrange in the prepared baking dish. Brush the top sheet evenly with some of the butter. Layer with 2 additional sheets of the pastry and brush the top sheet with some of the butter. Repeat the process 1 more time for a total of 6 sheets of pastry. Sprinkle 1/2 of the nuts and 1/2 of the sugar mixture over the top.

Layer the prepared layers with the remaining pastry sheets, brushing every other sheet with butter. Using a sharp serrated knife, cut through the layers into 2-inch diamonds or squares. This is a very important step as it is impossible to cut baked baklava and this also allows the syrup to soak around each piece.

Bake at 325 degrees for 30 minutes. Reduce the oven temperature to 300 degrees. Bake for 45 minutes longer or until golden brown.

For the syrup, combine the sugar, water, honey, lemon juice and orange zest in a saucepan. Bring to a gentle boil; reduce the heat. Simmer for 15 minutes, stirring occasionally. Strain the syrup and pour the hot syrup evenly over the hot baklava. Let stand for 4 hours or until cool.

Serves 12 to 16

The League ladies felt that River Road Recipes I *would eventually slide off in sales and that a new book should already be on the market to make up for and sustain sales when that day occurred. Thus, work began on* River Road Recipes II: A Second Helping *in 1972. That day never did come.* River Road Recipes I *still continues to outsell both* River Road Recipes II *and* River Road Recipes III: A Healthy Collection, *which debuted in 1994.*

A SOUTHERN TREE TRIMMING

A white Christmas in bayou country is unlikely, but the spirit of the season is alive when family and friends gather to decorate the tree and celebrate the holiday. This hearty menu is just right for a small group.

8 Guests

WHISKEY SOUR PUNCH

CRAWFISH BISQUE

ROASTED CORNISH GAME HENS

CREAMY NUTMEG POTATOES

EGGNOG CRÈME BRÛLÉE

Optional Menu Item
SEAFOOD GUMBO
(RRRI page 14)

WHISKEY SOUR PUNCH

This can also be referred to as "loud" punch because it turns up the volume at a party! Southern bourbon aged in charred wood barrels gives this a smoky quality.

   1 (12-ounce) can frozen pink lemonade concentrate
   1 (6-ounce) can frozen orange juice concentrate
   3 cups water
   3 cups orange juice
   1 to 2 cups Jack Daniel's whiskey
   1/4 to 1/2 cup fresh lemon juice
   1/4 cup maraschino cherry juice
   1 (12-ounce) can lemon-lime soda

Combine the lemonade concentrate, orange juice concentrate, water, orange juice, whiskey, lemon juice and cherry juice in a large pitcher and mix well. Stir in the soda just before serving and pour over ice in glasses. Garnish each with a skewer threaded with assorted fruit.

Serves 8 to 12

*R*iver Road Recipes II: A Second Helping *was named by Sue Turner, who served as the Baton Rouge Junior League president from 1965 to 1966. Sue entered a contest to name the second cookbook in 1975. She says that the title immediately came to mind. No pondering over what to write on her entry slip was needed. She modestly adds that other people made the same entry; she was just the first to submit the name. A gift for coming up with good titles must run in the family. Sue's cousin, Ann Arbour, came up with the original title,* River Road Recipes, *in 1959.*

A good roux is the start of many Creole and Cajun recipes. Learning to slowly transform flour and oil into a rich, nutty concoction is an art, but one that can be mastered by anyone with patience and a cast-iron skillet. A good roux requires thirty to forty minutes of the cook's constant whisking, because if the roux burns, it must be thrown out. Roux is a labor of love, but this precious blend of two simple ingredients is part of what gives Louisiana foods their authentic taste.

Try your hand with our favorite **Roux** recipe. Heat one-half cup vegetable oil in a large cast-iron skillet over medium heat. Gradually add two cups flour to the hot oil, whisking constantly. Cook for about thirty minutes or until the roux is dark mahogany in color, whisking constantly. The roux may be prepared in advance and stored, covered, in the refrigerator for up to one week.

CRAWFISH BISQUE

Crawfish Stuffing
1 king size loaf sliced bread
7 pounds fresh crawfish tails
4 ribs celery, finely chopped
4 small white onions, finely
  chopped
2 bunches parsley, trimmed
  and chopped
2 bell peppers, finely chopped
7 garlic cloves, chopped
2 bunches green onions (bulbs
  and tops), chopped
2 tablespoons seasoned pepper
1 teaspoon salt

Fried Stuffed Crawfish Heads
100 medium (about) crawfish
  heads, cleaned
4 cups sifted flour
2 tablespoons Creole seasoning
2 quarts vegetable oil for frying

Bisque
2^1/2 cups flour
2 cups vegetable oil
2 onions, chopped
2 bunches green onions (bulbs
  and tops), chopped
2 ribs celery, chopped
1 bell pepper, chopped
2 bunches parsley, trimmed and
  chopped
12 cups (or more) water
2 (14-ounce) cans stewed tomatoes
2 (12-ounce) cans tomato paste
2 (8-ounce) cans tomato sauce
Salt and pepper to taste

For the stuffing, arrange the bread slices on a baking sheet. Toast at 300 degrees until light brown. Coarsely crumble the bread into a large bowl. Place the crawfish tails in a food processor and pulse until finely chopped. Add the chopped crawfish, celery, onions, parsley, bell peppers, garlic, green onions, seasoned pepper and salt to the bread crumbs and mix well.

For the fried crawfish, stuff the crawfish heads with the stuffing and coat with a mixture of the flour and Creole seasoning. Heat the oil in a 6-quart fryer over medium-high heat. Fry the stuffed crawfish in batches in the hot oil until brown on all sides; drain on paper towels. Leftover stuffing may be whisked into the bisque for added thickening and flavor.

For the bisque, whisk the flour into the oil in a stockpot until blended. Cook over medium heat for 30 minutes, whisking constantly or until the roux is golden brown. Stir in the onions, green onions, celery and bell pepper. Cook for 10 minutes, stirring constantly. Add the parsley, water, undrained tomatoes, tomato paste, tomato sauce, salt and pepper.

Simmer, covered, for 4 hours, stirring occasionally to prevent the bisque from sticking. Ladle into soup bowls and top each serving with 4 to 6 fried stuffed crawfish heads. Serve with a mixed green salad and crusty bread. You may freeze for future use.

Makes 10 quarts

ROASTED CORNISH GAME HENS

Cornish game hens make a more elegant presentation than the usual roasted chicken. The whole house smells warm, homey, and reassuring while these tender hens roasting in garlic, herbs, and vermouth are in the oven.

8 Cornish game hens, cleaned
1 cup (2 sticks) butter, softened
4 garlic cloves, minced
2 tablespoons chopped fresh rosemary
2 teaspoons salt
2 teaspoons cracked pepper
1 1/2 cups dry vermouth

Rinse the game hens and pat dry. Beat the butter in a mixing bowl until creamy. Add the garlic, rosemary, salt and pepper to the butter and beat until mixed.

Loosen the skin carefully from the breast and legs of each game hen, taking care not to tear the skin. Spread 1/8 of the butter mixture under the skin and over the breast and legs of each game hen.

Arrange in a single layer in a roasting pan and pour the vermouth over the top. Roast, covered, at 375 degrees for 45 minutes, basting with the pan juices every 15 minutes; remove the cover. Roast for 10 to 15 minutes longer or until the juices run clear and the game hens are golden brown. Let stand for 5 minutes. To serve, cut each game hen into halves.

Serves 8

CREAMY NUTMEG POTATOES

Nutmeg and cream bring out the natural sweetness of the potatoes in this mild, yet decadent dish.

6 cups water
2 pounds medium red potatoes
2 tablespoons butter, softened
4 cups heavy cream
Salt and pepper to taste
Nutmeg to taste

Bring the water to a boil in a large pot. Add the potatoes and boil for 5 minutes or until tender; drain. Cool slightly. Peel and slice the potatoes.

Coat a 9×13-inch baking dish with the butter. Layer the potatoes and heavy cream (just to cover each layer) alternately in the prepared baking dish until all of the ingredients are used, sprinkling the potatoes each time with salt, pepper and nutmeg. Bake at 350 degrees for 20 to 30 minutes or until brown and bubbly.

Serves 8

In 1909, the Standard Oil Refinery constructed in Baton Rouge what was then the largest refinery in the world, becoming the impetus for what is now a ninety-mile-long industrial corridor along the Mississippi, stretching to New Orleans. Agricultural products such as soybeans and sugar and, in recent history, petroleum, chemicals, and nuclear power are important contributors to the economy of the area. The port of Baton Rouge is currently ranked tenth in the nation in terms of tonnage shipped.

Eggnog Crème Brûlée

Crème brûlée is a French term for what the English refer to as "burnt cream" and generally means a dessert that has been finished with a sugar glaze. Miniature kitchen torches, available at kitchen specialty shops, can be used to caramelize the sugar.

>   4 cups heavy cream
>   2/3 cup sugar
>   8 egg yolks
>   1/4 cup bourbon or brandy
>   1 tablespoon vanilla extract
>   1/2 teaspoon nutmeg
>   1/8 teaspoon (heaping) salt
>   1/3 cup packed brown sugar

Place an 8×11-inch (8-cup) shallow ceramic baking dish in a roasting pan. Bring the heavy cream and sugar to a simmer in a saucepan, stirring occasionally. Simmer until the sugar dissolves, stirring frequently. Whisk the egg yolks in a bowl until blended. Whisk a small amount of the hot cream mixture into the egg yolks. Whisk the egg yolk mixture into the hot cream mixture. Whisk the bourbon, vanilla, nutmeg and salt into the custard until blended.

Pour the custard into the baking dish. Add enough hot water to the roasting pan to reach halfway up the sides of the dish. Bake at 350 degrees for 40 minutes or until the center jiggles slightly when gently shaken. Remove the baking dish from the roasting pan. Chill on a wire rack in the refrigerator for 3 hours or longer.

Press the brown sugar through a sieve over the custard until completely covered. Broil 4 to 6 inches from the heat source for 2 minutes or until the sugar caramelizes. Chill for 1 to 3 hours or until the topping hardens. Serve cold.

Serves 8

'ROUND MIDNIGHT

*New Year's Eve for some people means an all-night party, but others
know that a low-key evening of fine food and a little something bubbly
with dear friends is the perfect beginning to a wonderful New Year.*

6 Guests

OYSTERS ON THE HALF SHELL
WITH PEPPER MIGNONETTE

ENDIVE SALAD WITH BLUE CHEESE
AND ROASTED PEPPERS

TILAPIA EN PAPILLOTE WITH
CITRUS BUTTER

SQUASH ROCKEFELLER

STRAWBERRY AMARETTO TRIFLE

Optional Menu Item
CRAB MEAT LIAISON

One of the most widely followed pieces of advice given when it comes to eating raw oysters is to enjoy them only in months that contain the letter "r." It is true that warmer weather produces warmer water, which affects the taste and health of oysters and can contribute to an increased risk of bacterial growth that can be harmful when consumed. Thus, it is generally recommended that oysters be eaten in the cooler months, September through February, which all happen to have an "r" in their names.

Oysters on the Half Shell with Pepper Mignonette

For a gorgeous and unusual presentation, arrange the oysters on a large serving platter on a bed of rock salt or wet play sand. Arrange sprigs of fresh dill weed or fennel tops over the oysters to resemble seaweed.

3 dozen oysters in shells
2 cups red wine vinegar
2 tablespoons minced red bell pepper
2 tablespoons minced green bell pepper
2 tablespoons minced red onion
1 1/2 teaspoons cracked black pepper
1 teaspoon crushed red pepper
1 teaspoon sugar

Clean and scrub the oysters. Shuck with a dull knife and release the oyster flesh from the bottom shells. Arrange the shucked oysters on a platter.

Combine the vinegar, bell peppers, onion, black pepper, red pepper and sugar in a bowl and mix well. Serve with the oysters.

Serves 6

Endive Salad with Blue Cheese and Roasted Peppers

Dijon Vinaigrette
3 tablespoons sherry vinegar
1 tablespoon Dijon mustard
1 teaspoon minced shallots
1/4 cup walnut oil
1/4 cup vegetable oil
Salt and pepper to taste

Salad
8 heads endive
1 red bell pepper, julienned
8 ounces blue cheese, crumbled
3/4 cup coarsely chopped toasted walnuts

For the vinaigrette, whisk the vinegar, mustard and shallots in a bowl. Add the walnut oil and vegetable oil gradually, whisking constantly until incorporated. Season with salt and pepper.

For the salad, remove the outside spears from the endive and discard. Separate the heads into spears and tear each spear into thirds. Divide the endive evenly between 8 chilled salad plates. Top each with the bell pepper and blue cheese. Drizzle with the vinaigrette and sprinkle with the walnuts. Serve immediately.

Serves 8

Louisiana Cajuns are descendants of the Acadians, who were expelled from Canada for refusing to sign allegiances to the British and denounce Catholicism for the Church of England. They settled in the swamplands and prairies and were eventually referred to as Cajuns, which is the slang term for Acadians. Cajun food mirrors the characteristics of its people throughout their history. . . peppery, fiery, hot country food that is cooked altogether in one big pot, usually consisting of whatever ingredients happen to be available from the land, water, or their own gardens. Staples from the bayou areas include crawfish, alligators, frogs, fish, and wild birds. From the Gulf of Mexico comes shrimp, oysters, and still more fish. The limitations of the ingredients that were available in this area in the 1700s have resulted in imaginative culinary creations that have been passed down from one generation to the next.

The Cajun cooking craze that swept throughout the United States in the 1980s was started with the introduction of the blackened redfish, a spicy fish that was cooked quickly at a high temperature until completely black. This tasty recipe was not a traditional Cajun dish, but its enormous popularity resulted in it becoming a symbol of Cajun cooking for those outside the area. Over-fishing to meet the consequent demand resulted in an alarming shortage of redfish that forced the state of Louisiana to put a temporary ban on the sale of redfish from the Gulf of Mexico. A positive outcome of the trend was the eventual worldwide introduction and acceptance of different types of Creole and Cajun food.

Tilapia en Papillote with Citrus Butter

Pompano from Florida is the fish traditionally used in this dish. However, it can be difficult to obtain. Try using tilapia, a widely available farm-raised fish with a delicate taste and flaking texture.

Tilapia
2 pounds tilapia fillets, cut into
   6 portions
Salt and pepper to taste
1 cup sliced red onion
2 tomatoes, sliced
12 sage leaves
6 sprigs of fresh thyme
12 tablespoons fresh rosemary
   leaves

Citrus Butter
3 oranges
1 grapefruit
3 lemons
3 limes
2 tablespoons honey
1 tablespoon minced shallots
2 teaspoons minced garlic
1/2 cup (1 stick) butter, chilled
   and cubed
3 tablespoons chopped fresh parsley
1/4 cup julienned fresh chives

For the tilapia, cut 6 pieces of baking parchment paper large enough to enclose the fillets. Season the fillets with salt and pepper. Arrange 1 fillet on half of 1 piece of the parchment paper. Layer the fillet with onion slices, tomato slices, 2 of the sage leaves, 1 sprig of the thyme and 2 tablespoons of the rosemary. Fold the parchment paper over the fillet and fold the edges to seal, forming a pouch. Repeat the process with the remaining fillets, remaining onion slices, remaining tomato slices, remaining sage leaves, remaining sprigs of thyme and remaining rosemary. Arrange the pouches on a baking sheet. Bake at 375 degrees for 25 minutes or until the fillets flake easily.

For the butter, grate 1 teaspoon of zest from each of the four citrus fruits. Juice the oranges, grapefruit, lemons and limes into a bowl, discarding the seeds. Combine the citrus juice, citrus zest, honey, shallots and garlic in a saucepan and mix well. Bring to a simmer; reduce the heat. Add the butter gradually, whisking constantly. Stir in the parsley.

To serve, make a slit in each pouch and drizzle the fillets with some of the butter. Sprinkle with the chives and garnish with citrus wedges. Serve with a fresh green vegetable or mixed green salad and boiled new potatoes.

Serves 6

CRAB MEAT LIAISON

A liaison is a culinary method for thickening a cream sauce with egg yolks.

1/2 cup (1 stick) butter
2 ribs celery, finely chopped
1 cup finely chopped onion
2 green onions, chopped
6 tablespoons flour
1 (12-ounce) can evaporated milk
2 tablespoons whole milk

2 egg yolks, lightly beaten
3/4 teaspoon seasoned pepper
1/8 teaspoon salt
2 tablespoons crème sherry
1 pound jumbo lump crab meat, drained
    and shells removed
6 ounces sharp Cheddar cheese, shredded

Heat the butter in a saucepan over medium heat. Sauté the celery, onion and green onions in the butter until tender. Stir in the flour gradually. Cook until bubbly, stirring constantly. Add the evaporated milk and whole milk gradually, stirring constantly. Stir in the egg yolks, seasoned pepper and salt.

Cook over low heat for 5 minutes or until thickened, stirring frequently. Stir in the crème sherry. Remove from the heat. Pour the sauce over the crab meat in a bowl and mix gently. Spoon the crab meat mixture into a greased 8×10-inch baking dish and sprinkle with the cheese. Bake at 375 degrees for 10 to 15 minutes or until light brown and bubbly. Broil until brown if desired. Garnish with additional chopped green onions and serve immediately.

Serves 6

SQUASH ROCKEFELLER

Oyster liquor is the term for the liquid surrounding commercially packed oysters. Anisette liqueur, or Pernod, has a sweet licorice flavor that goes well with spinach.

3 large yellow summer squash or mirliton,
    cut into halves and seeded
Salt to taste
1 pound fresh spinach, stems removed
3 tablespoons oyster liquor or clam juice
3 tablespoons anisette
1/2 cup (2 ounces) grated Parmesan cheese

1 teaspoon chopped fresh tarragon
1/2 teaspoon chopped fresh basil
Coarsely ground black pepper to taste
Cayenne pepper to taste
1 cup seasoned bread crumbs
1/2 cup (2 ounces) grated Parmesan cheese

Cook the squash in boiling salted water in a saucepan for 5 minutes or until tender; drain. Cook the spinach in boiling water in a saucepan for 3 minutes or until tender-crisp; drain. Press the excess moisture from the spinach and finely chop. Combine the spinach, oyster liquor, liqueur, 1/2 cup cheese, tarragon, basil, black pepper, cayenne pepper and salt in a bowl and mix well. Add the bread crumbs gradually, stirring until the mixture has the consistency of a stuffing and is firm enough to adhere. Arrange the squash halves cut side up on a baking sheet. Stuff the squash halves with equal portions of the spinach mixture and sprinkle with 1/2 cup cheese. Bake at 350 degrees for 10 to 12 minutes or until heated through.

Serves 6

Strawberry Amaretto Trifle

1 (12-ounce) round angel food cake
1 quart fresh or frozen strawberries, sliced
1 cup amaretto
3 tablespoons sugar
8 ounces cream cheese, softened

1/2 cup confectioners' sugar
1 cup amaretto
1 teaspoon vanilla extract
16 ounces whipped topping
1/2 cup sliced almonds

Slice the cake horizontally into 3 equal layers. Combine the strawberries, 1 cup liqueur and sugar in a bowl and mix gently. Chill, covered, in the refrigerator.

Beat the cream cheese and confectioners' sugar in a mixing bowl until creamy. Add 1 cup liqueur and vanilla and beat until blended. Add 8 ounces of the whipped topping gradually and beat at low speed until smooth. Add the remaining 8 ounces whipped topping and beat until blended.

Arrange 1 layer of the cake in the bottom of a round trifle dish. Spoon 1/3 of the strawberry mixture over the cake, allowing the juice to soak into the cake. Spread with 1/3 of the cream cheese mixture. Layer the prepared layers with the remaining cake layers, remaining strawberry mixture and remaining cream cheese mixture 1/2 at a time. Sprinkle with the almonds. Chill, covered, until serving time. Seasonal fruits such as mangoes, kiwifruit, blueberries and raspberries may be substituted for the strawberries, or a combination of the fruits may be used for additional color.

Serves 6 to 8

The Deluxe Edition of RRR, issued to commemorate the printing of the 200,000th copy in 1969, arrived at my home on the same day that my family and I were leaving for a vacation to Key Biscayne, Florida.

When we arrived at the Key Biscayne Hotel, we discovered that President and Mrs. Nixon were currently staying in their summer home, which was two blocks away. My Miami cousins convinced me that Mrs. Nixon should have the number-one copy of the new RRR. A note was written to her, and my cousins reassured me that I should pay no attention to the large forbidding blockade at the entrance to the home. I went right on through and immediately received the guard's undivided attention, with his hand on the gun in the holster at his side.

Apparently, a pregnant little lady with a cookbook to deliver was not too threatening, so I was allowed to proceed to the next barricade, where a repeat of the first scene took place. This time, the cookbook was actually put into the hands of the security guard, who promised that Mrs. Nixon would receive the gift. Upon our return to Baton Rouge, the league received a gracious note from Mrs. Nixon, expressing her appreciation for the work of the league, as well as for the marvelous recipes contained in our outstanding cookbook.

—Judy Powers, Chairman 1969

SUPER BOWL GET-TOGETHER

*Whether it is the Super Bowl, Election Day coverage, or the Oscars,
inviting a crowd over to view it together makes a big televised event more fun.
Even guests who are not interested in watching the featured program
will enjoy this hearty menu and visiting with friends.*

12 to 16 Guests

BLACK BEAN HUMMUS

BAKED CORN DIP

CHICKEN POCKETS

PICADILLO

CHOCOLATE-COATED PECAN TOFFEE

BEER NUT COOKIES

BLACK BEAN HUMMUS

Tahini, a thick paste made of ground sesame seeds, may be purchased in the specialty section of some grocery stores, in Middle Eastern markets, or in health food stores. Hummus is usually prepared with chick-peas, but this version made with black beans has a nice Creole-style flavor and color.

Pita Toasts
12 pita bread rounds
Garlic salt to taste

Black Bean Hummus
2 (15-ounce) cans black beans, drained and rinsed
3/4 cup tahini
1/4 cup fresh lemon juice
1/4 cup packed chopped fresh cilantro
4 green onions, sliced
2 tablespoons olive oil
2 large garlic cloves, minced
1 teaspoon cumin
1/2 teaspoon cayenne pepper
Salt and black pepper to taste
8 ounces carrots, cut into sticks
2 cucumbers, sliced

For the toasts, split the pita rounds into halves and cut each half into triangles. Arrange the triangles in a single layer on a baking sheet sprayed with nonstick olive oil cooking spray. Sprinkle with garlic salt and bake at 400 degrees for 5 to 10 minutes or until crisp.

For the hummus, reserve 2 tablespoons of the beans. Process the remaining beans, tahini, lemon juice, chopped cilantro, green onions, olive oil, garlic, cumin and cayenne pepper in a food processor until smooth. Season with salt and black pepper.

Spoon the hummus into a bowl. Chop the reserved beans by hand and sprinkle over the top. Garnish with a sprig of cilantro. Serve with the pita toasts, carrot sticks and cucumber slices.

Makes 3 1/2 cups

BAKED CORN DIP

There are countless renditions of this old favorite. Prepare in advance and bake just before game time.

8 ounces cream cheese
2 (11-ounce) cans Shoe Peg corn, drained
1 (4-ounce) can chopped green chiles
1 cup (4 ounces) shredded Cheddar cheese
1/4 cup chopped jalapeño chiles, or to taste

Microwave the cream cheese in a microwave-safe dish just until softened. Stir in the corn, undrained green chiles, 1/2 cup of the cheese and jalapeño chiles. Spoon the cream cheese mixture into a 9×13-inch baking dish sprayed with nonstick cooking spray and sprinkle with the remaining 1/2 cup cheese.

Bake at 350 degrees for 15 to 25 minutes or until bubbly. Garnish with additional chopped jalapeño chiles. Serve warm with tortilla chips.

Serves 12 to 16

CHICKEN POCKETS

Little packets of food seem to fascinate children, and kids and adults alike love these fun, easy Chicken Pockets. They freeze well in resealable plastic freezer bags and can be thawed and heated for a quick meal or snack.

3 ounces low-fat cream cheese, softened
2 tablespoons unsalted butter, softened
2 tablespoons milk or chicken broth
2 cups shredded cooked chicken
Chopped chives or minced onion to taste
Salt and pepper to taste
2 (8-count) cans reduced-fat crescent rolls

Beat the cream cheese and butter in a mixing bowl until creamy. Add the milk and beat until blended. Stir in the chicken, chives, salt and pepper.

Unroll the roll dough from 1 can onto a baking sheet. Separate into 4 rectangles and press the perforations to seal. Spoon 1/8 of the chicken mixture in the center of each rectangle. Bring the corners of each rectangle together over the center of the filling. Twist and pinch to resemble a hobo's bundle. Repeat the process with the remaining can of crescent rolls and remaining chicken mixture.

Arrange the packets on a baking sheet sprayed with nonstick cooking spray. Bake at 350 degrees for 20 to 25 minutes or until golden brown.

Makes 8 chicken pockets

In Cuba, picadillo is usually served with rice and black beans, while in Mexico, it is commonly used as a filling in various dishes such as tacos or burritos. In Louisiana, it is often combined with rice to use as a stuffing for eggplant, bell peppers, or mirlitons. By itself, picadillo can become a dip for tostados or corn chips. Setting up a South American-inspired Picadillo Bar is a good way to serve a crowd. Provide condiments such as shredded queso fresco, chopped green onions, chopped avocados, chopped fresh tomatoes, sour cream, and/or plantain chips, allowing guests to pick and choose according to their taste.

PICADILLO

Pronounced "pee-kah-DEE-yoh," this spicy dish has its origins in Spain. Recipes and uses vary by nation and region, but it is usually made from some combination of pork, beef, or veal with tomatoes, onions, or garlic. Picadillo is traditionally served on wide noodles, but here in Louisiana, we like it over locally grown rice.

1 pound ground turkey
1/4 cup fresh lemon juice
3 tablespoons dry white wine
1 cup finely chopped yellow onion
1 small green bell pepper, finely chopped
3 garlic cloves, minced
2 tablespoons extra-virgin olive oil
1 (8-ounce) can tomato sauce
1/2 cup loosely packed golden raisins
1/2 cup drained pimento-stuffed green olives, sliced crosswise into halves
1 tablespoon drained capers
1 tablespoon Worcestershire sauce
Freshly ground pepper to taste

Combine the ground turkey, lemon juice and wine in a stainless or ceramic bowl and mix well. Marinate, covered with plastic wrap, in the refrigerator for 1 hour. Sauté the onion, bell pepper and garlic in the olive oil in a large skillet for 3 minutes. Add the turkey mixture and mix well.

Cook for 5 minutes over medium heat, stirring constantly. Stir in the tomato sauce, raisins, olives, capers, Worcestershire sauce and pepper; reduce the heat. Simmer, covered, for 25 minutes, stirring occasionally. Spoon the picadillo over hot cooked rice on dinner plates. You may also use as a stuffing for eggplant, mirlitons or bell peppers.

Serves 4

Chocolate-Coated Pecan Toffee

Any kind of nut may be substituted for the pecans. This recipe makes a large amount of toffee, so share with friends and neighbors during the holidays or send home with your guests as a party favor.

>   1 cup (2 sticks) butter
>   2 cups packed brown sugar
>   1 cup chopped pecans
>   4 cups (24 ounces) semisweet, milk or white chocolate chips

Bring the butter and brown sugar to a boil in a saucepan over medium heat, stirring frequently. Reduce the heat to low. Cook for 10 minutes, stirring occasionally. Remove from the heat and stir in the pecans. Pour the pecan mixture into a greased baking pan and let stand until set. You may chill or freeze to speed up the process. Break into irregular pieces.

Microwave the chocolate chips in a microwave-safe bowl until melted and stir. Dip the toffee into the melted chocolate and arrange on a sheet of waxed paper. Let stand until set. Store in an airtight container. Do not substitute margarine for the butter.

Serves 12 to 16

Beer Nut Cookies

Despite their name, beer nuts are not flavored with beer. Originally called "redskins," beer nuts are peanuts with the red husk left on, then glazed to taste salty and slightly sweet. They are usually served in bars and taverns, or with beer, hence the moniker. If your grocery store does not carry them, try a convenience store.

>   3 cups flour
>   1 teaspoon salt
>   1 teaspoon baking soda
>   1 cup (2 sticks) butter, softened
>   1¹/4 cups sugar
>
>   3/4 cup packed brown sugar
>   1¹/2 teaspoons vanilla extract
>   2 eggs
>   1¹/2 cups beer nuts

Mix the flour, salt and baking soda together. Beat the butter, sugar, brown sugar and vanilla in a mixing bowl until light and fluffy, scraping the bowl occasionally. Add the eggs 1 at a time, beating well after each addition. Add the flour mixture gradually, beating until a soft dough forms. Stir in the beer nuts.

Drop by rounded teaspoonfuls onto a parchment-lined cookie sheet. Bake at 325 degrees for 12 to 15 minutes or until light brown. Cool on the cookie sheet for 2 minutes. Remove to a wire rack to cool completely. Store in an airtight container.

Makes 3 to 4 dozen cookies

BRIDGE LUNCH

A bridge lunch is a pleasant way to spend a day, whether with three or thirty friends. Louisiana ladies also love to play Cajun bouree and pochino. Whatever game you prefer, set up the card table by a window with a view and treat everyone to a light menu of "lady" foods.

8 Guests

WHITE SHRIMP RÉMOULADE SALAD

HERBED CORN CRACKERS

ICEBOX LIME CHEESECAKE

Optional Menu Item
BARBECUED CHICKEN AND GRAPE SALAD

WHITE SHRIMP RÉMOULADE SALAD

Rémoulade sauce is usually pink, but it is believed that the first version of this sauce from our French ancestors was white and made with capers or French gherkins.

White Rémoulade Sauce
1 (16-ounce) jar Creole mustard
1 onion, coarsely chopped
1/2 cup coarsely chopped fresh parsley
1/2 cup coarsely chopped green onions
3 ribs celery, coarsely chopped
3 dill pickles, drained, squeezed dry and coarsely chopped
6 garlic cloves, minced
1 quart mayonnaise
2 (3-ounce) jars capers, drained

Salad
6 cups baby lettuce leaves, torn
3 pounds deveined peeled boiled shrimp

For the sauce, process the mustard, onion, parsley, green onions, celery, pickles and garlic 1/3 at a time in a blender until blended. Combine the mustard mixture and mayonnaise in a bowl and mix well. Stir in the capers. You may store, covered, in the refrigerator for up to 2 weeks.

For the salad, line 8 salad plates with the lettuce leaves. Add the shrimp to the sauce and mix until coated. Mound the shrimp mixture evenly on the lettuce-lined plates. Or, spoon the shrimp mixture into a bowl and serve as an appetizer with wooden picks.

Serves 8

Louisiana is a center of abundance for shrimp, which accounts for over eighty-five percent of the state's fish production. While fresh shrimp can be found year-round in Louisiana, there are typically two shrimp seasons during the year. The spring season, in which mainly brown shrimp are harvested, lasts from mid-May to July. The fall season, which yields mostly white shrimp, lasts from August to December.

Make fancy butter curls by holding a butter curler under hot tap water for a few seconds, then pulling lightly over a stick of chilled butter. Before making additional curls, hold the curler under hot water. Chill the butter curls until serving time.

BARBECUED CHICKEN AND GRAPE SALAD

1 teaspoon onion powder
1 teaspoon paprika
1 teaspoon chili powder
1/2 teaspoon salt
1 pound boneless skinless chicken breasts
1 teaspoon olive oil
3/4 cup green grape halves

3/4 cup red grape halves
2/3 cup chopped celery
1/2 cup sliced red onion
1/4 cup low-fat mayonnaise
1 tablespoon red wine vinegar
1 tablespoon orange juice
1/4 teaspoon salt
1/4 cup chopped walnuts, toasted

Mix the onion powder, paprika, chili powder and 1/2 teaspoon salt in a small bowl. Sprinkle the paprika mixture over both sides of the chicken. Heat the olive oil in a cast-iron skillet over medium-high heat. Sauté the chicken in the hot oil for 2 minutes per side or until brown. Bake at 350 degrees for 10 minutes. Remove the chicken to a platter and chill. Cut into bite-size pieces.

Combine the grapes, celery, and onion in a bowl and mix well. Stir in the mayonnaise, vinegar, orange juice and 1/4 teaspoon salt. Add the chicken and mix well. Sprinkle with the walnuts. Chill, covered, until serving time.

Serves 8

HERBED CORN CRACKERS

Freshly baked homemade crackers make even a simple meal seem extra special. Roll the dough into one big sheet and bake. Break the baked sheet into large geometric shapes to pass at the table or use as a garnish to add height and drama to a salad.

2 cups cornmeal
2 cups flour
1/4 cup chopped fresh herbs of choice

1/2 cup shortening, chilled
2 egg whites, chilled
1 cup water
Kosher salt to taste

Mix the cornmeal, flour and herbs in a bowl. Add the shortening to the cornmeal mixture and mix well. Make a well in the center of the cornmeal mixture. Beat the egg whites with the water in a mixing bowl. Add the egg white mixture to the well and mix gently.

Knead the dough on a lightly floured surface until smooth. Roll 1/8 to 1/4 inch thick on the backs of baking sheets covered with baking parchment. Sprinkle with salt. Bake at 350 degrees for 20 minutes or until light brown. Cool for 5 minutes and break into geometric shapes.

Serves 8

ICEBOX LIME CHEESECAKE

Light and refreshing, this cheesecake, with its garnish of fresh limes, is also pretty and feminine. An ideal cake for Mother's Day, this can also be baked in a jelly roll pan and cut into squares.

Graham Cracker Crust

1 1/4 cups graham cracker crumbs
1/4 cup sugar
1/3 cup butter, melted

Lime Filling

1 envelope unflavored gelatin
2 to 4 tablespoons cold water
1/4 cup hot water
16 ounces cream cheese, softened
1 (14-ounce) can sweetened condensed milk
1 (6-ounce) can frozen limeade concentrate
2 cups whipping cream
1/4 cup confectioners' sugar, sifted
1 tablespoon vanilla extract

For the crust, combine the graham cracker crumbs, sugar and butter in a bowl and mix well. Press the crumb mixture over the bottom of a 9-inch springform pan. Bake at 350 degrees for 7 minutes. Let stand until cool.

For the filling, soften the gelatin in the cold water in a small bowl. Add the hot water and stir until the gelatin dissolves. Beat the gelatin mixture, cream cheese, condensed milk and limeade concentrate in a mixing bowl until smooth, scraping the bowl occasionally. Beat the whipping cream in a mixing bowl until soft peaks form. Add the confectioners' sugar and vanilla to the whipped cream and mix well. Fold the whipped cream mixture into the cream cheese mixture. Spoon the cream cheese mixture over the baked layer. Chill for 2 hours or longer.

Serves 6 to 8

In the South, iced tea is served year-round, whether the temperature outside is ninety-five degrees in the shade or freezing. Sweetened tea, fondly called "sweet tea," has sugar added before serving, while unsweetened lets each person decide whether and how much sweetener to add. Try this recipe for **Sweet Tea**. Pour one quart boiling water over three family-size or six regular-size tea bags in a heatproof pitcher. Steep for five minutes. Discard the tea bags. Stir in one cup sugar and add one quart tap water. Let stand until room temperature and pour the tea over ice in glasses. Garnish with lemon slices, lime slices, orange slices, and/or maraschino cherries.

CINCO DE MAYO

Cinco de Mayo, the fifth of May, marks the Mexican Army's victory over the French in 1862. This holiday has become popular recently and is now widely observed throughout the United States to celebrate the food, customs, music, and culture of Mexico.

12 Guests

PERFECT MARGARITAS

FRESH SALSA
(RRRIII page 20)

CHUNKY GUACAMOLE

TEX-MEX DEVILED EGGS

MARGARITA SEAFOOD SALAD

CHICKEN AND BLACK BEAN ENCHILADAS

MEXICAN FUDGE

PERFECT MARGARITAS

Our perfect margaritas are known as "top shelf." Using premium bottled lime juice makes it extra special.

>5 pints Roses lime juice
>3 to 4 pints Triple Sec
>2 pints tequila
>1 pint Cointreau
>Splash of Grand Marnier

Mix the lime juice, Triple Sec, tequila, Cointreau and Grand Marnier in a large pitcher. Pour over ice in margarita glasses.

Serves 4 to 6

CHUNKY GUACAMOLE

Pick avocados that are heavy but soft to the touch. Be creative and serve with assorted types of chips, such as black bean or sweet potato.

>1 pound ripe avocados, cut into quarters
>1/2 cup fresh cilantro, chopped
>1/2 cup chopped white onion
>1 serrano chile, minced
>2 teaspoons lime juice
>1 1/2 teaspoons kosher salt

Combine the avocados, cilantro, onion, serrano chile, lime juice and salt in a bowl and mash with a fork. Add water as needed for the desired consistency. Chill, covered, for 1 hour. Serve with assorted chips. Process the ingredients in a blender for a smoother consistency.

Makes 2 cups

For **Perfect Hard-Cooked Eggs,** place the desired amount of eggs with enough cold water to cover in a saucepan. Bring to a boil and remove from the heat. Let stand, covered, for 8 minutes; drain. Rinse the eggs under cold water until cool to the touch. The eggs will be cooked through without a trace of the blue sulfur color that results from overcooking.

TEX-MEX DEVILED EGGS

Serving a dish with eggs, or huevos, is a Mexican custom that is often overlooked at parties.

6 hard-cooked eggs
1 tablespoon minced green onion
1 small jalapeño chile, seeded and chopped
1/4 cup mayonnaise

1/4 cup (1 ounce) shredded Cheddar cheese
1 teaspoon prepared mustard
1/2 teaspoon salt
Chili powder to taste

Cut the eggs lengthwise into halves and remove the yolks, reserving the whites. Mash the yolks in a bowl. Stir in the green onion and jalapeño chile. Add the mayonnaise, cheese, prepared mustard and salt and mix well.

Mound the egg yolk mixture in the reserved egg whites and sprinkle with chili powder. Arrange the deviled eggs on a platter and chill, covered, until serving time.

Serves 6

MARGARITA SEAFOOD SALAD

Wow your guests by serving this salad in margarita glasses with salted rims. If you are familiar with the Spanish dish seviche, you will love this adaptation for its pungent lime flavor and appetizing texture.

Margarita Dressing
1/2 cup chopped purple onion
1/2 cup chopped green onions
1/2 cup chopped fresh parsley
1/4 cup chopped fresh cilantro
2 tablespoons grated lime zest
3/4 cup vegetable oil
1/2 cup tequila
1/3 cup fresh lime juice
2 teaspoons Creole seasoning

Salad
1 pound jumbo lump crab meat, drained and shells removed
1 pound boiled crawfish tails
1 pound deveined peeled boiled shrimp

For the dressing, mix the purple onion, green onions, parsley, cilantro and lime zest in a bowl. Add the oil, tequila, lime juice and Creole seasoning and whisk until mixed.

For the salad, mix the crab meat, crawfish tails and shrimp in a bowl. Add the dressing and toss to coat. Marinate, covered, in the refrigerator for 30 minutes. Taste and adjust the seasonings. Spoon the salad into 6 chilled margarita glasses.

Serves 6

CHICKEN AND BLACK BEAN ENCHILADAS

Whole wheat tortillas are relatively new on the market. The aroma and flavor are wonderful, and the texture is smoother than traditional corn tortillas.

6 cups chopped cooked chicken	Salt and pepper to taste
2 tablespoons minced garlic	2 bunches green onions, chopped
6 cups salsa	2 dozen whole wheat flour tortillas
2 (15-ounce) cans black beans	12 ounces reduced-fat Monterey
2 red bell peppers, chopped	Jack cheese, shredded
2 teaspoons cumin	

Sauté the chicken and garlic in a skillet sprayed with nonstick cooking spray for 3 minutes. Stir in the salsa, undrained beans, bell peppers, cumin, salt and pepper; reduce the heat. Simmer for 7 minutes or until thickened, stirring occasionally. Stir in the green onions.

Spoon 1/4 cup of the chicken mixture in the center of each tortilla and sprinkle with 1 tablespoon of the cheese. Roll to enclose the filling. Arrange seam side down in a 9×13-inch baking dish sprayed with nonstick cooking spray. Spoon the remaining chicken mixture evenly over the enchiladas and sprinkle with the remaining cheese. Bake at 350 degrees for 15 minutes or until the cheese melts.

Makes 12 enchiladas

MEXICAN FUDGE

Mexican Fudge is usually not chocolate. This caramel-flavored dessert literally melts in your mouth.

4 1/2 cups sugar	1/2 cup (1 stick) plus 2 tablespoons
1 (14-ounce) can sweetened	butter
condensed milk	4 cups chopped pecans
1/2 teaspoon salt	1 tablespoon vanilla extract
2/3 cup sugar	

Bring 4 1/2 cups sugar, condensed milk and salt to a boil in a saucepan over low heat, stirring occasionally. Boil for 3 minutes. Caramelize 2/3 cup sugar in a heavy skillet over medium-high heat, stirring constantly. Remove from the heat and gradually stir in the condensed milk mixture.

Return to the heat and continue cooking to 240 to 248 degrees on a candy thermometer, firm-ball stage. Add the butter just before removing from the heat. Beat until the mixture thickens and loses its luster. Stir in the pecans and vanilla and pour onto a buttered marble slab. Let stand until set. Cut into squares.

Serves 12

Every Mexican party needs a piñata. Surprise your guests with one that is just for the adults. Bring out the kid in everyone by stuffing the piñata with grown-up goodies, such as key chains, golf tees, and small packages of fine-quality chocolates, nuts, mints, or cookies.

WEDDING DAY JAZZ BRUNCH

One wonderful tradition of Southern weddings is a small brunch for the bridal party and out-of-town guests the day of or the day after the ceremony. Guests staying in hotels get a taste of home cooking and a relaxed visit with the bride, groom, and hostess. This elegant brunch menu features typical Louisiana cuisine.

16 to 20 Guests

ORANGE CHAMPAGNE COCKTAIL

BLOODY MARY ON A STICK

SMOKED OYSTER ROLL

CHICKEN GRILLADES OVER GRITS AND GREENS

SAUSAGE AND MUSHROOM STRUDEL

PECAN PIE MUFFINS

APPLE ROSEMARY CAKE

Optional Menu Item
BRUNCH CASSEROLE

Orange Champagne Cocktail

This festive drink is a cross between a mimosa and Bellini. For a nonalcoholic version, use sparkling apple cider or sparkling French lemonade.

2 quarts Champagne, chilled
2 quarts ginger ale, chilled
1 quart orange juice, chilled
2 pints fresh strawberries, sliced

Combine the Champagne, ginger ale and orange juice in a large pitcher and mix well. Pour into Champagne flutes and top each serving with some of the sliced strawberries.

Makes 15 (4-ounce) servings

Bloody Mary on a Stick

1 cup vodka, chilled
2 pounds cherry tomatoes
1 cup seasoned salt

Pour the vodka into a caviar server or chilled bowl. Arrange the tomatoes around the vodka and place the seasoned salt and wooden skewers in small bowls. Instruct your guests to spear a tomato, dip in the vodka and roll in the seasoned salt.

Serves a crowd

SMOKED OYSTER ROLL

This creamy spread has a smoky seafood flavor that goes nicely with brunch-type foods.

16 ounces cream cheese, softened
2 tablespoons mayonnaise
1 tablespoon Worcestershire sauce
1 tablespoon grated onion
1 teaspoon salt

1 teaspoon garlic salt
Hot sauce to taste
2 (4-ounce) cans smoked oysters, drained
1/2 cup dried chives

Line a 10×15-inch baking sheet with sides with waxed paper and spray lightly with nonstick cooking spray. Mix the cream cheese, mayonnaise, Worcestershire sauce, onion, salt, garlic salt and hot sauce in a bowl until blended. Spread the cream cheese mixture evenly on the prepared baking sheet. Chill until firm.

Mash the oysters in a bowl and spread over the chilled layer. Roll as for a jelly roll, discarding the waxed paper. Smooth the ends and chill, covered with plastic wrap, until firm. To serve, roll in the chives and arrange on a serving platter surrounded with assorted party crackers.

Serves 12 to 15

BRUNCH CASSEROLE

2 pounds Monterey Jack cheese, shredded
1 pound Cheddar cheese, shredded
8 ounces Pepper Jack cheese, shredded
2 (or more) packages thinly sliced ham, chopped
1 (4-ounce) can chopped green chiles, drained

1 (2-ounce) jar pimento, drained and chopped
10 eggs
3/4 cup milk
Salt and pepper to taste

Mix the Monterey Jack cheese, Cheddar cheese, Pepper Jack cheese, ham, green chiles and pimento in a bowl. Spread the cheese mixture evenly in a 9×13-inch or 11×14-inch baking dish. Whisk the eggs and milk in a bowl until fluffy and season with salt and pepper. Pour the egg mixture over the prepared layer. Bake at 350 degrees for 40 to 45 minutes or until brown. Let stand for 5 minutes before serving.

Serves 6 to 8

Chicken Grillades

Grillades is a hearty dish that can be served day or night, but somehow always ends up on a brunch menu. This is a lighter version of the traditional southern grillades prepared with round steak.

6 pounds boneless skinless chicken breasts, chopped
2/3 cup vegetable oil
Salt and pepper to taste
2/3 cup flour
2 onions, chopped
2 bell peppers, chopped

1 cup chopped celery
3 tablespoons chopped garlic
4 (10- to 15-ounce) cans tomatoes with green chiles
4 cups reduced-sodium chicken broth
1 tablespoon chopped fresh thyme

Brown the chicken in the oil in a large skillet. Remove the chicken to a bowl using a slotted spoon, reserving the pan drippings. Season the chicken with salt and pepper. Add the flour to the reserved pan drippings and mix well.

Cook over medium heat until brown and bubbly, stirring constantly. Stir in the onions, bell peppers, celery and garlic. Sauté for 3 to 5 minutes. Stir in the undrained tomatoes, broth and thyme. Add the chicken and simmer, covered, for 1 hour, stirring occasionally. Taste and adjust the seasonings. Serve over Grits and Greens.

Serves 12 to 16

Grits and Greens

6 cups water
2 teaspoons garlic
1 teaspoon pepper
1/2 teaspoon salt
1 1/2 cups grits

2 cups chopped mixed greens, such as mustard greens, turnip greens, collards, kale, chard and/or spinach
8 ounces cream cheese, cubed

Bring the water, garlic, pepper and salt to a boil in a saucepan over medium heat. Add the grits gradually, whisking constantly.

Cook for 20 minutes or until tender, stirring occasionally. Stir in the greens and cook for 10 minutes longer, stirring occasionally. Add the cream cheese to the grits mixture and cook until incorporated, stirring constantly. Serve immediately.

Serves 12

SAUSAGE AND MUSHROOM STRUDEL

This savory pastry takes the place of plain sausage or bacon for breakfast or brunch. The unbaked strudel may be frozen for future use.

2 pounds sweet Italian sausage, casings
   removed
2 pounds fresh mushrooms
1/4 cup minced shallots or green onions
6 tablespoons butter

2 tablespoons vegetable oil
16 ounces cream cheese, softened
Salt and freshly ground pepper to taste
8 sheets phyllo pastry
3/4 cup (1 1/2 sticks) butter, melted

Bake the sausage in a baking pan at 350 degrees until cooked through. Drain and crumble. Mince the mushrooms and squeeze dry using a tea towel. Sauté the mushrooms and shallots in a mixture of 6 tablespoons butter and oil in a skillet until the liquid evaporates. Remove from the heat. Blend in the sausage, cream cheese, salt and pepper. Divide the sausage mixture into 2 equal portions. Shape each portion into a 10-inch log.

Unroll the phyllo and cover with waxed paper topped with a damp towel to prevent it from drying out, removing 1 sheet at a time. Layer 4 sheets of the phyllo on a hard surface 1 sheet at a time, brushing each layer with some of the melted butter. Arrange 1 of the sausage logs on the narrow side of the pastry stack, leaving a 2-inch border. Fold in the sides and roll to enclose the filling. Brush the surface with some of the melted butter and arrange the roll on a buttered baking sheet. Repeat the process with the remaining phyllo, remaining sausage log and remaining melted butter. Bake at 400 degrees for 30 to 35 minutes or until golden brown. Serve with scrambled eggs and fresh fruit.

Serves 12 to 16

PECAN PIE MUFFINS

It is like biting into a pecan pie when you eat these muffins, a welcome change from the usual banana nut bread. A basket full of these warm muffins makes a wonderful gift for a friend.

1 cup packed brown sugar
1 cup chopped pecans
1/2 cup flour
2/3 cup butter, melted
2 eggs

Mix the brown sugar, pecans and flour in a bowl. Whisk the butter and eggs in a bowl until blended. Pour the butter mixture into the brown sugar mixture and stir just until moistened.

Fill greased or paper-lined miniature muffin cups 2/3 full. Bake at 350 degrees for 20 to 25 minutes or less. Serve warm.

Makes 2 to 2 1/2 dozen muffins

APPLE ROSEMARY CAKE

It is always nice to have a little something with fruit at a brunch.

1 1/2 cups flour
1 1/2 teaspoons baking powder
1/4 teaspoon salt
1 1/2 teaspoons minced fresh
  rosemary
1/2 cup packed brown sugar
3 tablespoons butter
1 tablespoon rum
2 or 3 apples, peeled and cut
  into quarters

3/4 cup sugar
6 tablespoons butter, softened
1 egg
1 egg yolk
3/4 teaspoon vanilla extract
2/3 cup milk
Sweetened whipped cream

Sift the flour, baking powder and salt into a bowl and mix well. Stir in the rosemary. Heat the brown sugar and 3 tablespoons butter in a saucepan over medium heat until the butter melts, stirring frequently. Remove from the heat and stir in the rum. Pour the rum mixture into a buttered 9-inch cake pan. Cut the apple quarters lengthwise into 1/4-inch slices and arrange the slices in a single layer in a decorative pattern over the prepared layer.

Beat the sugar and 6 tablespoons butter in a mixing bowl until light and fluffy. Add the egg, egg yolk and vanilla and beat until blended. Add the flour mixture alternately with the milk, beating just until combined after each addition. Pour the batter over the prepared layers and spread evenly. Bake at 375 degrees on the middle oven rack for 30 to 35 minutes or until the cake tests done. Cool in the pan on a wire rack for 5 minutes. Invert onto a cake platter. Serve warm with whipped cream.

Serves 6 to 8

Louisiana natives are born parade-lovers, and a second-line parade is very popular at both funerals and weddings. The folks in the procession are considered the first line, and the dancing spectators following the parade are the second line. A jazz trio leads the way for the bridal couple and attendants to strut their stuff, followed by dancing wedding guests brandishing decorated umbrellas and handkerchiefs, weaving their way through the party and encouraging others to join in.

I got a divorce, and my ex-husband had the nerve to take the River Road Recipes. *Please send an order form with prices and what books you have available now.*

—*Genie XXX, 1984, Norcross, Georgia*

In the Dining Room

*I*n certain parts of the country, dining rooms are used so rarely that some new homes are being built without them. But in the South, the dining room is still an essential part of the home. It's the one room in a house that is built solely for entertaining, a sort of showroom used most often for company or special occasions.

Since the dining room is designed for guests, much thought is put into its furnishings. It is usually the showplace for a family's cherished silver and crystal and is decorated to draw people in and make them want to linger. Even if the furnishings are less than grand and the table is a little scarred, every piece brings back memories of those who dined before. After all, what's on the table is not nearly as important as those gathered around it.

Menus

Tuscan Rehearsal Dinner

Sip and See

A Baton Rouge Thanksgiving

Graduation Dinner

Happy Birthday

Bridesmaids' Luncheon

Bloody Mary Brunch

New Year's Day Buffet

Before the Dance

Silver Anniversary Dinner

TUSCAN REHEARSAL DINNER

At-home wedding parties and rehearsal dinners are quite common in the South. With our strong sense of family, history, and tradition, it seems only natural to celebrate our most special rites of passage at home. Since weddings are often held in the summer, a Tuscan feast featuring summer's bounty is an easy choice.

8 Guests

BELLINI

GRILLED GARLIC FLATBREAD

ITALIAN PEPPERS

ITALIAN SHRIMP

TUSCAN MOZZARELLA SALAD

ZUPPA DI FAGIOLI

PASTA WITH PESTO

FRESH BERRY SORBET

BRACIUOLITINI

TIRAMISÙ

Bellini

An Italian favorite. Toast the bride and groom with this festive combination of Champagne and peach schnapps.

3 cups (about) crushed ice
2 cups chopped fresh or frozen peaches
2 cups Champagne

1¹/2 cups peach schnapps
1¹/2 cups sugar

Fill the blender ³/4 full with the ice. Add the peaches, Champagne, schnapps and sugar and process until smooth. Pour into glasses.

Serves 8

Grilled Garlic Flatbread

Prepare the dough balls in advance and store in the refrigerator for up to six hours before grilling. For an outdoor party, guests can have fun arranging the dough balls on the grill and watching them puff.

3¹/2 cups flour
2 envelopes dry yeast
1¹/2 cups warm water
1 tablespoon salt

1 tablespoon extra-virgin olive oil
¹/4 cup minced garlic
Extra-virgin olive oil to taste

Combine 1 tablespoon of the flour, yeast and warm water in a bowl and mix well. Let stand for 5 minutes. Mix the remaining flour and salt in a mixing bowl. Add the yeast mixture to the flour mixture and beat at low speed until blended. Add 1 tablespoon olive oil and beat until the dough begins to pull from the side of the bowl. Knead on a lightly floured surface until smooth and elastic. Shape into a ball and place in a greased bowl, turning to coat the surface.

Let rise, covered with a damp tea towel, for 45 minutes or until doubled in bulk. Punch the dough down and knead in the garlic. Shape the dough into softball-size balls.

Preheat the grill and coat the hot grill rack with additional olive oil. Stretch 1 dough ball into a pizza round and arrange on the hot grill rack. Grill for 2 minutes. Loosen the round with tongs and turn. Grill for 2 minutes longer or until light brown. Brush with additional olive oil and cut into wedges.

Serves 8

ITALIAN PEPPERS

Serve this colorful appetizer with crackers, or take it a step further and serve with the Grilled Garlic Flatbread on page 107. The "sweating" time in the paper or plastic bag allows the steam to condense, making the peppers' charred skin easier to remove.

6 yellow bell peppers
6 red bell peppers
1/2 teaspoon salt
1/2 cup extra-virgin olive oil
2 large garlic cloves, minced
6 anchovy fillets, minced

Line a baking sheet with foil, allowing enough overhang to form a rim. Arrange the bell peppers in a single layer on the foil. Broil until the skin is charred and blistered on all sides, turning frequently. Place the bell peppers in a brown paper bag immediately and seal tightly. Steam for 5 minutes. Peel and seed the peppers and cut into narrow strips. Sprinkle with the salt.

Heat the olive oil in a skillet over medium heat. Sauté the roasted peppers in the hot oil for 2 minutes. Stir in the garlic and anchovies and cook for 2 minutes or until heated through, stirring frequently. Serve immediately.

Serves 8

The "How Men Cook" section of RRRI was added because the committee decided that some of the most popular cooks in Baton Rouge were men and that any collection of representative recipes from the area had to include some recipes from them. Martha Bowlus, chairman of that section, soon discovered that while the male population may make up some of our greatest cooks, they seldom write down how they cook. The committee decided that rather than try to standardize the recipes to conform to the rest of the cookbook, they would leave the recipes in that section in their original language. What resulted is one of the best-loved and most unique sections of River Road Recipes. *All of the recipes make for a great read, even if the recipes aren't actually cooked.*

Italian Shrimp

This is really barbecued shrimp with Italian herbs, garlic, and olive oil. Typically in Louisiana, the shells are left on when preparing barbecued shrimp. In this recipe, the shrimp are peeled to make it neater to eat. Serve as an appetizer in a chafing dish with wooden picks or as a main course with a mixed green salad and crusty French bread.

1/2 cup (1 stick) butter
1/3 cup Worcestershire sauce
1 tablespoon olive oil
2 teaspoons rosemary
2 teaspoons crushed garlic
1 teaspoon black pepper

1 teaspoon thyme
1/2 to 1 teaspoon cayenne pepper
1/2 teaspoon salt
1/2 teaspoon celery salt
3 pounds medium shrimp, peeled and
   deveined

Heat the butter in a large skillet. Stir in the Worcestershire sauce, olive oil, rosemary, garlic, black pepper, thyme, cayenne pepper, salt and celery salt. Simmer for 8 to 10 minutes, stirring occasionally; do not boil. Remove from the heat. Let stand until cool.

Add the shrimp to the marinade and toss to coat. Spoon into a 4-quart baking dish. Marinate, covered, in the refrigerator for 4 to 10 hours, stirring occasionally. Bring the shrimp mixture to room temperature and bake at 400 degrees for 15 to 18 minutes or until the shrimp turn pink. Serve with wooden picks.

Serves 8

Tuscan Mozzarella Salad

The mild and milky flavor of fresh mozzarella cheese makes this salad extra special.

4 cups mixed salad greens
3 (14-ounce) cans artichoke hearts, drained and
   cut into halves
2 pints grape tomatoes
6 ounces fresh baby mozzarella cheese,
   cut into bite-size pieces
Coarsely ground salt and cracked pepper
3/4 cup extra-virgin olive oil
1/4 cup light balsamic vinegar
1/2 cup julienned fresh basil

Place 1/2 cup of the salad greens on each of 8 chilled salad plates. Arrange the artichoke hearts, tomatoes and cheese evenly over the salad greens and sprinkle with salt and pepper.

Whisk the olive oil and vinegar in a bowl and drizzle over the salads. Sprinkle evenly with the basil and serve immediately.

Serves 8

Zuppa di Fagioli

Zuppa di Fagioli is the Italian term for bean soup, and this mélange of beans and veggies is healthy and hearty. This is a simpler version of a classic Tuscan soup. Double the recipe and store in the freezer for unexpected company.

2 tablespoons olive oil
1/2 teaspoon chili powder
2 small red onions, chopped (about 11/4 cups)
2 or 3 carrots, sliced
1 rib celery with tops, chopped
1/4 cup chopped fresh parsley
3 garlic cloves, minced
2/3 cup dry red wine
1 (14-ounce) can cannellini beans, drained
1 (14-ounce) can diced tomatoes
2 cups homemade chicken stock
1 to 2 cups fresh spinach leaves
Salt and pepper to taste

Heat the olive oil and chili powder in a heavy 5-quart stockpot over medium heat. Sauté the onions, carrots, celery and parsley in the hot oil until the vegetables are tender-crisp. Stir in the garlic. Cook for 3 to 5 minutes longer, stirring frequently. Increase the heat and stir in the wine. Cook until the liquid evaporates, stirring frequently. This entire process should take approximately 30 minutes.

Mash 1/3 of the beans in a bowl with a fork. Add the mashed beans, remaining beans, undrained tomatoes and stock to the stockpot and mix well. Simmer for 45 minutes, stirring occasionally. Toss the spinach on top of the soup; do not stir. Simmer, covered, for 5 minutes longer and stir. Season with salt and pepper. Ladle into heated soup bowls. Garnish with ciabatta croutons, a drizzle of olive oil, snipped fresh basil, freshly grated Parmesan cheese and chopped red onion. Serve immediately.

Makes 8 cups

PASTA WITH PESTO

Freeze pesto in ice cube trays for future use in all types of recipes. Add chopped cooked chicken or steamed shrimp for a hearty entrée.

2 cups fresh basil leaves
4 garlic cloves, chopped
1 cup pine nuts, walnuts or pecans, toasted
3/4 cup good-quality olive oil
1/2 cup (2 ounces) freshly grated Parmesan cheese
1/2 cup (2 ounces) freshly grated Romano cheese
Salt and freshly ground pepper to taste
1 pound hot cooked pasta

Process the basil, garlic and pine nuts in a food processor fitted with a steel blade or in batches in a blender until finely chopped. Add the olive oil gradually, processing constantly until incorporated. Add the Parmesan cheese, Romano cheese, salt and a generous grinding of pepper and process just until combined. Spoon approximately 1/2 to 3/4 cup of the pesto over the hot cooked pasta on a serving platter. Store the leftovers, covered, in the refrigerator.

Makes 2 cups

FRESH BERRY SORBET

In Italy, this course is called "sorbetto."

2/3 cup sugar
2/3 cup water
2 pints fresh strawberries
1 pint fresh blueberries
1 pint fresh raspberries or blackberries
1 tablespoon grated lemon zest
1/2 cup framboise

Combine the sugar and water in a medium saucepan. Cook over low heat until the sugar dissolves, stirring occasionally.

Process the strawberries, blueberries and raspberries in a food processor until puréed. Strain the berry mixture through a sieve into a bowl, discarding the seeds. Stir the syrup, lemon zest and brandy into the berry purée. Pour the berry mixture into an ice cream freezer container and freeze using the manufacturer's directions. Store in the freezer.

Serves 8

A formal Italian dinner is usually served in courses. The first course is the antipasto course, followed by the soup course, pasta course, sorbetto course, and finally the entrée. The meal ends with a cheese plate and dessert.

BRACIUOLITINI (VEAL ROLLS)

This recipe is a streamlined method for making Brocioluni, an Italian veal dish that is very labor intensive and normally takes days to prepare.

20 (3-ounce) veal scaloppine or thinly
  pounded veal
1 cup (2 sticks) butter, melted
2 cups Italian-seasoned bread crumbs
10 (1/2-inch) slices salami, cut into
  rectangles
10 (1/2-inch) slices cooked ham,
  cut into rectangles

20 slices mozzarella cheese
6 hard-cooked eggs, each cut into
  8 wedges
2 cups (8 ounces) grated Romano cheese
  or Parmesan cheese
2 onions, cut into wedges
10 to 15 bay leaves
Fresh lemon juice to taste

Cut the scaloppine into uniform 3×4-inch slices. Dip in the butter and coat with the bread crumbs. Layer each scaloppine with 1 salami slice, 1 ham slice, 1 mozzarella cheese slice and 1 egg wedge. Reserve the remaining egg wedges for another recipe. Sprinkle with the Romano cheese and roll to enclose the filling. Secure with wooden picks.

Thread the veal rolls, onion wedges and bay leaves alternately onto wooden skewers, arranging 2 to 4 veal rolls per skewer depending on the size of the skewer. Arrange the skewers in a single layer in a baking pan. Bake at 325 to 350 degrees for 20 to 30 minutes or until the scaloppine is cooked through and brown, turning halfway through the baking process. Discard the bay leaves and drizzle with lemon juice. Serve immediately. Serve with hot cooked pasta and red sauce. You may omit the skewers and arrange the veal rolls in a baking pan. Top with the bay leaves and onion wedges. Bake as directed above.

Serves 4 to 5

TIRAMISÙ (TUSCAN TRIFLE)

1 quart whipping cream
1/16 teaspoon salt
Sugar to taste
8 ounces mascarpone cheese
1 (14-ounce) package ladyfingers

Strong brewed coffee to taste
Kahlúa to taste
Baking cocoa to taste
Chocolate syrup to taste

Beat the whipping cream and salt in a mixing bowl until soft peaks form. Add sugar and mix well. Beat the cheese into the whipped cream until blended.

Dip the ladyfingers quickly in a mixture of the coffee and liqueur; do not soak. Layer 1/2 of the ladyfingers and 1/2 of the whipped cream mixture in a 9×13-inch dish and sprinkle with baking cocoa. Repeat the process with the remaining ladyfingers, remaining whipped cream mixture and baking cocoa. Chill, covered, until serving time. Drizzle chocolate syrup on a dessert plate and top with a slice of tiramisù. Garnish each serving with mint leaves and fresh strawberries.

Serves 8

SIP AND SEE

*One of the biggest pleasures a new baby brings is the
joy of sharing this new life with those who are near and dear.
A "sip and see" is a southern "debut" for the baby,
usually given by one or both of the grandmothers, proud to
introduce friends to the newest angel.*

12 Guests

GREEN TEA SPRITZER

ROSY CHEEK WINE SLUSH

SPINACH SALAD SANDWICHES

DILL SHRIMP SALAD SANDWICHES

STRAWBERRY BREAD

ROSE WATER CREAM WITH FRESH FRUIT

PETITS FOURS

SAND TARTS
(RRRI page 198)

Instead of serving from the usual punch bowl, look around the house for a fun, innovative alternative. A large colored glass salad bowl, old-fashioned candy jar, extra large trifle bowl, or silver Revere bowl would all look pretty filled with punch. Float lady apples for an autumnal garnish, or lemon slices for a summery look. Ice down soft drinks, bottled water, or kid's juice boxes in a new baby bathtub that can be given to the new mother or kept as a spare for grandmother's house.

Green Tea Spritzer

The consumption of green tea has been an important part of Japanese culture for thousands of years. Its popularity has spread to the United States, where it is also valued for its purported medicinal benefits.

> 4 cups water
> 4 green tea with lemon tea bags
> 1/3 cup honey
> 4 cups ginger ale
> 2 lemons, sliced
> Sprigs of fresh mint

Bring the water to a simmer in a saucepan; do not boil. Remove from the heat and add the tea bags. Let steep for 5 to 7 minutes; discard the tea bags. Stir in the honey and let stand until cool.

Combine the sweetened green tea and ginger ale in a large pitcher and mix well. Add the lemon slices. Pour over ice in glasses and garnish with fresh mint.

Serves 12

Rosy Cheek Wine Slush

A potent punch that may be served at an afternoon party or evening soiree.

> 3 cups frozen pink lemonade concentrate
> 9 cups rosé

Combine the lemonade concentrate and wine in a freezer container and mix well. Freeze for 1 hour or until slushy. Spoon into glasses.

Serves 12 to 14

Spinach Salad Sandwiches

Ingredients normally found in a spinach salad are combined to make this green party sandwich spread.

 1 (10-ounce) package frozen chopped spinach, thawed and drained
 1/2 cup crumbled crisp-cooked bacon
 1/4 cup (about) sour cream
 3 tablespoons (about) mayonnaise
 2 tablespoons chopped green onions
 1 hard-cooked egg, finely chopped
 1/2 teaspoon Creole seasoning
 1/8 teaspoon hot sauce
 1 loaf pumpernickel bread

Press the excess moisture from the spinach. Mix the spinach, bacon, sour cream, mayonnaise, green onions, egg, Creole seasoning and hot sauce in a bowl, adding additional sour cream and/or mayonnaise for the desired consistency.

Spread the spinach mixture over 1/2 of the bread slices and top with the remaining bread slices. Trim the crusts and cut the sandwiches into quarters.

Serves 12

Dill Shrimp Salad Sandwiches

Fancy petite sandwiches made with spicy boiled shrimp.

 3 pounds peeled cooked seasoned shrimp
 1/2 cup chopped celery
 1/2 cup chopped green onions
 2 tablespoons lemon juice
 2 tablespoons lime juice
 1 tablespoon chopped fresh dill weed
 1 cup mayonnaise
 1 loaf sourdough bread, sliced

Combine the shrimp, celery, green onions, lemon juice, lime juice and dill weed in a food processor. Pulse until finely chopped. Spoon the shrimp mixture into a stainless steel bowl and fold in the mayonnaise. Chill, covered, until serving time.

Spread the shrimp mixture on 1/2 of the bread slices and top with the remaining bread slices; trim the crusts. Cut as desired. Serve immediately.

Serves 12

To make perfect finger sandwiches, spread the filling on the bread all the way to the edge of the crusts. Stack four sandwiches together and trim the crusts, preferably using an electric knife, being careful not to mash the bread. It is acceptable to use slightly stale bread that is less likely to crush and is easier to slice.

Strawberries may be frozen with or without sugar, although the texture and flavor is usually better when sugar is added. Do not add sugar to berries that will be used to make preserves or jams. If freezing with sugar, rinse the berries, remove the caps and slice if desired. Place four to five cups of the berries in a large bowl. In another bowl, place one-half to three-fourths cup sugar. If desired, one teaspoon ascorbic acid mixture may be added to the sugar to help the strawberries retain their bright red color. Sprinkle the sugar over the berries and gently mix until coated. Let stand for about ten minutes to allow the berries to make juice. Pour the berries and juice into freezer bags or containers, leaving a one-half-inch headspace. If freezing without sugar, rinse the berries and remove the caps. Place the whole berries in a single layer on a baking sheet and cover loosely with plastic wrap or waxed paper and freeze just until firm. Pack the frozen berries in freezer bags or containers.

STRAWBERRY BREAD

A sweet quick bread, great for a breakfast buffet or to keep on hand for a snack. A gift of strawberry bread is always welcome.

Creamy Strawberry Spread
1 (20-ounce) package frozen strawberries, thawed
8 ounces cream cheese, softened

Bread
3 cups flour
2 cups sugar
1 tablespoon cinnamon
1 teaspoon baking soda
1 teaspoon salt
1 1/4 cups vegetable oil
4 eggs, lightly beaten

For the spread, drain the strawberries, reserving the juice and strawberries. Process the reserved juice and cream cheese in a food processor until creamy. Store, covered, in the refrigerator until serving time.

For the bread, mix the flour, sugar, cinnamon, baking soda and salt in a bowl. Make a well in the center of the flour mixture. Add the reserved strawberries, oil and eggs to the well and stir until combined.

Spoon the batter into two 4×8-inch loaf pans sprayed with nonstick cooking spray. Bake at 350 degrees for 1 hour or until the loaves test done. Cool in the pans for 10 minutes. Invert onto a wire rack to cool completely. Slice and serve with the spread.

Makes 2 loaves

ROSE WATER CREAM WITH FRESH FRUIT

Rose water, found at most specialty gourmet shops, is a flavoring made up of a distillation of rose petals. This essence of rose flavoring is popular in Middle Eastern and European cooking and adds a sweet floral flavor to the whipped cream.

8 ounces cream cheese, softened
3/4 cup heavy cream
1/4 cup confectioners' sugar

2 teaspoons rose water
2 drops of red food coloring
Assorted fresh fruit

Combine the cream cheese, heavy cream and confectioners' sugar in a mixing bowl. Beat at medium speed until light and fluffy, scraping the bowl occasionally. Fold the rose water and food coloring into the cream cheese mixture. Chill, covered, until serving time. Serve with fresh fruit.

Serves 12

PETITS FOURS

Petits Fours are a well-loved pick-up dessert that originated in Louisiana. These tiny iced cakes may be decorated to suit any occasion, such as a baby shower, wedding, or tea party.

Petits Fours
1 teaspoon baking soda
1 cup buttermilk
1 cup (2 sticks) unsalted butter,
  softened
1 1/2 cups sugar
4 egg yolks
1 tablespoon vanilla extract
2 1/2 cups flour
4 egg whites

Confectioners' Sugar Icing
2 cups sifted confectioners' sugar
1/4 cup warm water
1 tablespoon light corn syrup

For the petits fours, dissolve the baking soda in the buttermilk. Beat the butter and sugar in a mixing bowl until creamy, scraping the bowl occasionally. Add the egg yolks 1 at a time, beating well after each addition. Beat in the vanilla. Add the buttermilk mixture alternately with the flour, beating well after each addition. Beat the egg whites in a mixing bowl until soft peaks form and fold into the batter.

Spoon the batter into a greased and floured 9×13-inch cake pan. Bake at 350 degrees for 20 to 25 minutes or until the cake tests done. Cool in the pan on a wire rack. Remove the cake to a wire rack.

For the icing, mix all the ingredients in a bowl. Pour the icing over the top of the cake. Chill for 20 minutes. Cut into small squares using a knife dipped in hot water.

Serves 12 to 14

Have a question about types of flour? Refer to this short glossary for some of those answers. All-purpose flour is a combination of hard winter wheat and soft spring wheat and is useful in everything from baking to thickening. Self-rising flour is all-purpose flour or, in some cases, a soft spring wheat blend that also has salt and baking powder added for convenience. Recipes that call for self-rising flour generally do not call for baking powder, but many call for baking soda. Unbleached flour is similar to all-purpose flour except that it has not been bleached white. Instead, it retains the original creamy color of the wheat grains. Cake flour is a special flour that is taken from the first, finest sifting of the freshly ground flour. It produces a light-textured cake. Bread flour is ground from special high-gluten strains of wheat to produce bread with fine body and springy texture.

A BATON ROUGE THANKSGIVING

*Family traditions are a cherished part of Thanksgiving everywhere.
Whether your family has served the same dishes for years or tries something new
each year, Thanksgiving is a culinary feast everyone remembers. In
Baton Rouge, the temperature outside can vary between "sweater weather" or
"shorts weather," but the feeling around the table is always warm and cozy.*

12 or more Guests

TOMATO JUICE COCKTAIL

CRANBERRY COMPOTE

ROAST TURKEY WITH BOURBON GRAVY

NEW ORLEANS-STYLE OYSTER AND
FRENCH BREAD DRESSING

DOWN HOME DRESSING

CORN PUDDING

SMOTHERED GREEN BEANS

SWEET POTATO BAKE

SPINACH MADELINE
(RRRIII page 114)

REFRIGERATOR ROLLS

AMBROSIA

PUMPKIN PANNA COTTA

PECAN PIE

TOMATO JUICE COCKTAIL

Instead of loading up on appetizers, try serving a tomato-based drink to your guests to stop those hunger pangs until the time comes to sit down for the big meal.

2 (46-ounce) cans tomato juice, chilled
1/2 cup fresh lemon juice
1/4 cup finely chopped celery
2 tablespoons grated onion
4 teaspoons Worcestershire sauce
2 teaspoons sugar
1 1/2 teaspoons prepared horseradish
12 lemon wedges

Combine the tomato juice, lemon juice, celery, onion, Worcestershire sauce, sugar and prepared horseradish in a large container and mix well. Chill, covered, for 2 hours or longer before serving. Strain, if desired, and pour over ice in glasses. Garnish each serving with a lemon wedge.

Serves 12

CRANBERRY COMPOTE

Turkey would not be the same without the cranberry sauce. Make sure that you prepare enough to go with the leftover turkey.

2 1/2 cups cranberry juice
1 (6-ounce) package dried cranberries
1/4 cup sugar
3/4 cup crème de cassis

Combine the juice, cranberries and sugar in a medium saucepan and mix well. Bring to a boil and stir in the liqueur. Reduce the heat. Simmer for 20 minutes, stirring occasionally. Remove from the heat and let stand until cool. For variety, spoon the compote over sliced fresh pineapple.

Serves 12

Roast Turkey with Bourbon Gravy

No matter what state you hail from, turkey is a seasonal necessity, and always the centerpiece of every Thanksgiving celebration. A touch of southern bourbon makes a rich gravy that pairs well with the apple flavor from the turkey.

1 (17-pound) turkey
1 onion, chopped
2 ribs celery, chopped
2 Granny Smith apples, chopped
1 tablespoon poultry seasoning
2 tablespoons salt
2 tablespoons pepper
3 cups water
1/2 cup flour
1/4 cup bourbon

Place the oven rack in the bottom 2/3 of the oven. Remove the neck and giblet bag from the turkey, discarding the liver. Rinse the turkey with cool water and pat dry.

Combine the onion, celery, apples and poultry seasoning in a bowl and mix well. Stuff the turkey with the apple mixture. Rub the salt and pepper over the outer surface of the turkey.

Arrange the turkey, neck and giblets in a roasting pan. Roast at 350 degrees for 2 hours in a convection oven or 4 hours in a conventional oven or until a meat thermometer registers 180 degrees. Remove the turkey to a platter, reserving the pan drippings. Add the water to the reserved warm drippings and stir to loosen any crusty browned bits. Pour into a saucepan and bring to a simmer.

Mix the flour and bourbon in a bowl and whisk into the pan drippings mixture. Cook over medium-high heat for 10 minutes or until thickened and of a gravy consistency, stirring frequently. Serve with the turkey.

Serves 12

New Orleans-Style Oyster and French Bread Dressing

It is not uncommon to find more than one type of dressing on a Baton Rouge holiday table. Oyster, ground meat, sausage, and mirliton are other popular varieties of dressing.

2 large loaves stale French bread, cubed
1 quart fresh oysters
1 bunch parsley, trimmed and chopped
2 bunches green onions, chopped
1 large bell pepper, chopped
1 large onion, chopped

4 ribs celery, chopped
3 garlic cloves, chopped
1 tablespoon (heaping) bacon drippings
1 cup (2 sticks) butter
1/8 to 1/4 teaspoon thyme
Salt and red pepper to taste

Dry the bread cubes on a baking sheet at 200 degrees. Drain the oysters, reserving the liquor and discarding any shells. Cut large oysters into halves if desired. Soak the bread cubes in the reserved oyster liquor in a bowl.

Sauté the parsley, green onions, bell pepper, onion, celery and garlic in a mixture of the bacon drippings and 1/2 cup of the butter in a large skillet until the vegetables are tender. Combine the sautéed vegetables, bread cubes, remaining 1/2 cup butter, oysters, thyme, salt and red pepper in a bowl and mix well. Spoon the dressing into a baking dish. Bake at 350 degrees until brown and bubbly.

Serves 10 to 12

Down Home Dressing

A dressing containing some combination of ground meat and sausage is a southern holiday staple.

1 pound ground pork
1 pound ground beef
1 pound bulk pork sausage
1 onion, chopped
2 bunches green onions, chopped
1 bunch parsley, trimmed and chopped

4 ribs celery, chopped
3 tablespoons olive oil
3 cups herb-seasoned bread crumbs
1 egg, lightly beaten
1 envelope onion soup mix, prepared and
   cooled

Brown the ground pork, ground beef and sausage in a skillet, stirring until crumbly; drain. Sauté the onion, green onions, parsley and celery in the olive oil in a large skillet until tender.

Combine the ground pork mixture, sautéed onion mixture, bread crumbs, egg and soup in a large bowl and mix well. Spoon into a baking dish or stuff the dressing into a turkey. Bake at 350 degrees for 45 minutes. For variety, add dried cranberries and/or chopped walnuts to the dressing.

Serves 12

CORN PUDDING

Individual molds of corn pudding look elegant on the table.

3/4 cup heavy cream
3/4 cup milk
2/3 cup unsalted butter, melted and cooled
1 1/2 tablespoons sugar
3/4 teaspoon salt
1/4 teaspoon freshly ground pepper
5 eggs, lightly beaten
3 cups fresh or frozen corn

Coat the bottoms and sides of twelve 1/2-cup ramekins with butter. Whisk the heavy cream, milk, 2/3 cup butter, sugar, salt, pepper and eggs in a bowl until blended. Stir in the corn. Divide the corn mixture evenly between the prepared ramekins.

Arrange the ramekins in a baking pan just large enough to hold them. Add enough hot water to the baking pan to reach halfway up the sides of the ramekins. Bake at 350 degrees for 50 minutes or until the tops are slightly puffed, golden brown and firm to the touch. Remove the ramekins to a wire rack and let stand for 5 minutes. Run a sharp knife around the edges of the ramekins and invert the puddings onto individual dinner plates. Serve immediately.

Serves 8

When picking fresh corn at the market, look for tightly wrapped, vivid green husks with shiny, moist-looking silk. Peel back the husk just a tad and peek in to make sure that the rows are full. It is not necessary to peel the husk all the way down. Husks should be left on until just before cooking. To remove the corn from the ear, stand the husked ears on one end inside a large baking pan and use a sharp knife to slice down, cutting close to the cob. It is best to cook corn quickly at high heat. Corn that is cooked too long loses its sweetness.

In 1975, Ladies' Home Journal *magazine chose RRR to be featured in their series on community cookbooks. We selected three typical Baton Rouge homes for the photography sessions. At the first home, one of the dishes to be photographed was Crab Meat Mornay. However, so much of it had been snitched by the time they were ready to shoot that there wasn't enough to fill the chafing dish. The managing editor and photographer from the* Journal *simply filled the bottom of the chafing dish with crumpled foil and mounded the Crab Meat Mornay on top. It looked gorgeous.*

At another home, the photographer wanted to shoot under a large oak tree, but the camellia bushes under the tree had only a few flowers on them. Across the yard, in a sunnier location, were camellia bushes loaded with flowers. The committee was instructed to cut camellias off those bushes and wire them onto the bushes that would be in the picture. If you look at the photograph that appeared in the Journal, *you will see some lovely but unusual camellia bushes with several different varieties of camellias "growing" on them!*

—*Mary Lilley McNamara, Chairman 1975*

SMOTHERED GREEN BEANS

These are green beans prepared the old-fashioned way, cooked down with onions and bacon until very tender and flavorful.

> 3 tablespoons chopped bacon
> 2 small onions, chopped
> 2 pounds fresh green beans, trimmed and snapped
> Salt and pepper to taste

Sauté the bacon in a large heavy saucepan until brown and crisp. Remove the bacon to a bowl using a slotted spoon, reserving the pan drippings. Sauté the onions in the reserved pan drippings until tender. Add the green beans and enough water to cover to the saucepan. Season with salt and pepper. Bring to a boil; reduce the heat.

Simmer until the beans are tender or the desired degree of crispness, stirring occasionally. Spoon into a serving bowl and sprinkle with the bacon.

Serves 12

SWEET POTATO BAKE

A classic Thanksgiving side dish, especially in Louisiana, where huge sacks of locally grown sweet potatoes or yams are often given to friends and family during the holidays. Prepare without the topping one day in advance and store, covered, in the refrigerator. Sprinkle with the pecan topping just before baking.

Sweet Potatoes
10 sweet potatoes or yams, chopped
6 tablespoons butter
1/2 cup sugar
3 eggs
1 1/2 teaspoons vanilla extract
1 or 2 drops of milk

Pecan Topping
1 cup packed brown sugar
1/2 cup flour
1/3 cup butter, melted
1 cup chopped pecans

For the potatoes, cook the sweet potatoes in enough water to cover in a saucepan until tender; drain. Beat the sweet potatoes in a mixing bowl until smooth. Add the butter and sugar and beat until blended. Add the eggs, vanilla and milk and beat until smooth. Spoon into a baking dish sprayed with nonstick cooking spray.

For the topping, combine the brown sugar, flour and butter in a bowl and mix until crumbly. Stir in the pecans and spoon over the prepared layer. Bake at 350 degrees for 25 to 30 minutes or until brown and bubbly.

Serves 12

When making homemade bread, lightly flour the work surface before rolling out the dough. Once you find a brand of flour that works with a particular recipe, note that brand on the recipe. Different brands can give unpredictable results and may not work as well. Bread making is a process that should not be rushed. Bake at the proper time indicated and allow enough time to rise and bake.

REFRIGERATOR ROLLS

This basic recipe may also be used to make cinnamon rolls. Pat the dough into a rectangle, drizzle with melted butter, and sprinkle with cinnamon and sugar. Roll as for a jelly roll, cut into one-half-inch slices, and bake until light brown. Makes a good pizza crust too.

6 cups flour	1 cup sugar
1 tablespoon salt	1 cup boiling water
2 envelopes dry yeast	2 eggs
1 cup warm water	Melted butter to taste
1 cup shortening	

Sift the flour and salt together. Sprinkle the yeast over the warm water in a small bowl. Let stand for 5 minutes. Beat the shortening and sugar in a mixing bowl until creamy. Add the boiling water and beat until blended. Beat the eggs in a bowl until thickened and add to the creamed mixture. Beat until smooth. Add the yeast mixture to the lukewarm egg mixture and mix well. Beat in the flour mixture and chill, covered, in the refrigerator for 8 hours or for up to 1 week.

Roll the dough 1/2 inch thick on a lightly floured surface and cut into rounds with a biscuit cutter. Brush the rounds with melted butter and fold over, pinching the edges to seal. Arrange in lightly greased baking pans and brush with melted butter. Let rise for 2 to 3 hours or until doubled in bulk. Bake at 375 degrees for 10 minutes or until light brown. Serve immediately.

Makes 3 dozen rolls

AMBROSIA

According to Greek mythology, ambrosia means "immortality" and is referred to as food of the gods. Ambrosia is an old southern favorite that completes a holiday menu.

12 large oranges	1/2 cup sugar
6 Ruby Red grapefruit	2 tablespoons maraschino cherry
3/4 cup flaked coconut	juice
1/2 cup drained maraschino cherries	

Peel the oranges and grapefruit and remove the membranes; separate into sections. Combine the orange sections, grapefruit sections, coconut, cherries, sugar and cherry juice in a bowl and toss gently. Chill, covered, for 8 to 10 hours before serving.

Serves 10 to 12

Pumpkin Panna Cotta

Panna Cotta is a cooked cream custard that is very light and served cold. Serve with the Ambrosia on page 124 or any fresh fruit for a new twist on the traditional pumpkin pie.

2 envelopes unflavored gelatin	1 cup sugar
3 cups milk	1/2 teaspoon cinnamon
2 cups heavy cream	1/4 teaspoon salt
2 cups pumpkin purée	Whipped cream (optional)

Sprinkle the gelatin over 1/2 cup of the milk in a 2-quart saucepan. Let stand for 5 minutes. Combine the remaining 2 1/2 cups milk, heavy cream, pumpkin purée, sugar, cinnamon and salt in a blender and process until smooth.

Cook the gelatin mixture over low heat until the gelatin dissolves, stirring occasionally. Add the pumpkin mixture and mix well. Increase the heat to medium and cook until the steam rises, stirring occasionally. Pour the custard into individual dessert bowls. Chill for 2 to 3 hours or until set. Top each serving with a dollop of whipped cream.

Serves 6 to 8

Pecan Pie

A holiday must. Serve with whipped cream on the side.

6 eggs	2 teaspoons vanilla extract
2 cups dark corn syrup	1/4 teaspoon salt
1 cup sugar	1 1/2 cups pecan pieces
1 cup packed dark brown sugar	2 unbaked (9-inch) pie shells
1/4 cup (1/2 stick) butter, melted	

Whisk the eggs lightly in a bowl. Stir in the corn syrup, sugar, brown sugar, butter, vanilla and salt. Fold in the pecans. Spoon the pecan mixture evenly into the pie shells. Bake at 350 degrees for 1 hour. Remove the pies to a wire rack to cool.

Serves 12 to 16

GRADUATION DINNER

After years of homework hassles, test stress, and parent-teacher conferences, the big day has finally arrived. Show the graduate how proud you are with a special dinner. Invite all the friends and relatives who helped your graduate attain this milestone.

8 Guests

SALAD WITH DRESSING-IN-A-JAR
(RRRII page 38)

SEAFOOD LASAGNA

ROASTED ASPARAGUS

RED VELVET CAKE

Optional Menu Item
VEAL SCALOPPINE

SEAFOOD LASAGNA

A divinely delicious dish that can be prepared in advance and frozen.

6 lasagna noodles
1 cup chopped onion
1 cup sliced mushrooms
1/4 cup (1/2 stick) butter or margarine
8 ounces cream cheese, cubed and softened
1 1/2 cups cottage cheese
1/2 cup (2 ounces) grated Parmesan cheese
1 egg, beaten
1 tablespoon parsley flakes
2 teaspoons basil
Salt and pepper to taste
1 (10-ounce) can cream of mushroom soup
1/3 cup dry white wine
1 pound deveined peeled boiled shrimp
1 pound lump crab meat, drained and shells removed
1 cup (4 ounces) shredded mozzarella cheese

Cook the noodles using the package directions; drain. Sauté the onion and mushrooms in the butter in a large skillet until tender. Remove from the heat. Add the cream cheese and mix well. Stir in the cottage cheese, Parmesan cheese, egg, parsley flakes, basil, salt and pepper. Combine the soup and wine in a bowl and mix well. Fold the shrimp and crab meat into the soup mixture.

Layer the noodles, cream cheese mixture and shrimp mixture 1/2 at a time in a greased 9×13-inch baking dish and sprinkle with the mozzarella cheese. Bake at 350 degrees for 45 minutes.

Serves 8

When decorating for a graduation party, line the driveway or walkway with balloons in the graduate's high school colors or pennants from their chosen college or university. Incorporate hobbies, sports, or interests into the decorating theme. Soccer balls, ballet shoes, musical notes, and the like are good ideas, or just pictures of the guest of honor through the years. Create a keepsake by setting up a guest book at the front door for guests to write out a prediction for the honoree's future. Another fun idea is to make autograph shirts by providing all the graduate's friends with plain tee shirts and permanent markers.

Veal Scaloppine

A very easy and scrumptious dish that also looks impressive. The white lemony sauce makes the veal outstanding.

1 cup (4 ounces) grated Parmesan cheese
1/2 cup flour
2 teaspoons salt
1/4 teaspoon pepper
3 pounds veal scaloppine, cut into
   3-inch strips
2 tablespoons olive oil

2 garlic cloves, minced
1 cup dry white wine
1 cup beef stock or beef bouillon
2 tablespoons lemon juice
Capers to taste
Chopped fresh parsley to taste

Mix the cheese, flour, salt and pepper in a shallow dish. Coat the veal with the flour mixture, shaking off the excess. Pound the flour coating into the veal with a potato masher or the edge of a plate.

Heat the olive oil and garlic in a skillet. Brown the veal lightly on both sides in the hot oil mixture; discard the garlic. Stir in the wine, stock and lemon juice. Simmer, covered, for 20 minutes, stirring occasionally. Stir in capers.

Simmer for 10 minutes longer, stirring occasionally. Sprinkle with parsley just before serving. Serve with hot cooked angel hair pasta mixed with minced garlic, olive oil and pepper along with steamed asparagus or sugar snap peas drizzled with lemon butter.

Serves 8

Roasted Asparagus

Sometimes the simplest pleasures in life are also the most enjoyable. What could be simpler than tender asparagus, roasted to perfection?

2 bunches asparagus
1/3 cup olive oil
2 teaspoons kosher salt

Snap off the woody ends of the asparagus spears and arrange in a single layer on a baking sheet. Brush the spears with the olive oil and sprinkle with the salt.

Broil until tender but firm. The cooking time will vary depending on the size of the spears. Small spears take approximately 3 to 5 minutes, while thicker spears take approximately 5 to 7 minutes.

Serves 8

RED VELVET CAKE

Cake

1 (2-layer) package butter-recipe
   cake mix
1 teaspoon baking cocoa
1 cup buttermilk
1/2 cup (1 stick) margarine, melted
3 eggs
1 teaspoon vanilla extract
1 bottle red food coloring
1 teaspoon baking soda
1 teaspoon vinegar

Velvet Frosting

1 1/2 cups milk
4 1/2 tablespoons flour
1 1/2 cups sugar
1 1/2 cups (3 sticks) margarine
1 1/2 teaspoons vanilla extract

For the cake, combine the cake mix and baking cocoa in a mixing bowl and stir until mixed. Add the buttermilk, margarine, eggs, vanilla and food coloring and beat until moistened. Add a mixture of the baking soda and vinegar and beat at medium speed for 4 minutes, scraping the bowl occasionally. Pour the batter into 2 greased and floured cake pans. Bake at 375 degrees for 25 to 30 minutes or until the layers test done. Cool in the pans for 10 minutes. Remove to a wire rack to cool completely. Cut each layer horizontally into halves.

For the frosting, whisk the milk and flour in a saucepan until blended. Cook over medium heat for 3 minutes or until thickened, stirring constantly. Cool for 1 hour. Beat the sugar, margarine and vanilla in a mixing bowl until light and fluffy. Add the thickened flour mixture and beat until smooth. Spread the frosting between the layers and over the top and side of the cake.

Serves 12

Lining the bottom of a cake pan with waxed paper will ensure that a cake turns out perfect every time. Invert the cake pan and place waxed paper on top of the bottom of the pan, cutting around the edge to make a circle or square exactly the same size as the pan. Return the cake pan to the upright position and place the cut piece of waxed paper in the bottom of the pan.

HAPPY BIRTHDAY

*Now that going to a restaurant is an ordinary event,
a home-cooked meal in the dining room is a real birthday treat.
The food is always prepared with love, exactly the way the
birthday person likes it, and the company, naturally, incomparable.*

8 Guests

Fall/Winter

BACON CHEESE SPREAD

MIXED GREENS WITH PEARS AND CHÈVRE

CHICKEN POTPIE

CHOCOLATE SHEET CAKE
(RRRII page 204)

Optional Menu Item
OSSO BUCO

Spring/Summer

CRAWFISH MOUSSELINE
(RRRIII page 20)

AVOCADOS WITH CILANTRO VINAIGRETTE

LOUISIANA SEAFOOD PAELLA

MILK CHOCOLATE BAR CAKE

Optional Menu Item
PECAN-CRUSTED CATFISH WITH HONEY GLAZE

BACON CHEESE SPREAD

Spoon into a crock or a decorative mold to serve.

    8 ounces cream cheese, softened
    4 slices bacon, crisp-cooked and crumbled
    1 bunch green onions, chopped
    1/2 teaspoon Worcestershire sauce
    Salt and pepper to taste
    3/4 cup (about) chopped pecans

Beat the cream cheese in a mixing bowl until creamy. Stir in the bacon, green onions, Worcestershire sauce, salt and pepper. Shape the cream cheese mixture into a ball and coat with the pecans. Chill, wrapped in plastic wrap, for several hours. Serve with assorted party crackers.

Serves 8

MIXED GREENS WITH PEARS AND CHÈVRE

Use fresh ripe pears for this salad. A mild goat cheese may be substituted for the chèvre.

    1 cup walnuts
    1/3 cup balsamic vinegar
    1/4 cup canola oil
    3 large ripe pears, peeled and sliced
    1 package European-style mixed salad greens
    2 ounces chèvre, crumbled

Spread the walnuts in a single layer on a baking sheet. Toast at 350 degrees for 3 minutes and stir. Turn off the oven. Let the walnuts stand in the oven with the door closed until cool.

Whisk the vinegar and canola oil in a bowl. Add the pears and toss to coat. Marinate for 30 minutes. Remove the pears to a bowl using a slotted spoon, reserving the vinaigrette. Toss the salad greens with the vinaigrette in a bowl until coated. Arrange the salad greens evenly on each of 8 salad plates. Top with the pears, chèvre and walnuts.

Serves 8

Osso Buco

An Italian phrase meaning "to jump in the mouth." Osso Buco is a home-style smothered veal shank dish. This Italian-inspired dish may also be prepared with lamb.

Bouquet Garni
1 bay leaf
1 tablespoon cracked peppercorns
Sprig of rosemary
Parsley stems

Osso Buco
10 to 12 small veal shanks (at least
   1/2 from lower shank)
Salt and pepper to taste
Olive oil
1 cup coarsely chopped onion
1/2 cup coarsely chopped carrots
2 tablespoons coarsely chopped garlic
1 cup coarsely chopped fennel bulb
1/2 cup coarsely chopped celery
3 cups white wine
2 cups reduced-sodium chicken broth
2 cups reduced-sodium beef broth
1 cup caper berries
1/2 cup (1 stick) butter, chilled
   and cubed
Juice of 1 lemon
1 cup coarsely chopped flat-leaf
   parsley

For the bouquet garni, tie the bay leaf, peppercorns, rosemary and parsley in a cheesecloth bag.

For the osso buco, sprinkle the shanks liberally with salt and pepper. Brown the shanks in batches on all sides in the olive oil in a large Dutch oven. Remove the shanks to a plate, reserving the pan drippings.

Brown the onion, carrots and garlic in the reserved pan drippings, stirring as little as possible. Add the fennel and celery and sauté for 2 minutes. Return the shanks to the Dutch oven. Add the wine and bring to a boil. Cook for 8 minutes or until the wine is reduced to a sweet flavor, stirring occasionally. Stir in the chicken broth, beef broth, caper berries and bouquet garni. Bring to a boil.

Bake, covered, at 350 degrees for 1 1/2 hours or until the veal is tender. Discard the bouquet garni and remove the shanks to a bowl using a slotted spoon, reserving the pan juices. Cover to keep warm. Bring the reserved juices to a boil. Cook for 15 minutes or until of a sauce consistency, stirring frequently. Remove from the heat. Add the butter, lemon juice and parsley and stir until the butter melts. Spoon the sauce over the shanks in shallow bowls.

Serves 8

Chicken Potpie

4 or 5 boneless skinless chicken breasts
1 large onion, coarsely chopped
1 cup coarsely chopped celery
1 bay leaf
Salt and pepper to taste
1/2 cup (1 stick) butter
1/2 cup flour

1 cup frozen pearl onions
1 cup milk
1 cup chopped fresh or frozen carrots
1 cup frozen peas
1 tablespoon chopped fresh parsley
1 tablespoon chopped fresh thyme
2 refrigerator pie pastries

Combine the chicken, onion, celery, bay leaf, salt and pepper with enough water to cover in a stockpot. Bring to a boil; reduce the heat. Cook until the chicken is tender. Strain, reserving the chicken and 2 cups of the broth, discarding the vegetables and bay leaf. Chop enough of the chicken to measure 4 cups.

Heat the butter in a saucepan. Add the flour and stir until blended. Cook until bubbly, stirring constantly. Stir in the pearl onions and cook until the onions are tender, stirring frequently. Season with salt and pepper. Add the reserved broth and milk gradually and cook until thickened, stirring constantly. Stir in the chicken, carrots and peas. Add the parsley and thyme and mix well. Taste and adjust the seasonings.

Spoon the chicken mixture into a greased 9×13-inch baking pan. Unfold the pie pastries and place overlapping on a lightly floured hard surface. Roll to fit the 9×13-inch baking pan, allowing a slight overhang. Arrange the pastry over the top of the chicken mixture. Flute the edges and cut vents in the top of the pastry. Bake at 450 degrees until light brown. Reduce the oven temperature to 350 degrees and bake for 30 minutes longer.

Serves 8 to 12

Avocados with Cilantro Vinaigrette

Not your typical salad course, these are absolutely delicious, easy, and so innovative. The avocado pit is simply scooped out to make little cups to hold the vinaigrette.

1 cup rice wine vinegar
1 cup canola oil or grapeseed oil
1/2 cup packed chopped cilantro
Juice of 2 large limes

1/2 jalapeño chile, chopped
Salt and pepper to taste
4 avocados

Process the vinegar, canola oil, cilantro, lime juice, jalapeño chile, salt and pepper in a blender or food processor until blended. Cut the avocados into halves and twist the halves in opposite directions to separate. Strike the pits with the side of a chef's knife and twist; the pits should release easily.

To serve, place 1 avocado half on each of 8 chilled salad plates and fill the centers with some of the vinaigrette. Instruct the guests to scoop the avocado with the vinaigrette.

Serves 8

Louisiana Seafood Paella

This is similar to a Louisiana jambalaya with the distinct flavor of saffron rice.

8 ounces andouille, sliced
2 tablespoons extra-virgin olive oil
8 ounces boneless skinless chicken breasts, cut into strips
1 cup chopped yellow onion
1 cup drained chopped canned tomato
1/2 cup chopped peeled carrots
1 tablespoon chopped garlic
2 cups long grain white rice
1 cup dry white wine
2 teaspoons saffron
1 1/2 cups chicken stock or broth

1 1/2 cups shrimp stock (made from shrimp shells)
Salt and pepper to taste
1 pound large white shrimp, peeled
12 ounces speckled trout fillets
8 ounces crawfish tails
1 cup oysters with liquor
2/3 cup frozen green peas, thawed
Juice of 1 lemon
1/4 cup chopped fresh basil
1 lemon, cut into wedges
1/4 cup black olives

Brown the sausage in the olive oil in a large Dutch oven or roasting pan. Remove the sausage to a plate, reserving the pan drippings. Brown the chicken on all sides in the reserved pan drippings. Remove the chicken to a plate, reserving the pan drippings. Sauté the onion, tomato, carrots and garlic in the reserved pan drippings until the vegetables are tender. Stir in the rice. Cook until heated through, stirring frequently. Add the wine and saffron and mix well. Bring to a boil; reduce the heat.

Simmer for 3 minutes, stirring occasionally. Add the chicken stock, shrimp stock, salt and pepper and bring to a boil. Bake, covered, at 375 degrees for 15 minutes.

Layer the shrimp, trout, crawfish and undrained oysters over the rice mixture. Layer with the chicken and sausage. Bake for 30 to 40 minutes longer or until the rice is tender and the seafood is cooked through; do not overcook. Remove from the oven and fold in the peas; fluff the rice. Taste and season with salt and pepper. Drizzle with the lemon juice. Top with the basil, lemon wedges and olives.

Serves 8

PECAN-CRUSTED CATFISH WITH HONEY GLAZE

8 (7- to 8-ounce) catfish fillets
3 cups pecans
Salt and pepper to taste
1 cup flour
1 teaspoon paprika
1/2 cup water

2 eggs
Peanut oil for frying
1/2 cup honey
1/4 cup (1/2 stick) butter
1/2 cup chopped fresh parsley

Remove the fatty skin and bones from the fillets. Place the pecans in a food processor and pulse until the consistency of coarse meal. Season with salt and pepper and spread in a shallow dish. Mix the flour and paprika in a shallow dish. Whisk the water and eggs in a shallow bowl until blended.

Coat the fillets with the flour mixture and shake off the excess. Dip in the egg mixture and shake off the excess. Coat with the ground pecans and press lightly to adhere. Pour enough peanut oil into a large skillet to measure 1/4 inch. Pan-fry the fillets in the hot oil for 2 to 3 minutes per side or until the fillets flake easily and are light brown. Drain on paper towels.

Combine the honey and butter in a microwave-safe bowl. Microwave for 1 minute and stir. Drizzle the glaze over the fillets and sprinkle with the parsley.

Serves 8

MILK CHOCOLATE BAR CAKE

People who love candy will adore this cake.

1 (2-layer) package Swiss chocolate
  cake mix
8 ounces cream cheese, softened
1 cup confectioners' sugar
1/2 cup sugar
8 (1.5-ounce) milk chocolate candy bars
  with almonds, finely chopped

12 ounces frozen whipped topping,
  thawed
2 (1.5-ounce) milk chocolate candy bars
  with almonds, chopped

Prepare the cake mix using the package directions. Divide the batter evenly between 3 greased and floured 8-inch cake pans. Bake at 325 degrees for 20 to 25 minutes or until a wooden pick inserted in the center comes out clean. Cool in the pans on a wire rack for 10 minutes. Invert onto the wire rack to cool completely.

Beat the cream cheese, confectioners' sugar and sugar in a mixing bowl at medium speed until creamy, scraping the bowl occasionally. Fold the cream cheese mixture and 8 chopped candy bars into the whipped topping in a bowl. Spread the frosting between the layers and over the top and side of the cake. Sprinkle 1 of the chopped candy bars over the top of the cake and press the remaining chopped candy bar along the bottom edge of the cake. Store, covered, in the refrigerator.

Serves 12

BRIDESMAIDS' LUNCHEON

A bridesmaid luncheon brings together the ladies in the wedding party and the favorite friends of the bride-to-be. Whether there's one attendant or twelve, the event is an opportunity for the bride to spend time with and thank those women in her life who are important to her.

12 Guests

LEMON DROPS

ASPARAGUS SANDWICHES

POTATO AND LEEK SOUP WITH CRAB MEAT

WEDDING DAY SALAD

SESAME CHIVE BISCUITS

FRENCH CREAM PIE

LEMON DROPS

For a final touch, add lemon twists to each drink. First cut a lemon into one-eighth-inch slices. Then cut halfway through each slice and twist both sections in opposite directions to make a twist.

2 (6-ounce) cans frozen lemonade concentrate
2 lemonade cans Absolut Citron or vodka
1 cup Lemoncello or Lemoncino (Italian lemon liqueur)
Ice cubes

Combine the lemonade concentrate, Absolut Citron and liqueur in a blender and add enough ice to fill. Process at high speed until the ice is finely crushed. Pour into glasses and garnish with lemon twists.

Serves 12

ASPARAGUS SANDWICHES

Dainty little pinwheels made from rolled up slices of white bread.

1 loaf thinly sliced white bread
1/2 cup (1 stick) unsalted butter, softened
2 bunches fresh asparagus, trimmed and blanched
Creole seasoning to taste

Flatten the bread slices with a rolling pin on a hard surface. Spread 1 side of the bread slices with butter and top with 1 or 2 asparagus spears. Sprinkle with Creole seasoning and roll to enclose the asparagus. Chill, covered, until serving time. Cut each roll into 6 equal slices and arrange cut side up on a serving platter.

Serves 12

Potato and Leek Soup with Crab Meat

This rich and delicious soup may be served as a prelude to a meal or as a light main course all on its own.

2 leek bulbs, cut into halves lengthwise and chopped	1 cup heavy cream
2 teaspoons chopped garlic	3 tablespoons grated asiago cheese
2 pounds potatoes, peeled and chopped	1 tablespoon minced fresh sage
1 quart chicken broth	Salt and pepper to taste
	1 pound lump crab meat, drained and shells removed

Sauté the leeks and garlic in a medium stockpot sprayed with nonstick cooking spray over medium heat for 2 minutes. Stir in the potatoes and broth and bring to a simmer.

Simmer until the potatoes are tender, stirring occasionally. Process the potato mixture in a food processor until puréed. Return the purée to the stockpot and stir in the heavy cream, cheese and sage. Bring to a simmer, stirring occasionally. Taste and season with salt and pepper.

To serve, divide the crab meat evenly among 12 soup bowls. Ladle the soup over the crab meat and garnish with fresh sage leaves.

Serves 12

Wedding Day Salad

Add chopped cooked chicken breast for a hearty entrée salad.

Apricot Vinaigrette
2/3 cup olive oil
1/4 cup white wine vinegar
1/4 cup orange juice
1/4 cup apricot jam
1 teaspoon salt
1/2 teaspoon coriander
1/2 teaspoon pepper

Salad
2 (10-ounce) packages baby spinach
2 pints grape tomatoes, halved
1 large red onion, thinly sliced
1 cup chopped dried apricots
1 cup (4 ounces) crumbled feta cheese
2 ripe avocados, chopped
1 cup chopped pecans, toasted
2 (11-ounce) cans mandarin oranges, drained

For the vinaigrette, whisk the olive oil, vinegar, orange juice, jam, salt, coriander and pepper in a bowl until mixed.

For the salad, toss the spinach, tomatoes, onion, apricots, feta cheese, avocados, pecans and mandarin oranges in a bowl. Add the vinaigrette and toss gently until coated.

Serves 12

Sesame Chive Biscuits

A sprinkling of sesame seeds adds an extra nutty aroma and crunch.

2 cups flour, sifted
1/3 cup chopped fresh chives
1 tablespoon baking powder
1 teaspoon salt
1 garlic clove, minced
3/4 cup sour cream
1/3 cup half-and-half

1 teaspoon vegetable oil
1/2 teaspoon sesame oil
1 egg, beaten
1 to 2 teaspoons water
Sesame seeds to taste
Kosher salt to taste

Mix the flour, chives, baking powder, salt and garlic in a bowl. Combine the sour cream, half-and-half, vegetable oil and sesame oil in a bowl and mix well. Add the sour cream mixture to the flour mixture gradually and stir until the mixture begins to adhere. Knead about 30 times. Let rest for 5 minutes.

Roll the dough 1/2 inch thick on a lightly floured surface and cut with a biscuit cutter dipped in flour. Arrange the rounds on a baking sheet lined with baking parchment. Brush the rounds with a mixture of the egg and water and sprinkle with sesame seeds and kosher salt. Bake at 375 degrees for 25 to 30 minutes or until golden brown. Serve immediately.

Makes 12 to 16 biscuits

French Cream Pie

1 (8-ounce) package vanilla wafers
1 tablespoon butter, softened
1 cup confectioners' sugar
1/2 cup (1 stick) butter, softened
2 eggs

1 tablespoon vanilla extract
3/4 cup chopped pecans or walnuts
1 (4-ounce) jar maraschino cherries,
    drained and finely chopped
1 pint whipping cream, whipped

Process the vanilla wafers in a food processor until crushed. Mix the vanilla wafer crumbs and 1 tablespoon butter in a bowl. Reserve 1/2 of the crumb mixture. Press the remaining crumb mixture over the bottoms and up the sides of 2 generously buttered pie plates.

Beat the confectioners' sugar, 1/2 cup butter, eggs and vanilla in a mixing bowl until creamy, scraping the bowl occasionally. Spread 1/2 of the creamed mixture in each of the prepared pie plates. Fold the pecans and cherries into the whipped cream in a bowl and spread the whipped cream mixture equally over the prepared layers. Sprinkle with the reserved crumbs. Chill, covered, for 8 to 24 hours before serving. If you are concerned about using raw eggs, use eggs pasteurized in their shells, which are sold at some specialty food stores, or use an equivalent amount of pasteurized egg substitute.

Serves 12

Garnishing with **Chocolate Leaves** can turn any dessert into a show-stopper. They can be made at home using rinsed and dried nontoxic leaves such as mint, rose, lemon, or strawberry. In a small microwave-safe dish, place a handful of semisweet chocolate chips and microwave on High for fifteen seconds or until melted. Use a clean, small paint brush to brush the melted chocolate onto the underside of the leaves. Wipe off any extra chocolate, that seeps onto the front of the leaves. Build up several layers of chocolate, then place the leaves, chocolate side up, onto a baking sheet lined with waxed paper. Freeze until hardened, and then separate by carefully peeling off the real leaves. Try to avoid touching the chocolate leaves so they will not begin to melt. Store in the refrigerator on waxed paper.

BLOODY MARY BRUNCH

A mixed drink before eleven in the morning may seem strange in other parts of the country, but a mid-morning Bloody Mary in Louisiana just seems natural. This is a great menu for a big morning crowd, so invite everyone over late morning, put on some Dixieland jazz, and laissez le bon temps roulez!

8 Guests

RED STICK BLOODY MARY

MILK PUNCH

CREOLE CRAB CAKES WITH
ROASTED GARLIC AïOLI

BACON-WRAPPED OYSTERS

MINT JULEP MELON SALAD

HERB WALDORF SALAD

OVEN-BAKED NUTMEG FRENCH TOAST

GRITS SOUFFLÉ

PRALINE COOKIES
(RRRII page 218)

RASPBERRY-ICED BROWNIES

RED STICK BLOODY MARY

Set up a Bloody Mary bar and allow your guests to create their own drinks. Provide peppers, limes, string beans, onions, okra, and, of course, plenty of celery.

2 cups vegetable juice cocktail
1 1/2 cups vodka citron
1 cup cocktail sauce
Juice of 1/2 large lemon
Juice of 1 small lime
2 teaspoons cracked pepper
1 teaspoon Tabasco sauce

1 teaspoon celery seeds
1/4 teaspoon cumin seeds, ground
Celery salt to taste
Celery heart spears
12 pickled okra
12 spicy pickled green beans

Combine the vegetable juice cocktail, vodka, cocktail sauce, lemon juice and lemon, lime juice and lime, pepper, Tabasco sauce, celery seeds and cumin seeds in a large container and mix well.

Moisten the rims of 6 glasses with water and rotate the rims in celery salt to cover evenly. Fill the glasses with ice and strain the Bloody Mary mixture into the glasses. Serve with celery hearts, pickled okra and pickled green beans.

Serves 6

MILK PUNCH

Typically, people think of punch as something that is served at a gathering of ladies or children. However, this is one of those classic southern drinks enjoyed by both men and women.

1 gallon whole milk
1 (750-milliliter) bottle Jack Daniel's whiskey
1 (16-ounce) package confectioners' sugar
1 (1-ounce) bottle vanilla extract
Freshly grated nutmeg

Combine the milk, whiskey, confectioners' sugar and vanilla in a large freezer container and mix well. Freeze, covered, until firm. Let stand at room temperature for 30 minutes or until slushy and ladle into punch cups. Sprinkle each serving with nutmeg.

Serves 8 to 12

CREOLE CRAB CAKES WITH ROASTED GARLIC AÏOLI

Roasted Garlic Aïoli

1 head garlic, roasted (refer to sidebar)
3/4 cup mayonnaise
1 tablespoon lemon juice
Salt and pepper to taste

Crab Cakes

1 cup bread crumbs
4 egg whites, lightly beaten
2 tablespoons minced red bell pepper
2 tablespoons minced red onion
1 tablespoon lemon juice
2 teaspoons minced jalapeño chile
2 pounds jumbo lump crab meat, drained and shells removed
Peanut oil

For the aïoli, squeeze the garlic pulp into a bowl. Stir in the mayonnaise, lemon juice, salt and pepper.

For the crab cakes, combine the bread crumbs, egg whites, bell pepper, onion, lemon juice and jalapeño chile in a bowl and mix well. Fold in the crab meat. Shape the crab meat mixture gently into 8 round cakes.

Pour enough peanut oil into a skillet to measure 1/4 inch. Sauté the crab cakes in the hot oil for 3 minutes per side; drain. Serve with the aïoli.

Serves 8

In the best-selling novel, Divine Secrets of the Ya-Ya Sisterhood, *author Rebecca Wells writes that Vivi Walker, the main character, becomes so enraged at her daughter, Sidda, that she throws out all photographs and mementos of her, except for the one remaining photo she keeps secretly tucked away in her* River Road Recipes *cookbook, on page 103, next to Mrs. Hansen Scobee's recipe for Crawfish Étouffée, Sidda's favorite. The producers of the movie version of this story chose to leave out this part, a fact that baffled most members of the Junior League of Baton Rouge since most can fully understand why Vivi chose the cookbook for safe-keeping in the first place.*

Bacon-Wrapped Oysters

Easy to prepare and delightful to pick up and eat. These cocktail bites consist of raw oysters and water chestnuts wrapped in bacon, secured with wooden picks, and broiled.

> 1 (1-pound) package thinly sliced bacon
> 3 dozen oysters, shucked
> 1 (8-ounce) can water chestnuts, drained, rinsed and sliced
> 1 bottle Pickapeppa sauce

Wrap 1 slice of bacon around 1 oyster and 1 water chestnut slice and secure with a wooden pick. Repeat the process with the remaining bacon, remaining oysters and remaining water chestnut slices.

Arrange the oysters in a single layer in a large baking pan and drizzle with the sauce. Broil until the bacon is cooked through, turning once.

Serves 8 to 12

Mint Julep Melon Salad

Melon balls, simple syrup, and fresh mint are combined in this recipe. Serve as an individual side salad or in one large bowl with wooden picks.

> 1/2 cup sugar
> 1/2 cup water
> 1 tablespoon fresh mint leaves
> 2 cups fresh cantaloupe balls
> 2 cups fresh honeydew balls
> 2 cups fresh watermelon balls

Mix the sugar and water in a small saucepan. Cook over low heat until the sugar dissolves, stirring occasionally. Stir in the mint. Let stand for 30 minutes or longer; strain, discarding the mint. Let stand until cool. Toss the melon balls with the syrup in a salad bowl. Garnish with sprigs of fresh mint. You may store the mint syrup in an airtight container in the refrigerator for up to 2 weeks.

Serves 8 to 12

Herb Waldorf Salad

This is a delightful salad, especially for those who love to grow herbs or have access to an herb garden.

5 cups baby lettuce leaves
1 cup fresh basil
1/2 cup chopped fresh fennel weed
1/2 cup arugula
1 tablespoon olive oil
Salt and pepper to taste
1 Granny Smith apple, chopped
1 Red Bartlett pear, chopped
2 cups toasted pita chips

1 cup sliced celery
1 cup sliced fennel bulb
1/2 cup walnuts, toasted
1/2 cup pecans, toasted
1/4 cup minced fresh tarragon
1/2 cup olive oil
3 tablespoons white wine vinegar
2 tablespoons sugar
1 teaspoon salt

Mix the lettuce, basil, fennel weed and arugula in a large salad bowl. Add 1 tablespoon olive oil and toss to coat. Season with salt to taste and pepper.

Toss the apple, pear, pita chips, celery, sliced fennel, walnuts, pecans and tarragon in a bowl. Whisk 1/2 cup olive oil, the vinegar, sugar and 1 teaspoon salt in a bowl until blended. Drizzle the vinaigrette over the fruit mixture and mix well. Taste and season with salt to taste and pepper. Divide the lettuce mixture evenly among salad plates and top each serving with some of the fruit mixture. Serve immediately.

Serves 8 to 12

Oven-Baked Nutmeg French Toast

This is a sophisticated version of regular French toast that does not involve standing over a hot griddle cooking one piece at a time.

16 (3/4-inch) slices Italian or French bread
8 eggs
2 cups milk or half-and-half
1/4 cup sugar
1/4 cup orange juice
1 teaspoon vanilla extract

1 teaspoon nutmeg
1 teaspoon salt
2/3 cup butter
1 cup chopped pecans
1/2 cup packed light brown sugar
2 tablespoons butter, melted

Arrange the bread slices in a single layer in a 9×13-inch baking dish. Whisk the eggs, milk, sugar, orange juice, vanilla, nutmeg and salt in a bowl until blended. Pour the egg mixture evenly over the bread slices, turning to coat. Chill, covered, for 2 to 10 hours.

Heat 2/3 cup butter in a 10×15-inch baking pan in a 400-degree oven until melted, tilting the pan to ensure even coverage. Arrange the bread slices in a single layer in the prepared pan. Bake for 25 minutes or until firm and golden brown.

Mix the pecans, brown sugar and 2 tablespoons butter in a bowl. Sprinkle the pecan mixture over the baked layer and broil 5 inches from the heat source for 1 minute or until bubbly. Serve immediately.

Serves 8

GRITS SOUFFLÉ

Serving some type of grits dish at every brunch is part of our Louisiana heritage.

4 cups water
1 cup grits
1 teaspoon salt
1/4 cup (1/2 stick) butter
1 cup (4 ounces) shredded jalapeño cheese
1 cup (4 ounces) shredded sharp Cheddar cheese
1/4 cup chopped jalapeño chiles
3 egg yolks, lightly beaten
4 egg whites
1/2 teaspoon cream of tartar

Combine the water, grits and salt in a saucepan and mix well. Cook using the package directions. Remove from the heat and stir in the butter, cheese and jalapeño chiles. Cool slightly and stir in the egg yolks.

Beat the egg whites and cream of tartar in a mixing bowl until stiff peaks form. Fold the egg whites into the grits mixture and spoon into 8 to 12 greased ramekins. Arrange the ramekins on a baking sheet. Bake at 350 degrees for 25 to 30 minutes. Serve immediately.

Serves 8 to 12

RASPBERRY-ICED BROWNIES

For a quick bar cookie, brownies cannot be beat. The raspberry icing adds a little pizzazz.

1 (22-ounce) package brownie mix
1/2 (10-ounce) package raspberry chips or toffee chips

Prepare the brownie mix using the package directions. Spread the batter in a 9×13-inch baking pan sprayed with nonstick cooking spray. Sprinkle with the raspberry chips. Bake at 350 degrees for 27 minutes. Cool in the pan on a wire rack and cut into squares. Serve with vanilla ice cream. The brownies may be frozen for future use.

Makes 2 to 3 dozen brownies

NEW YEAR'S DAY BUFFET

A buffet on New Year's Day is an excellent way to entertain without conflicting with December's many other social and family obligations. Different generations can mingle at a buffet-style gathering and make a gala celebration of "the morning after."

8 to 12 Guests

CAVIAR CRISPS

BAKED OYSTERS

TANGY APPLE SALAD WITH MAPLE DRESSING

STANDING RIB ROAST

MARCHAND DE VIN SAUCE

BLACK-EYED PEA MAQUE CHOUX

NEW YEAR'S DAY SAUTÉED CABBAGE

BRANDIED MUSHROOMS

OVEN RICE PILAF

CREAMY SHERRY TRIFLE

CAVIAR CRISPS

Caviar eggs from the choupique fish from Louisiana's waters make Cajun caviar an excellent example of a creative product that uses local ingredients.

2 cups fat-free sour cream
3 tablespoons chopped fresh chives
2 tablespoons lemon juice

1 package unsalted "kettle-style"
   potato chips
1 jar Cajun caviar

Combine the sour cream, chives and lemon juice in a bowl and mix well. Spoon 1 teaspoon of the sour cream mixture on each potato chip and top with 1/2 teaspoon of the caviar. Arrange on a serving platter.

Serves 8 to 12

BAKED OYSTERS

Serve from a chafing dish at a buffet or cocktail party, or bake in individual gratins for a seated dinner.

1 cup chopped green onions
1 cup chopped celery
1/2 cup chopped fresh parsley
1/4 cup (1/2 stick) butter
1 1/2 tablespoons Worcestershire
   sauce
1 teaspoon seasoned salt
3 1/2 cups Italian-style bread crumbs
1/2 cup (1 stick) butter, melted
6 to 8 dozen large oysters
5 tablespoons milk
2 tablespoons butter

Sauté the green onions, celery and parsley in 1/4 cup butter in a large skillet until the vegetables are tender. Stir in the Worcestershire sauce and seasoned salt. Toss the bread crumbs and 1/2 cup butter in a bowl and stir into the green onion mixture. Taste and adjust the seasonings.

Spread 1/3 of the bread crumb mixture in a greased shallow baking dish. Cover with a layer of closely packed oysters. Layer with 1/2 of the remaining bread crumb mixture and the remaining oysters. Top with the remaining bread crumb mixture. Drizzle with the milk and dot with 2 tablespoons butter. Bake at 400 degrees for 35 to 40 minutes or until brown and bubbly. Serve hot with crusty French bread for dipping.

Serves 8 to 12

A buffet is probably the easiest type of party to throw. It can always be expanded to include more people, and there is no need to worry about having an uneven number of guests. Since people tend to eat in shifts, it does not matter whether or not all of the guests can be seated at the same time. Set up the buffet in the most convenient location. That may be the dining room table, kitchen counter, picnic table, or even on several smaller groups of tables or stations that guests can get to from all sides. If the group is especially large, consider setting up two lines with the same foods.

For quickly **Toasted Walnuts,** spread the walnuts in a single layer on a microwave-safe rimmed plate. Microwave on High until crisp and brown, stirring every thirty seconds.

Tangy Apple Salad with Maple Dressing

Maple syrup and sugar combined with seasonal fruits make this dressing sweet and tangy. Craisins may be substituted for the dried cherries.

Maple Dressing
3/4 cup mayonnaise
1/3 cup maple syrup
2 tablespoons Champagne vinegar
1 tablespoon sugar
3/4 cup vegetable oil
Salt and freshly ground pepper
    to taste

Salad
3/4 cup coarsely chopped walnuts,
    toasted
2 (5-ounce) packages mixed baby
    salad greens
3 Granny Smith apples, peeled and
    julienned
3/4 cup dried tart cherries

For the dressing, whisk the mayonnaise, maple syrup, vinegar and sugar in a bowl until smooth. Add the oil gradually, whisking constantly until slightly thickened. Season with salt and pepper. Chill, covered, until serving time. You may prepare several days in advance and store, covered, in the refrigerator.

For the salad, reserve 1/4 cup of the walnuts. Toss the remaining walnuts, salad greens, apples and cherries in a bowl. Stir the dressing and add just enough to lightly coat the greens. Arrange the salad on salad plates and sprinkle with the reserved walnuts.

Serves 8 to 12

Standing Rib Roast

Always impressive looking, a standing rib roast makes a magnificent centerpiece for the buffet table.

1 (7- to 8-pound) rib roast, at room temperature
Salt and freshly ground pepper to taste

Rub the roast generously with salt and sprinkle with pepper. Arrange the roast fat side up in a shallow roasting pan. Do not cover or add water.

Bake at 375 degrees for 1 hour. Turn off the oven. Let the roast stand in the oven with the door closed for at least 2 hours. Turn the oven to 375 degrees 30 to 40 minutes before serving and continue to roast. The roast should be medium-rare at the end of the roasting process. Slice as desired. Serve with Marchand de Vin Sauce on page 149.

Serves 12

Marchand de Vin Sauce

A French phrase that means "wine merchants," this sauce is made from reduced red wine and is served with roasted or grilled meats.

<table>
<tr><td>1/2 cup minced ham</td><td>2 tablespoons flour</td></tr>
<tr><td>1/2 cup finely chopped onion</td><td>1/2 teaspoon salt</td></tr>
<tr><td>1/3 cup chopped fresh mushrooms</td><td>1/8 teaspoon black pepper</td></tr>
<tr><td>1/3 cup chopped green onions</td><td>1/8 teaspoon cayenne pepper</td></tr>
<tr><td>2 tablespoons minced garlic</td><td>3/4 cup beef stock</td></tr>
<tr><td>3/4 cup (1 1/2 sticks) butter</td><td>1/2 cup red wine</td></tr>
</table>

Sauté the ham, onion, mushrooms, green onions and garlic in the butter in a 9-inch skillet until the onions are brown. Stir in the flour, salt, black pepper and cayenne pepper.

Cook for 7 to 10 minutes or until all of the ingredients are brown, stirring frequently. Stir in the stock and wine; reduce the heat. Simmer for 35 to 45 minutes, stirring occasionally. Serve warm with Standing Rib Roast on page 148.

Serves 8 to 12

Black-Eyed Pea Maque Choux

A black-eyed pea and corn relish that tastes great at room temperature or chilled. Also perfect for tailgating.

<table>
<tr><td>1 cup chopped onion</td><td>2 cups frozen Shoe Peg corn, thawed</td></tr>
<tr><td>2 tablespoons chopped garlic</td><td>2 cups frozen black-eyed peas, thawed</td></tr>
<tr><td>2 tablespoons peanut oil</td><td>1 cup chopped seeded tomato</td></tr>
<tr><td>1/2 cup chopped red bell pepper</td><td>Salt and pepper to taste</td></tr>
<tr><td>1/2 cup chopped green bell pepper</td><td></td></tr>
</table>

Sauté the onion and garlic in the peanut oil in a saucepan until the onion is tender. Stir in the bell peppers, corn and black-eyed peas. Cook for 3 minutes, stirring frequently. Add the tomato, salt and pepper and mix well. Cook for 1 minute longer or until heated through, stirring frequently. Spoon into a serving bowl.

Serves 12

NEW YEAR'S DAY SAUTÉED CABBAGE

It is a southern tradition to eat cabbage on New Year's Day to ensure good health and wealth for the New Year. A seasonal tradition, cabbage is plentiful in the winter and goes well with spicy Louisiana cuisine.

4 slices bacon
1 cup chopped green onions
1 cup chopped onion
1 cup chopped bell pepper
1 cup chopped celery
1 head cabbage, trimmed and shredded

1 teaspoon salt
1 teaspoon celery seeds
1/4 teaspoon hot sauce
1/8 teaspoon pepper
3 tablespoons chopped pimento

Fry the bacon in a large cast-iron skillet until brown and crisp. Drain, reserving the drippings. Crumble the bacon.

Sauté the green onions, onion, bell pepper and celery in the reserved pan drippings until the onion is tender. Stir in the cabbage and sauté just until the cabbage is tender-crisp. Season with the salt, celery seeds, hot sauce and pepper, adding additional hot sauce if desired for a spicier flavor. Stir in the pimento. Spoon into a serving bowl and top with the crumbled bacon.

Serves 8 to 12

BRANDIED MUSHROOMS

Mushrooms are an excellent side dish that goes especially well with a rib roast.

1 cup (2 sticks) butter
3 tablespoons minced garlic
4 cups button mushrooms, trimmed and cut into halves
1 cup brandy
Salt and pepper to taste

Heat the butter in a large sauté pan until melted. Sauté the garlic in the butter for 1 minute. Stir in the mushrooms and sauté for 2 minutes longer. Add the brandy and mix well.

Bring the mushroom mixture to a boil; reduce the heat. Simmer for 5 minutes, stirring occasionally. Season with salt and pepper. Serve over sliced beef tenderloin.

Serves 12

OVEN RICE PILAF

Beef stock and onion add extra flavor to this simple side dish.

1 1/4 cups rice
2 green onions, chopped
1/4 cup chopped fresh parsley
2 ribs celery, chopped
1/2 cup (1 stick) butter
8 ounces fresh mushrooms, cut into halves
2 (10-ounce) cans beef consommé

Pour the rice into a baking dish. Sauté the green onions, parsley and celery in the butter in a skillet until the green onions and celery are tender. Spoon the green onion mixture over the rice. Add the mushrooms and consommé to the rice mixture and mix well.

Bake, covered, at 350 degrees for 30 minutes and stir. Bake, covered, for 15 minutes longer or until the rice is tender, stirring as needed.

Serves 8 to 12

CREAMY SHERRY TRIFLE

Trifle is such a southern dessert and makes a wonderfully light finale to a big meal.

1 envelope unflavored gelatin
1/2 cup milk
4 egg yolks
3/4 cup sherry
1/2 cup sugar
4 egg whites
1/16 teaspoon salt
1/2 cup sugar
2 cups whipping cream, whipped
1 small angel food cake, torn
Toasted slivered almonds

Soften the gelatin in the milk in a small bowl. Beat the egg yolks in a mixing bowl until thick and pale yellow. Add the sherry and 1/2 cup sugar and beat until blended. Cook in a double boiler until the egg mixture coats a spoon, stirring frequently. Add the gelatin mixture to the custard and mix well. Let stand until cool.

Beat the egg whites and salt in a mixing bowl until stiff peaks form. Add 1/2 cup sugar and 1/2 of the whipped cream to the egg whites and mix well. Fold the egg white mixture into the cooled custard.

Line the bottom of a 9×13-inch dish with waxed paper. Layer 1/2 of the cake pieces, the custard and remaining cake pieces in the prepared dish. Chill, covered, for 12 hours or longer. Spread with the remaining whipped cream and sprinkle with almonds. Cut into squares to serve.

Serves 12

BEFORE THE DANCE

Dinner at home before the prom or homecoming dance is much more affordable for teens than an expensive restaurant. The atmosphere is more relaxed, too, which is a bonus for teens with limited dating experience.

6 Guests

SPINACH AND ARTICHOKE DIP

SHRIMP AND TASSO PASTA

FRENCH BREAD

FRUIT COMPOTE
(RRRIII page 76)

BROWNIE PUDDING

Spinach and Artichoke Dip

All teenagers love this tried and true classic.

1¹/2 teaspoons butter
¹/2 cup finely chopped green onions
1 garlic clove, minced
10 ounces fresh spinach, trimmed, cooked and drained
¹/2 (14-ounce) can water-pack artichoke hearts, drained, rinsed and chopped
4 ounces light cream cheese, cubed
2 ounces mozzarella cheese, shredded
¹/4 cup light sour cream
1 teaspoon Worcestershire sauce
¹/8 teaspoon Tabasco sauce, or to taste
¹/4 cup (1 ounce) finely grated Romano cheese
1 teaspoon dill weed
¹/2 cup (2 ounces) shredded Monterey Jack cheese

Heat the butter in a large saucepan. Sauté the green onions and garlic in the butter until the onions are tender. Remove from the heat. Stir in the spinach and artichokes. Add the cream cheese, mozzarella cheese, sour cream, Worcestershire sauce, Tabasco sauce, Romano cheese and dill weed and mix well.

Spoon the spinach mixture into a baking dish and sprinkle with the Monterey Jack cheese. Bake at 350 degrees for 20 minutes or until the Monterey Jack cheese melts, or microwave on Medium for 8 minutes. Serve with assorted chips. You may substitute 2 (10-ounce) packages drained thawed frozen chopped spinach for the fresh spinach.

Serves 6 to 8

To make geometric butter shapes, line a rectangular, square, or other straight-edged dish with plastic wrap and fill with plain or infused butter. Use a ruler or other tool with a straight edge to smooth the butter in the dish so that it slopes down to resemble a butter "ramp." Place the pan in the refrigerator for several hours until the butter is firm. Unmold the butter by turning the pan upside down and remove the plastic wrap. Slice the butter into long strips and stack onto a small serving platter or onto individual butter plates.

SHRIMP AND TASSO PASTA

Tasso gives a smoky flavor to this seafood pasta dish. This freezes well and is an excellent dish to take to a friend with a new baby or a death in the family.

16 ounces fine or wide egg noodles
1 bell pepper, chopped
1 yellow onion, chopped
1 rib celery, chopped (optional)
1 bunch green onions, chopped
8 garlic cloves, chopped
1/2 cup (1 stick) margarine
2 pints heavy cream

1 pound deveined peeled shrimp
2 cups chopped tasso
Crushed red pepper to taste
Salt to taste
Creole seasoning to taste
Paprika to taste
3/4 cup (3 ounces) grated Parmesan cheese

Cook the pasta using the package directions until al dente; drain. Cover to keep warm. Sauté the bell pepper, onion, celery, green onions and garlic in the margarine in a large skillet until the vegetables are tender. Add the heavy cream and shrimp and mix well.

Cook for 2 minutes or until the shrimp turn pink, stirring frequently. Fold in the tasso and pasta. Season with red pepper, salt, Creole seasoning and paprika and sprinkle with the cheese.

Serves 6 to 8

BROWNIE PUDDING

Serve with ice cream or whipped cream.

3/4 cup flour
1/2 cup sugar
2 tablespoons baking cocoa
1 teaspoon baking powder
3/4 teaspoon salt
1/2 cup milk

1 1/4 tablespoons shortening, melted
1 teaspoon vanilla extract
3/4 cup chopped pecans
3/4 cup packed light brown sugar
1 1/2 tablespoons baking cocoa
1 cup boiling water

Sift the flour, sugar, 2 tablespoons baking cocoa, baking powder and salt into a bowl and mix well. Stir in the milk, shortening and vanilla and fold in the pecans. Spoon the batter into a greased 7×10-inch baking pan or dish.

Mix the brown sugar and 1 1/2 tablespoons baking cocoa in a bowl and sprinkle over the prepared layer. Pour the boiling water gradually over the top; do not stir. Bake at 350 degrees for 30 to 40 minutes or until firm to the touch. Let stand for 30 minutes before serving. Spoon the pudding into dessert bowls. Double the recipe for a large crowd and bake in a 9×12-inch pan.

Serves 6

SILVER ANNIVERSARY DINNER

*An invitation to this rare and special milestone is something to be cherished.
For this occasion, a sit-down dinner for a group of close friends and
relations can be more meaningful than a huge crowd of acquaintances.*

12 Guests

Crab Meat and Caviar Elegant

Fresh Mushroom Soup

Steak Chevillot

Rosemary Grilled Onions

Blue Cheese Mashed Potatoes

White Chocolate Cake with Silver Dragées

Optional Menu Item
Trout Sazerac over Wilted Greens

CRAB MEAT AND CAVIAR ELEGANT

A divine presentation of crab meat and caviar suitable for a special occasion.

16 ounces cream cheese, softened
1¹/3 cups sour cream
6 tablespoons mayonnaise
Juice of 1 lemon
¹/2 teaspoon hot sauce
¹/8 teaspoon garlic juice

1 pound lump crab meat, drained and
  shells removed
1 small jar black caviar
1 bunch green onion tops, thinly sliced
Sliced lemons

Combine the cream cheese, sour cream, mayonnaise, lemon juice, hot sauce and garlic juice in a mixing bowl and beat until smooth, scraping the bowl occasionally. Spread the cream cheese mixture on a large platter and smooth with a knife. Drop small bits of the crab meat over the prepared layer. Using a small spoon, drop bits of caviar and green onion tops artfully around the crab meat mounds. Arrange lemon slices around the edge of the platter. Serve with assorted party crackers.

Serves 12

FRESH MUSHROOM SOUP

A light cream-based soup. For a lighter version, reduce the butter to two tablespoons and substitute another eight to twelve ounces of broth for the cream.

16 ounces portobello mushrooms
¹/4 cup (¹/2 stick) butter or margarine
2 cups mushroom, chicken or beef broth
1 cup heavy cream or half-and-half
¹/4 cup water

1 tablespoon flour
2 cups cooked small pasta
1 teaspoon Creole seasoning
Salt and pepper to taste

Clean the mushrooms with a mushroom brush or damp paper towel and finely chop. Sauté the mushrooms in the butter in a saucepan over medium-high heat for 10 to 15 minutes or until the liquid evaporates. Add the broth and bring to a slow boil, stirring occasionally; reduce the heat.

Whisk the heavy cream, water and flour in a bowl until blended and add the cream mixture gradually to the mushroom mixture, stirring constantly to avoid lumps. Stir in the pasta. Add additional flour for a thicker consistency or additional water for a thinner consistency if desired.

Simmer just until heated through, stirring occasionally. Season with Creole seasoning, salt and pepper. Ladle into soup bowls. You may substitute any variety of mushrooms for the portobello mushrooms.

Serves 4

STEAK CHEVILLOT

Beef Fillet
1 tablespoon butter
1 (4- to 5-pound) beef fillet,
 trimmed and silver skin removed

Burgundy Sauce
1 tablespoon minced shallots
1 1/2 tablespoons butter
1 cup red burgundy
1 tablespoon flour
1 teaspoon plus 1 tablespoon butter
2 tablespoons red burgundy

For the beef, heat the butter in a large skillet. Brown the fillet on all sides in the butter for 6 to 8 minutes or until a meat thermometer inserted in the thickest portion registers 145 degrees for medium-rare, or to the desired degree of doneness. Remove the fillet to a heated platter.

For the sauce, sauté the shallots in 1 1/2 tablespoons butter in a skillet for 30 seconds. Add 1 cup burgundy and cook until the wine is reduced by 1/2. Stir in a mixture of 1 tablespoon flour and 1 teaspoon butter. Cook for 30 seconds. Swirl in the remaining 1 tablespoon butter and cook until the butter melts, stirring constantly. Stir in 2 tablespoons burgundy. Cut the fillet into individual steaks and serve approximately 2 tablespoons of the sauce with each steak.

Serves 8 to 10

TROUT SAZERAC OVER WILTED GREENS

Louisiana natives have enjoyed the Sazerac cocktail for generations, and it is widely believed to be the first cocktail served in New Orleans. The ingredients for this drink are used in this recipe to prepare the Cognac sauce that is served over mild white fish fillets.

3 pounds trout fillets
Salt and pepper to taste
2 teaspoons extra-virgin olive oil
6 ounces Cognac
1 cup beef stock or reduced-sodium
 beef broth

1/4 cup sugar
5 tablespoons butter, chilled
2 tablespoons chopped fresh parsley
2 teaspoons bitters
1 (16-ounce) package fresh baby
 spinach, blanched and seasoned

Season the fillets with salt and pepper. Sear the fillets presentation side down in the olive oil in a sauté pan. Reduce the heat and turn the fillets. Cook until the fillets are translucent and flake easily. Remove the fillets to a heated platter to keep warm.

Deglaze the pan with the Cognac; be careful as the pan might flame. Stir in the stock and sugar. Simmer for 3 minutes, stirring occasionally. Add the butter gradually, stirring constantly until incorporated. Stir in the parsley and bitters. Arrange the fillets over the spinach on dinner plates and drizzle with the sauce.

Serves 6 to 8

Silver skin is a layer of membrane that is sometimes found on the surface of a cut of meat. It should be removed since it is usually tough and can cause the meat to contract into an undesirable shape when cooking. Slip a thin, sharp knife (a paring knife or boning knife is preferred) just under the surface of the silver skin at the end of the cut of meat and make a short cut about an inch wide. Then, while trying not to cut into the meat, hold the silver skin up, slide the knife under it, and make long cuts, separating the skin from the meat. Angle the knife, keeping its edge right at the contact point of the silver skin and the meat. Avoid cutting into the silver skin since it will be easier to remove in long strips.

ROSEMARY GRILLED ONIONS

2 tablespoons chopped fresh rosemary
1/4 cup balsamic vinegar
2 pounds onions, sliced
1/4 cup olive oil

1 teaspoon kosher salt
1 teaspoon freshly cracked pepper
2 tablespoons chopped fresh parsley
Salt and pepper to taste

Heat the rosemary and vinegar in a saucepan over low heat until hot; do not boil. Remove from the heat and cover. Let stand for 20 minutes.

Brush the onion slices on both sides with the olive oil and arrange in a single layer on a baking sheet, keeping the slices intact. Sprinkle with 1 teaspoon salt and 1 teaspoon pepper.

Arrange the onion slices in batches on a lightly oiled grill rack. Grill for 4 to 6 minutes per side or until charred and tender. Place the grilled onions in a large bowl. Add the rosemary vinegar and parsley to the onions and toss to coat. Season with salt and pepper to taste.

Serves 6

BLUE CHEESE MASHED POTATOES

To prepare roasted garlic mashed potatoes, substitute garlic that has been roasted in the oven with olive oil for the blue cheese. This is also delicious as a filling for twice-baked potatoes.

10 red potatoes, peeled
Salt to taste
1 (12-ounce) can evaporated milk,
    evaporated skim milk or evaporated
    fat-free milk

3 tablespoons butter
4 to 6 ounces blue cheese, crumbled
Pepper to taste

Boil the potatoes in lightly salted water in a saucepan for 20 minutes or until tender; drain. Add the evaporated milk and butter to the potatoes and mash with a potato masher or fork until smooth. Stir in the blue cheese and season with salt and pepper. Serve immediately.

Serves 12

*W*ill you please send me a copy of the Louisiana River Road Recipes *cookbook? I saw an opossum, and I want to roast him.*

—B.H., 1969, Bothell, Washington

White Chocolate Cake with Silver Dragées

Dragées are shiny silver candy-coated almonds that can also be used to decorate cookies or cupcakes.

Cake

1 1/2 cups (3 sticks) butter
3/4 cup water
4 ounces Ghirardelli white chocolate, broken
1 1/2 cups buttermilk
4 eggs, lightly beaten
1 1/2 teaspoons vanilla extract
3 1/2 cups flour
1 cup chopped pecans, toasted
2 1/4 cups sugar
1 1/2 teaspoons baking soda

White Chocolate Cream Cheese Frosting

4 ounces Ghirardelli white chocolate, broken
8 ounces cream cheese, softened
3 ounces cream cheese, softened
1/3 cup butter
6 1/2 cups sifted confectioners' sugar
1 1/2 teaspoons vanilla extract
1 package silver dragées (optional)

For the cake, bring the butter and water just to a boil in a medium saucepan over medium heat, stirring occasionally. Remove from the heat. Add the chocolate and stir until blended. Stir in the buttermilk, eggs and vanilla.

Mix 1/2 cup of the flour and pecans in a bowl until coated. Combine the remaining 3 cups flour, sugar and baking soda in a bowl and mix well. Add the chocolate mixture to the flour mixture gradually, stirring constantly. Fold in the pecan mixture; the batter will be thin.

Pour the batter evenly into 3 greased and floured 9-inch cake pans. Bake at 350 degrees for 20 to 25 minutes or until the layers test done. Cool in the pans on a wire rack for 10 minutes. Remove the layers from the pans and cool completely on the wire rack.

For the frosting, heat the chocolate in a heavy saucepan over low heat until melted, stirring constantly. Cool for 10 minutes, stirring occasionally. Beat the cream cheese and butter in a mixing bowl at medium speed until creamy, scraping the bowl occasionally. Add the melted chocolate gradually, beating constantly until blended. Add the confectioners' sugar gradually, beating constantly until smooth. Stir in the vanilla. Spread the frosting between the layers and over the top and side of the cake. Sprinkle the dragées over the cake. Store, covered, in the refrigerator.

Serves 12

Throughout the Garden

When southerners build or buy a home, much consideration is put into how the outdoor areas will function for entertaining. Elaborate barbecue grills and outdoor kitchens are common, and almost everyone owns special equipment for boiling seafood and roasting or smoking large cuts of meat. Baton Rougeans are experts at outdoor entertaining, and many of the town's best hostesses are also the best gardeners.

Lucky Louisianans enjoy a mild climate, and outdoor parties are possible almost year-round. But, because the area also receives a lot of rain, outdoor entertaining can be tricky. The seasoned Baton Rouge party-giver always has a plan for bringing the party indoors, should a tropical storm blow in on the night of a poolside engagement supper.

Louisiana summers are long, and at the height of the season, the heat and humidity can be incredible. Yet Louisianans entertain outside even when the thermometer tops ninety degrees. This is the time we retreat to the shade of a porch, a huge oak tree, a gazebo, or even a large pool umbrella.

Menus

Indian Summer Dinner at Sunset

Pumpkin Carving

Cocktails in the Herb Garden

Early Supper with the Neighbors

Children's Backyard Party

Luncheon in the Sunroom

Easter Egg Hunt at Noon

Father's Day Outdoor Grill

Tropical Pool Party

Louisiana Crawfish Boil

INDIAN SUMMER DINNER AT SUNSET

*Autumn in the South nearly always includes a warm, summer-like
day late in the season, even in the early winter. This phenomenon of above-
average temperatures with dry and hazy conditions is referred to
as "Indian Summer." A warm day after weeks of cold weather is a thrill
and a good opportunity for inviting friends over for one
last warm evening in the garden before the cold sets in for good.*

6 Guests

LOUISIANA MARTINI
(RRRIV page 255)

WEST INDIES CRAB MEAT SALAD

PEPPERED BEEF TENDERLOIN

ROASTED GREEN BEANS

YELLOW PEPPER ORZO GRATIN

PROFITEROLES WITH CHOCOLATE GANACHE AND PEPPERMINT ICE CREAM

WEST INDIES CRAB MEAT SALAD

If available, use colored salad plates so that the beautiful white lump crab meat will be the shining star. If glass or white plates are used, line them first with a pretty leaf and garnish with lime wedges and commercially prepared bread sticks.

1¼ cups chopped yellow or red onions
½ cup extra-virgin olive oil
6 tablespoons white wine vinegar
¼ cup fresh lime juice
2 tablespoons chopped fresh parsley
2 teaspoons salt
1½ teaspoons freshly ground pepper
1½ teaspoons chopped fresh basil, or
   ½ teaspoon dried basil

1 teaspoon Dijon mustard
½ teaspoon sugar
⅛ teaspoon thyme
1 pound jumbo lump crab meat, drained
   and shells removed
1 head lettuce, separated
1 avocado, sliced
½ cucumber, sliced
1 tomato, sliced

Combine the onions, olive oil, vinegar, lime juice, parsley, salt, pepper, basil, mustard, sugar and thyme in a blender and pulse several times to combine. Combine the onion mixture and crab meat in a nonreactive bowl and mix gently. Marinate, covered, in the refrigerator for 8 to 10 hours.

    Spoon the crab meat mixture evenly onto lettuce-lined salad plates and surround with the sliced avocado, sliced cucumber and sliced tomato. You may serve as an appetizer with assorted party crackers.

Serves 6

PEPPERED BEEF TENDERLOIN

Serve on a large platter with the Roasted Green Beans on page 166 arranged along the side. Pass the hollandaise sauce at the table.

1 (6-pound) beef tenderloin (3 pounds trimmed)
¼ cup olive oil
Salt and freshly cracked pepper to taste
Hollandaise sauce

Have the butcher trim the tenderloin of chain, butt, silver skin and excess fat, or prepare the tenderloin yourself. Rub the outer surface with the olive oil and sprinkle with salt and pepper. Let stand until room temperature.

    Arrange the tenderloin on a baking sheet with sides and place on the middle oven rack. Roast at 425 degrees for 20 to 25 minutes or until a meat thermometer registers 145 degrees for medium-rare. Let rest for 5 minutes before slicing. Serve with hollandaise sauce.

Serves 6

Even in the late fall, Louisiana gardens have summer flowers and plants, such as zinnias, sunflowers, roses, and croton that still look fresh and make colorful, casual arrangements. Yellow peppers, found in abundance this time of year, are another inexpensive and colorful decoration. Set a table with a white cloth over a colorful cloth, then top with white tableware. For more color and soft light, place candles in colored jars suspended over the table with bark wire, a paper-covered wire resembling grapevine tendrils that is available at floral supply stores. Suspended lighting is a good solution for entertaining with limited table space.

ROASTED GREEN BEANS

Roasting green beans in the oven keeps them tender but still firm. This is a good dish for an outdoor party since it can be prepared in advance and held at room temperature.

2 pounds fresh green beans, trimmed, or 1 (16-ounce) package frozen whole green beans	1 tablespoon olive oil
	3/4 teaspoon salt
	1/2 teaspoon garlic powder
3 tablespoons slivered almonds	1/2 teaspoon basil
1 1/2 tablespoons lemon juice	1/2 teaspoon freshly ground pepper

Combine the green beans, almonds, lemon juice, olive oil, salt, garlic powder, basil and pepper in a bowl and mix well. Spread the bean mixture in a 10×15-inch baking pan. Roast at 450 degrees for 10 minutes or until tender and brown, stirring occasionally.

Serves 6

YELLOW PEPPER ORZO GRATIN

Very attractive when served in individual gratins but can also be prepared in a large baking dish. The yellow and red peppers lend a sweet, mild taste.

8 ounces orzo	1/2 teaspoon salt
3 yellow bell peppers, chopped	1 egg
1/4 cup minced shallots	1/2 cup (2 ounces) grated Parmesan cheese
1 garlic clove, minced	
1 tablespoon olive oil	1/4 cup chopped fresh chives
1/2 cup dry white wine	
1/2 cup reduced-sodium chicken broth	

Cook the pasta using the package directions until al dente; drain and rinse. Sauté the bell peppers, shallots and garlic in the olive oil in a skillet for 3 minutes. Stir in the wine, broth and salt.

Simmer, covered, for 10 minutes, stirring occasionally; remove the cover. Simmer until the liquid is absorbed, stirring occasionally. Remove from the heat and let stand until cool. Process the bell pepper mixture and egg in a food processor or blender until puréed. Fold the puréed mixture into the pasta. Stir in 1/4 cup of the cheese and chives.

Spoon the pasta mixture evenly into 6 greased ramekins and sprinkle with the remaining 1/4 cup cheese. Bake at 350 degrees for 20 minutes. You may prepare in advance and store, covered, in the refrigerator. Bake just before serving.

Serves 6

Profiteroles with Chocolate Ganache and Peppermint Ice Cream

Serve in a shallow rimmed bowl and drizzle at the last minute with the Chocolate Ganache. Garnish with a sprig of mint, crushed peppermint, and a peppermint stick.

Peppermint Ice Cream
1 quart whipping cream
1/2 cup sugar
1 (14-ounce) can sweetened condensed
   milk
1/2 cup crushed peppermint candies
2 egg yolks, beaten
1/2 teaspoon vanilla extract

Choux Pastry
1/2 cup (1 stick) unsalted butter
1/2 cup water
1/2 cup whole milk
1 teaspoon salt
1 cup sifted flour
4 eggs

Chocolate Ganache
3/4 cup half-and-half
8 ounces bittersweet or semisweet
   chocolate, chopped

For the ice cream, beat the whipping cream and sugar in a mixing bowl until soft peaks form and the sugar dissolves. Fold in the condensed milk, peppermint candies, egg yolks and vanilla. Pour the cream mixture into an ice cream freezer container and freeze using the manufacturer's directions. If you are concerned about using raw egg yolks, use eggs pasteurized in their shells, which are sold at some specialty food stores, or use an equivalent amount of pasteurized egg substitute.

For the pastry, bring the butter, water, milk and salt to a boil in a large saucepan, stirring occasionally. Add the flour all at once and stir vigorously with a wooden spoon until the dough pulls from the side of the pan. Continue to cook for 1 minute to cook out any excess moisture. The butter may sweat out, which means the moisture is evaporating. Place the dough in a bowl and let stand until cool. Add the eggs 1 at a time, stirring after each addition until thoroughly incorporated. The dough will become smooth and shiny.

Scoop the dough into a pastry bag fitted with a 1/2-inch plain tip. Pipe profiteroles onto an ungreased baking sheet or a baking sheet lined with baking parchment. Bake at 400 degrees for 15 minutes. Reduce the heat to 350 degrees. Bake for 15 minutes longer or until firm to the touch and golden brown. Turn off the oven. Turn the rolls and poke a hole in the bottom of each. Let stand in the oven with the door closed for 10 minutes to dry out.

For the ganache, bring the half-and-half to a boil in a saucepan. Remove from the heat and add the chocolate. Stir until smooth. Cover to keep warm. Cut the rolls horizontally into halves and remove any uncooked pastry. Arrange the bottom half in a shallow rimmed bowl and top with a scoop of peppermint ice cream. Cover with the remaining half and drizzle with the warm ganache. Repeat with the remaining rolls, remaining ice cream, and remaining ganache.

Serves 6

PUMPKIN CARVING

Reconnect with the neighbors over a light supper and pumpkin carving session before trooping off to trick-or-treat. Create a pumpkin patch by filling empty vegetable gardens and flowerbeds with an array of pumpkins in all shapes and sizes and let the guests "pick" a pumpkin. Spread newspapers over a picnic table, provide adults with knives and carving instruments, and let the occasion inspire the group to create the most elaborate jack-o-lanterns ever!

12 Guests

CITRUS PARTY SLUSH

GINGERSNAP DIP

PEPPER JELLY CHEESE PÂTÉ

BLACK BEAN AND SAUSAGE BAKE

GREEN CHILE CORN BREAD STICKS

POPCORN TREATS

GHOULISH SUGAR COOKIES

CITRUS PARTY SLUSH

Mashed bananas are the secret ingredient that gives this punch a thick, rich flavor.

4 cups water
2¹/2 cups sugar
1 (46-ounce) can pineapple juice
1 (6-ounce) can frozen orange juice
   concentrate

¹/2 cup lemon juice
5 bananas, mashed
2 liters ginger ale

Bring the water and sugar to a boil in a large saucepan. Boil until the sugar dissolves, stirring frequently. Remove from the heat and stir in the pineapple juice, orange juice concentrate, lemon juice and bananas.

Pour the mixture into 10 ice cube trays and freeze until firm. Transfer the frozen cubes to resealable plastic freezer bags and seal tightly. Just before serving, place the frozen cubes in a punch bowl. Pour the ginger ale over the cubes and ladle into punch cups.

Serves 12 to 14

GINGERSNAP DIP

16 ounces cream cheese, softened
4 teaspoons honey
4 teaspoons lemon juice
1 tablespoon amaretto
³/4 tablespoon grated lemon zest

¹/4 teaspoon almond extract
¹/4 cup apricot preserves
Sliced almonds
Gingersnaps

Beat the cream cheese, honey, lemon juice, liqueur and lemon zest in a mixing bowl until blended. Shape the cream cheese mixture into a rounded mound on a serving platter. Chill, covered, until firm.

Make an indentation large enough to hold the preserves in the center of the cream cheese mound and add the preserves to the indentation. Press the almonds evenly into the surface and serve with gingersnaps. You may prepare in advance and store, covered, in the refrigerator, making the final touches with the preserves and almonds just before serving. Bring to room temperature before serving.

Serves 18 to 20

Be practical and choose fall decorations that can have another life in the garden after the party. Fill unusual containers such as watering cans, metal buckets, and baskets with fall annuals such as mums, marigolds, and croton. After the party, plant the flowers in beds. In the south, straw is used instead of hay for fall decorations since it is more widely available and can be used as garden mulch after Halloween. Sugar cane stalks look great mixed with fall decorations, and the kids love to chew on them for a sweet fall treat.

Pepper Jelly Cheese Pâté

Commercially prepared pepper jelly is very southern and may be purchased in just about any grocery store or gourmet food store. Some are spicier than others, but any flavor pepper jelly may be used to top this cheese pâté. Serve with whole wheat crackers, water crackers, or any type of mild cracker.

1¹/2 cups (6 ounces) shredded
    Cheddar cheese
1 cup mayonnaise
1 cup pecans, chopped

¹/4 cup chopped green onions
Salt and pepper to taste
1¹/2 cups red pepper jelly
1 sleeve whole wheat crackers

Spray a 1-quart loaf pan with nonstick cooking spray. Line the prepared pan with plastic wrap, allowing enough overhang to cover the pâté and spray the plastic wrap with nonstick cooking spray. Mix the cheese, mayonnaise, pecans, green onions, salt and pepper in a bowl.

Pat the cheese mixture into the prepared pan and cover with the plastic wrap. Chill, covered, for 3 to 10 hours. Invert the pâté onto a serving platter and discard the plastic wrap. Spread the top of the pâté with the pepper jelly, allowing some of the jelly to drizzle down the sides. Serve with the whole wheat crackers.

Serves 12 to 14

Black Bean and Sausage Bake

Similar to black bean soup but with a thicker consistency, this casserole is loaded with sausage and may be served over rice or with the Green Chile Corn Bread Sticks on page 171.

1 pound dried black beans
2 quarts water
1 large onion, chopped
1 garlic clove, chopped
1 bay leaf
2 teaspoons salt

Pepper to taste
1 cup dry red wine
2 pounds link Italian, venison or smoked
    sausage, cut into ¹/2- to 1-inch slices
1 tablespoon butter or margarine
1 onion, sliced

Generously cover the beans with water in a stockpot. Let stand, covered, for 8 to 10 hours; drain and rinse. Combine the beans, 2 quarts water, chopped onion, garlic and bay leaf in the stockpot. Bring to a boil; reduce the heat. Simmer, covered, for 4 to 6 hours or until the beans are tender, stirring occasionally and removing the cover 2 hours before the end of the cooking process. Stir in the salt and pepper 30 minutes before the beans are tender. Add the wine and mix well.

Cook the sausage in the butter in a skillet. Add the sliced onion and continue to cook until the sausage is cooked through and the onion is tender, stirring frequently. Mash 1 cup of the beans in a bowl and stir into the sausage mixture. Add the mashed bean mixture to the beans and mix well. Cook until heated through; discard the bay leaf. Spoon the bean mixture into a large baking dish. Bake in a moderate oven for 45 minutes.

Serves 12

GREEN CHILE CORN BREAD STICKS

Mild-tasting green chiles give this corn bread a nice flavor without too much heat.

1¹/2 cups flour
1 tablespoon baking powder
1¹/2 teaspoons salt
¹/4 teaspoon chili powder
1 cup cornmeal
¹/2 cup (1 stick) butter
6 tablespoons sugar
4 eggs
1 (15-ounce) can cream-style corn
1 (4-ounce) can chopped green chiles, drained
²/3 cup shredded Pepper
    Jack cheese

Sift the flour, baking powder, salt and chili powder into a bowl and mix well. Beat the cornmeal, butter and sugar in a mixing bowl until creamy. Add the eggs 1 at a time, beating well after each addition. Add the flour mixture to the creamed mixture and beat until mixed. Fold in the corn, green chiles and cheese.

Fill 14 greased corn bread stick molds ³/4 full. Bake at 375 degrees for 15 to 20 minutes or until golden brown.

Makes 14 corn bread sticks

Stack up a tower of pumpkins outside the front door to welcome guests. Hunt for pumpkins in various colors that have a fat, flat shape and a short stem. Try out different shapes and sizes at the fruit stand to ensure that you get the look you want before you buy.

171

Reserve the pumpkin seeds after carving jack-o-lanterns and fry for a delicious, crunchy treat. Rinse the pumpkin seeds and remove the pulpy strings. Heat peanut oil in a skillet to 350 degrees. Fry the seeds in the hot oil for 5 to 8 minutes or until the seeds are puffed, crisp, and a brown chestnut color. Remove the seeds with a slotted spoon and drain on paper towels. Season with salt and pepper.

POPCORN TREATS

These fun treats may be shaped into balls, wrapped in plastic wrap, and given as party favors. Mix in candy corn, orange and black chocolate candies, or any other type of candy or nuts for a colorful, sweet treat.

8 cups popped popcorn	8 ounces roasted peanuts
1 (12-ounce) package "M & M's" Chocolate Candies	1/2 cup candy corn (optional)
	1 (10-ounce) package marshmallows
1/2 cup "M & M's" Peanut Chocolate Candies (optional)	1/2 cup (1 stick) butter, coarsely chopped

Layer the popcorn, chocolate candies, peanuts and candy corn 1/3 at a time in a large bowl; do not stir. Combine the marshmallows and butter in a microwave-safe dish and microwave on High for 2 minutes; stir. Microwave for 1 minute longer or until blended; stir. Pour the marshmallow mixture over the prepared layers and stir until coated.

Press the popcorn mixture into a lightly buttered bundt pan. Chill in the refrigerator. Invert onto a platter. To serve, either slice or pull pieces off as desired.

Serves 12

GHOULISH SUGAR COOKIES

Ideal for cutting out shapes, this cookie dough can be rolled again and again, without becoming overworked and tough like pastry dough.

3 cups flour	1 egg, lightly beaten
1/2 teaspoon baking powder	2 tablespoons milk
1/2 teaspoon baking soda	1 teaspoon vanilla extract
1/2 teaspoon salt	2 (16-ounce) cans white icing
1 cup (2 sticks) butter or margarine	Orange, black and green food coloring
1 cup sugar	

Sift the flour, baking powder, baking soda and salt together. Combine the butter and sugar in a bowl and mix with a fork until creamy. Add the egg to the creamed mixture and mix well. Stir in the milk and vanilla. Add the flour mixture and stir until blended.

Roll the dough on a lightly floured surface and cut with cutters into Halloween shapes. Arrange the cookies 2 inches apart on an ungreased cookie sheet. Bake at 400 degrees for 5 to 7 minutes or until light brown. Cool on the cookie sheet for 2 minutes. Remove to a wire rack to cool completely.

Tint the icing separately with the food colorings and spread over the cooled cookies. Let stand for 30 minutes or until set.

Makes 2 to 3 dozen cookies

COCKTAILS IN THE HERB GARDEN

Because of the state's semitropical climate, a Louisiana herb garden is filled year-round with color, texture, and aroma. Fresh herbs give ordinary foods a beautiful look and superior taste. Dining in the herb garden is a unique delight before going on to the theater, symphony, or other event.

8 Guests

Louisiana Mint Mojitos

Fresh Artichokes
with Garlic Tarragon Sauce

Tomato Basil Sandwiches

Shrimp Salad Verdi

Grilled Lamb Chops with Rosemary

Sweet Herb Shortbread

A bus station set up outside saves the host from constantly running in and out of the house during the meal to fetch things. Bring a small table or other piece of furniture outside, or think about using an old potting bench to set up any extra items that might be needed during the meal. Good things to have within reach are extra pitchers of water, additional napkins, additional utensils, an ice bucket filled with ice, a cork screw, lemons, and limes.

LOUISIANA MINT MOJITOS

Garnish this Cuban cocktail Louisiana-style with small stalks of sugar cane.

> 32 sprigs of mint, stems removed (about 1 bunch)
> 2 cups fresh lime juice
> 1 cup sugar
> 2 cups light rum
> 2 cups club soda

Combine the mint, lime juice and sugar in a large pitcher. Crush the mint mixture with a wooden spoon or pestle. Add the rum and club soda and mix well. Immediately pour over crushed ice in glasses. Garnish with sugar cane stalks.

Serves 8

Fresh Artichokes with Garlic Tarragon Sauce

Garlic Tarragon Sauce
1 1/2 cups (3 sticks) unsalted
   butter, melted
1/2 cup lemon juice
3 tablespoons chopped fresh
   tarragon
1 tablespoon minced garlic
Salt and pepper to taste

Artichokes
4 large artichokes
6 quarts water
1/2 cup lemon juice
2 teaspoons salt

For the sauce, whisk the butter, lemon juice, tarragon, garlic, salt and pepper in a bowl until mixed.

For the artichokes, cut off the stems to form a flat base and trim the prickly tips of the leaves. Bring the water, lemon juice and salt to a boil in a stockpot. Add the artichokes to the boiling water and boil for 20 to 25 minutes. Drain the artichokes upside down in a colander. Let stand until room temperature. Serve with the sauce.

Serves 4 to 6

Tomato Basil Sandwiches

Make these miniature sandwiches in the summertime, when tomatoes are at their peak. Serve along with a meal or as a canapé.

1/4 cup mayonnaise
3 ounces cream cheese, softened
2 teaspoons chopped fresh basil
1/4 teaspoon salt

1/4 teaspoon pepper
1 baguette, cut into 16 slices
4 plum tomatoes, sliced
1/2 cup chopped fresh basil

Combine the mayonnaise, cream cheese, 2 teaspoons basil, 1/8 teaspoon of the salt and 1/8 teaspoon of the pepper in a bowl and mix well. Chill, covered, for up to 8 hours if desired.

Spread the cream cheese mixture on 1 side of each of the bread slices. Top each with a tomato slice. Sprinkle with the remaining 1/8 teaspoon salt and remaining 1/8 teaspoon pepper. Just before serving, sprinkle with 1/2 cup chopped fresh basil.

Makes 16 appetizer servings

Muscadine grapes are sweet, musky, and widely grown in Louisiana backyards and vineyards. Since Louisiana's earliest history, they have been used to make jellies, jams, and wines. Muscadine wine makes a great summertime wine cooler to add to an outdoor party bar. Encourage your guests to mix up their own wine coolers by adding a splash of soda water and a teaspoon of sugar to their glass of Muscadine wine.

Dining en plain aire (in open air) should not mean you are limited to using the patio furniture. If the weather is nice enough to dine outside, there is no reason why indoor furniture cannot be brought outside. Imagine how beautiful your dining room table would look on your terrace. Look with fresh eyes at all of your indoor furniture and consider how each piece might work to create an outdoor setting.

Shrimp Salad Verdi

Loads of herbs and green onions give a fresh green color to the shrimp. Serve at a cocktail party with wooden picks or on top of a bed of tender salad greens as a side salad.

1/2 cup Italian-style bread crumbs
1 teaspoon salt
1 teaspoon cumin
1 teaspoon red pepper
3/4 cup chopped fresh parsley
1/2 cup lime juice
1/4 cup chopped green onions
2 tablespoons Creole mustard

1 teaspoon minced garlic
1 teaspoon prepared horseradish
3/4 cup fat-free Italian dressing
1/4 cup olive oil
1/4 cup finely chopped celery
3 pounds deveined peeled boiled shrimp
Iceberg lettuce leaves

Process the bread crumbs, salt, cumin and red pepper in a food processor until blended. Add the parsley, lime juice, green onions, mustard, garlic and horseradish and process until combined. Add the Italian dressing and olive oil gradually, processing constantly until incorporated. Add the celery and quickly pulse.

Toss the olive oil mixture with the shrimp in a bowl until coated. Spoon the shrimp mixture onto lettuce-lined salad plates or mix the shrimp mixture with the lettuce. Serve immediately.

Serves 8

Grilled Lamb Chops with Rosemary

Dishes containing lamb are perfect in the spring.

10 to 12 (3- to 4-ounce) lamb chops, trimmed
Salt and pepper to taste
3/4 cup olive oil
3 garlic cloves, chopped
2 tablespoons chopped fresh rosemary

Sprinkle both sides of the chops with salt and pepper and arrange in a single layer in a large shallow dish. Whisk the olive oil, garlic and rosemary in a bowl and drizzle over the chops, turning to coat. Let stand at room temperature for 30 minutes.

Arrange the chops on a grill rack over hot coals. Grill for 41/2 to 5 minutes per side for medium-rare, or 5 to 6 minutes per side for medium. Serve immediately. You may arrange the chops on a broiler rack in a broiler pan and broil to the desired degree of doneness.

Serves 5 to 6

SWEET HERB SHORTBREAD

2 cups flour
1 teaspoon salt
1/2 teaspoon baking powder
3/4 cup (11/2 sticks) butter, softened
1/2 cup confectioners' sugar
2 tablespoons honey
1/2 cup dried apricots, chopped
3 tablespoons chopped fresh herbs, such as rosemary, dill weed, lemon thyme, fennel and/or tarragon

Mix the flour, salt and baking powder in a bowl. Beat the butter, confectioners' sugar and honey in a mixing bowl until light and fluffy, scraping the bowl occasionally. Add the flour mixture gradually, beating well after each addition. Fold in the apricots and herbs.

Pat the dough into a greased 9-inch round baking pan. Bake at 350 degrees for 20 to 30 minutes or until light brown and puffy. Cool in the pan for 10 minutes before cutting into wedges. Serve warm with jam and/or lemon curd.

Serves 12

One of the highlights of my year had to be the cell phone call I received from a large discount store wanting to place a substantial order. I negotiated the deal while sitting in the car waiting for my daughter to finish softball practice. I tried to act cool, like I did this every day, assuring the distributor that RRR could fill their initial order and have books ready throughout the year to fill their projected quarterly orders. One quick glance at the inventory summary in my always-handy chairman's binder told me their needs exceeded our inventory on hand. I thanked them for their business and, like a good junior leaguer, ever resourceful, found a way before I left the ballpark to time the reprints and still have money to turn over to community projects.

—Martha Miller Rome, *Chairman 2001-2002 and* RRRIV *Chairman*

EARLY SUPPER WITH THE NEIGHBORS

Baton Rouge winters are generally mild and short. Still, there's rejoicing when spring finally begins to show itself in the yard. The patio is a charming spot to treat the book club or neighbors to a light dinner in the cool evening air.

8 to 12 Guests

BROCCOLI SOUP

CRAWFISH PIES

MIXED GREENS WITH
TANGY SOUTHERN SALAD DRESSING

CHOCOLATE STRAWBERRY SHORTCAKES

Optional Menu Item
CHOCOLATE FANTASY DESSERT

BROCCOLI SOUP

Fresh broccoli and carrots make a good combination for this winter vegetable soup.

1 onion, chopped	2 to 3 cups chopped fresh or frozen
1 red bell pepper, chopped	broccoli, including stems
1/2 cup (1 stick) butter or margarine	and florets
1/2 cup flour	2 bay leaves
6 cups chicken broth	1 cup milk or half-and-half
1 1/2 cups shredded carrots	1/4 teaspoon cayenne pepper
(optional)	Salt to taste

Sauté the onion and bell pepper in the butter in a stockpot until tender. Add the flour and mix well. Whisk in the broth to avoid lumps. Stir in the carrots, broccoli and bay leaves. Bring to a simmer over medium heat; reduce the heat to low.

Simmer until the broccoli and carrots are tender, stirring frequently. Discard the bay leaves. Stir in the milk, cayenne pepper and salt. Simmer just until heated through, stirring occasionally. Ladle into soup bowls.

Serves 12

CRAWFISH PIES

1 1/2 cups chopped onions	2 teaspoons cornstarch
1 1/2 cups chopped celery	1/2 cup chopped green onions
6 garlic cloves, minced	1 bunch parsley, trimmed and
1/2 cup (1 stick) butter	chopped or minced
1 (10-ounce) can cream of	3 pounds Louisiana crawfish tails
mushroom soup	8 ounces Parmesan cheese, grated
1 (12-ounce) can evaporated milk	Salt and pepper to taste
2 tablespoons cold water	6 refrigerator pie pastries

Sauté the onions, celery and garlic in the butter in a large saucepan until the vegetables are tender. Stir in the soup and evaporated milk. Mix the cold water and cornstarch in a small bowl and stir into the soup mixture. Add the green onions, parsley and crawfish and mix well. Cook over medium heat for 15 minutes, stirring occasionally. Stir in the cheese, salt and pepper.

Line three 9-inch plates with 3 of the pastries. Spoon the crawfish mixture evenly into the 3 pastry-lined pie plates. Top with the remaining pastries, fluting the edges and cutting vents. Bake at 350 degrees for 30 minutes or until light brown. Let stand for 15 minutes before serving. You may prepare and bake in advance and freeze for future use. Reheat at 325 degrees for 25 minutes or until heated through.

Serves 18

When preparing a cheese tray, choose a combination of three or four cheeses, each representing a different taste, texture, or appearance. A good basic combination to start with would be a soft, mild cheese such as Camembert or Brie, a hard nutty cheese such as asiago or Parmigiano-Reggiano, and a sharp blue cheese such as Gorgonzola or Stilton.

Cheeses look best when served on natural-looking pieces like wood, slate, or a woven tray, as long as the serving piece is large enough to accommodate the cheeses being displayed without touching. For a tropical look, line the serving piece with large banana or ginger leaves from the yard. Be creative when thinking about garnishes and accompaniments. Instead of the obligatory cluster of grapes or apples, consider adding sliced honeydew melon, plums, peaches, and/or pears.

Remove cheese from the refrigerator at least thirty minutes before serving so the flavors can develop fully. Remove the wrappers, but leave the rinds on, and do not pre-slice before serving, as it causes the cheese to dry out. Arrange the cheeses on a platter from the mildest to the most pungent. Provide a separate knife for each type of cheese, and serve with mild-flavor crackers or bread.

Mixed Greens with Tangy Southern Salad Dressing

Keep extras of the dressing in the refrigerator to enjoy anytime.

Tangy Southern Salad Dressing
1 beef bouillon cube
3 tablespoons boiling water
2/3 cup tarragon vinegar
1/2 small white onion, finely chopped
1 egg
1 large garlic clove, crushed
1 tablespoon Dijon mustard
1/2 teaspoon Worcestershire sauce
1/8 teaspoon Tabasco sauce
Freshly ground pepper to taste
2/3 cup olive oil
1 1/3 cups vegetable oil
Salt to taste

Salad
12 to 16 cups mixed salad greens

For the dressing, dissolve the bouillon cube in the boiling water in a heatproof bowl. Combine the vinegar, onion, egg, garlic, mustard, Worcestershire sauce, Tabasco sauce and pepper in a blender and process until blended. Add the olive oil gradually, processing constantly until incorporated. Add the bouillon and process until blended. Add the vegetable oil and salt gradually, processing constantly. Store, covered, in the refrigerator for up to 2 weeks. If you are concerned about using raw eggs, use eggs pasteurized in their shells, which are sold at some specialty food stores, or use an equivalent amount of pasteurized egg substitute.

For the salad, bring the dressing to room temperature. Toss the salad greens with approximately 1 1/2 cups of the dressing in a bowl until coated. Serve immediately.

Serves 12

CHOCOLATE STRAWBERRY SHORTCAKES

Shortcakes
3 cups self-rising flour
1 cup baking cocoa
2/3 cup sugar
1/2 teaspoon salt
2 cups heavy cream

Strawberry Filling
2 pints fresh strawberries, sliced
1/2 cup sugar
1/2 cup kirsch (optional)
1/2 cup baking cocoa
1/2 cup confectioners' sugar
4 cups whipping cream
1 teaspoon vanilla extract

For the shortcakes, sift the self-rising flour, baking cocoa, sugar and salt into a bowl and mix well. Add the heavy cream and mix until a dough forms. Knead gently on a lightly floured surface.

Divide the dough into 2 equal portions and shape each portion into a 3×6-inch log. Cut each log into 6 equal slices and arrange on a greased baking sheet. Bake at 400 degrees until light brown. Remove to a wire rack to cool.

For the filling, gently toss the strawberries with the sugar and liqueur. Sift the baking cocoa and confectioners' sugar into a mixing bowl and mix well. Add the whipping cream to the baking cocoa mixture and beat until soft peaks form. Add the vanilla and beat until blended.

To serve, cut the shortcakes horizontally into halves. Arrange the bottom halves on dessert plates and spoon 1 tablespoon of the strawberry mixture over each half. Top with the remaining halves and a dollop of the chocolate whipped cream. Serve immediately.

Serves 12

When choosing fresh strawberries, look for a solid red color and fresh green caps, which means they are freshly picked. A wilted top usually signals a berry that is past its prime and will quickly become soft. Strawberries do not ripen after picking, so avoid those that have a noticeable amount of white flesh at the top. Also look out for any moisture, mold, or decayed areas. Mold travels quickly among strawberries, so even one moldy berry can quickly ruin an entire batch. Be sure to inspect your berries immediately after purchase and discard any moldy ones that may have been hidden from view. Spread unrinsed berries in a flat container, cover with a paper towel, and chill until ready to use. Strawberries should be rinsed gently in cold water just before consuming.

CHOCOLATE FANTASY DESSERT

25 chocolate sandwich cookies
5 tablespoons butter, softened
1 (10-ounce) package marshmallows
1 cup (6 ounces) semisweet chocolate chips
1/2 cup milk
2 cups whipping cream
2 chocolate sandwich cookies, crushed

Crush 25 cookies into a bowl. Add the butter and mix well. Press the cookie crumb mixture over the bottom of an 8×8-inch or 9×9-inch dish. Freeze until firm.

Combine the marshmallows, chocolate chips and milk in a saucepan. Cook over low heat until blended, stirring constantly. Cool to room temperature. Beat the whipping cream in a mixing bowl until soft peaks form and fold into the marshmallow mixture. Spoon the marshmallow mixture over the prepared layer and sprinkle with 2 crushed cookies. Freeze for 15 minutes or longer. Cut into squares to serve.

Serves 6 to 8

Throughout the years, River Road Recipes *has developed such a loyal following that devotees can be found everywhere . . . even the White House! According to an article that appeared in* The New York Times *in 2001, the cookbooks are a favorite of First Lady Laura Bush. The article states, "Laura Bush has a collection of cookbooks that she dips into just for the pleasure of reading them. But when it's time to cook, she reaches for the tried and true." A particular favorite of the Bush family is the recipe for Pickled Shrimp that appears in the first* River Road Recipes *cookbook. The article went on to state that the first family is so fond of this special dish that Mrs. Bush plans to have the White House chef prepare it for Christmas.*

CHILDREN'S BACKYARD PARTY

These days, so many venues offer children' parties that hosting is as easy as writing a check. Still, what better way to teach a child hospitality than with a party he or she helps host? The excitement of helping shop and plan an event meant for his own peers is equal to the thrill of a mountain of gifts and the pleasure of being a year older.

18 to 20 Guests

CITRUS PARTY SLUSH
(RRRIV page 169)

PERKY PARTY MIX

CARAMEL APPLE DIP

LEMON YOGURT DIP WITH FRUIT KABOBS

SPINACH DIP
(RRRIII page 241)

HAM AND CHEESE NIBBLES

BIRTHDAY CAKE WITH ICE CREAM

PERKY PARTY MIX

Children can have fun preparing this mix, and adults love it too.

3 cups pretzel sticks, broken into halves
3 cups Cheddar cheese miniature bread sticks
1 cup "M & M's" Chocolate Candies
1 cup peanuts
1 cup golden raisins
1 cup dried cranberries

Mix the pretzels, bread sticks, chocolate candies, peanuts, raisins and cranberries in a bowl. Store, covered, in an airtight container.

Serves 18

CARAMEL APPLE DIP

Slice red or green apples to use as dippers with this cream cheese spread topped with caramel. Children love to eat this with graham crackers, pretzels, gingersnaps, or vanilla wafers.

4 Granny Smith apples, cut into wedges
4 Red Delicious apples, cut into wedges
2 liters lemon-lime soda
8 ounces cream cheese, softened
1/4 cup confectioners' sugar
1/2 (12-ounce) jar caramel ice cream topping
1/2 cup chopped pecans

Toss the apples with the soda in a bowl. Soak, covered, in the refrigerator for 8 to 10 hours. Beat the cream cheese and confectioners' sugar in a mixing bowl until creamy.

Mound the cream cheese mixture in the center of a serving platter. Drizzle with the caramel topping and sprinkle with the pecans. Surround with the apple wedges, alternating the colors.

Serves 12

Lemon Yogurt Dip with Fruit Kabobs

A bit of fresh fruit is always a good idea, and if a cool and refreshing dip is provided with it, the children will be more likely to partake.

1 1/2 cups lemon yogurt
1 1/2 cups whipped topping
2 teaspoons honey
1 teaspoon vanilla extract
1/2 watermelon, seeded and balled or cubed
1 cantaloupe, balled or cubed
1 bunch red grapes
1 pineapple, cut into chunks

Mix the yogurt, whipped topping, honey and vanilla in a serving bowl. Chill, covered, in the refrigerator. Skewer the watermelon, cantaloupe, grapes and pineapple alternately on wooden skewers. Serve with the yogurt dip.

Serves 18

Ham and Cheese Nibbles

These are easy for children to eat with one hand.

3 (24-count) packages party rolls
8 slices sandwich ham
9 ounces Monterey Jack cheese, sliced
1/2 cup (1 stick) margarine, melted
2 tablespoons minced onion
2 tablespoons sugar
2 tablespoons poppy seeds
3 tablespoons Durkee sauce

Quick-freeze the rolls for easy slicing. Slice the rolls horizontally into 2 layers and return the bottom layers to the disposable pans. Arrange the sliced ham and sliced cheese evenly over the bottom layers. Top with the remaining roll layers. Cut through the rolls to separate.

Combine the margarine, onion, sugar, poppy seeds and Durkee sauce in a saucepan and mix well. Cook just until heated through, stirring occasionally. Drizzle or brush the poppy seed mixture over the rolls. Bake at 400 degrees for 15 minutes. You may substitute miniature croissants cut into halves for the rolls. Reduce the baking time to 10 minutes.

Makes 6 dozen nibbles

Make ice cream balls from different flavor combinations of ice cream and freeze the balls on a cookie sheet in advance. At party time, simply transfer the frozen balls into fun bowls or other containers that relate to the party theme and serve. This is much easier than trying to scoop ice cream for impatient children during the party.

LUNCHEON IN THE SUNROOM

*In the late winter, when skies are sunny but it is too cold to eat outdoors,
move the table next to a bright window. The sunlight feels warm,
makes the food look beautiful, and reminds everyone that spring is coming.
If it is not too cold, open the windows a bit to feel and smell the fresh air.*

12 Guests

FRESH PEA SOUP WITH HERBED CRÈME FRAÎCHE

FESTIVE FALL SALAD

BRANDY ICE

CINNAMON-GLAZED OATMEAL COOKIES

Optional Menu Item
ASPARAGUS SOUP

FRESH PEA SOUP WITH HERBED CRÈME FRAÎCHE

Elegant but easy to prepare.

Herbed Crème Fraîche
1¹/2 cups whipping cream
1¹/2 cups sour cream
¹/2 cup chopped fresh herbs (such as parsley or chives)

Pea Soup
1¹/2 cups chopped onions
1¹/2 cups chopped green onions (white and green parts)
1¹/2 tablespoons minced garlic
¹/4 cup (¹/2 stick) butter
6 cups fresh or frozen green peas
6 cups reduced-sodium chicken broth
1¹/2 cups half-and-half
Salt and pepper to taste
1¹/2 cups fresh or frozen green peas, cooked and drained
1 loaf French bread, sliced and toasted

For the crème fraîche, heat the whipping cream in a saucepan to 100 degrees. Remove from the heat and whisk in the sour cream. Let stand at room temperature for 1 to 2 hours. Fold in the fresh herbs. Chill, covered, for 8 to 10 hours.

For the soup, sauté the onions, green onions and garlic in the butter in a saucepan over medium heat until the onions are tender. Add 6 cups peas and broth and mix well. Simmer for 10 to 15 minutes or until the peas are tender, stirring occasionally. Stir in the half-and-half. Remove from the heat.

Process the soup mixture in a blender until smooth. Strain the soup into the saucepan, discarding the solids. Cook just until heated through, stirring occasionally. Taste and season with salt and pepper. Ladle into soup bowls, top with a dollop of crème fraîche and sprinkle evenly with 1¹/2 cups peas. Serve with the French bread toasts.

Serves 12

Create a fresh tabletop that anticipates spring. Choose lightweight, crisp linens. Tie napkins with green or yellow ribbons, or even a length of shimmery organdy. For serving, gather all of the silver, crystal, and pastel pieces from around the house to create an atmosphere that feels bright and new and represents the coming of spring.

ASPARAGUS SOUP

2 pounds fresh asparagus, trimmed
2 tablespoons olive oil
2 tablespoons butter
1 cup chopped onion
1/2 cup chopped shallots
1 1/2 cups chopped peeled russet potatoes

1/2 cup chopped carrots (optional)
6 cups chicken stock
1 cup (about) heavy cream (optional)
Salt and freshly ground white pepper
  to taste
Red pepper to taste

Remove the tips from 1/2 of the asparagus spears, reserving the stalks. Blanch the tips in boiling water in a saucepan for 30 seconds or until bright green. Immediately plunge the tips into a bowl of ice water to stop the cooking process; drain. Chop the reserved stalks and remaining asparagus spears.

Heat the olive oil and butter in a large saucepan. Cook the onion and shallots in the olive oil mixture for 5 to 7 minutes or until tender, stirring constantly. Add the potatoes, carrots and unblanched asparagus to the onion mixture and mix gently. Cook until the asparagus turns bright green, stirring occasionally. Stir in the stock and bring to a boil; reduce the heat.

Simmer for 20 minutes or until the potatoes, carrots and asparagus are tender, stirring occasionally. Process the soup in batches in a food processor or blender until puréed. Return the soup to the saucepan and simmer just until heated through, stirring occasionally. Add the heavy cream until of the desired consistency and mix well. Cook until heated through, stirring occasionally. Season with salt, white pepper and red pepper. Ladle into soup bowls. Top with the reserved asparagus tips. Serve hot or chilled.

Serves 6

FESTIVE FALL SALAD

1 cup olive oil
1/4 cup balsamic vinegar
2 tablespoons honey
2 teaspoons Dijon mustard
1 teaspoon salt
1/4 teaspoon pepper
2 pounds boneless skinless chicken breasts

5 ounces each romaine, radicchio and
  mesclun
3/4 cup craisins
1 pound white grapes
4 ounces Gorgonzola cheese, crumbled
1 cup walnuts, toasted
Croutons

Whisk the olive oil, vinegar, honey, mustard, salt and pepper in a bowl until blended. Chill, covered, in the refrigerator. Arrange the chicken in a shallow dish and drizzle with 1/2 cup of the vinaigrette, turning to coat. Marinate, covered, in the refrigerator for 1 to 2 hours, turning occasionally. Grill the chicken over hot coals until cooked through, turning occasionally. Cool slightly and cut into strips.

Mix the romaine, radicchio, mesclun, craisins, grapes, cheese and walnuts in a salad bowl. Add 1/2 of the remaining vinaigrette and toss to coat. Spoon the salad evenly onto salad plates and top each salad with the grilled chicken and croutons. Store the remaining vinaigrette in the refrigerator.

Serves 12

Brandy Ice

A creamy, nutty drink similar to a milk punch.

1 to 1 1/2 quarts vanilla ice cream, softened
1 cup brandy
2/3 cup crème de cacao
1/2 cup hazelnut liqueur
1/2 teaspoon nutmeg

Process 1 quart of the ice cream, brandy and liqueurs in a blender until smooth. Add enough of the remaining 1/2 quart ice cream until a pourable consistency is achieved, processing constantly. Pour into glasses and sprinkle with the nutmeg.

Serves 12

Cinnamon-Glazed Oatmeal Cookies

Cookies
3 cups old-fashioned oats
2 cups flour
1 teaspoon baking soda
1 teaspoon cinnamon
1/2 teaspoon salt
1 cup (2 sticks) butter, softened
1 cup packed brown sugar
1/2 cup sugar
2 eggs
1 teaspoon vanilla extract
1 cup walnuts, chopped

Cinnamon Glaze
1 cup sugar
2 tablespoons skim or whole milk
1/2 teaspoon vanilla extract
1/2 teaspoon cinnamon
Food coloring (optional)

For the cookies, combine the oats, flour, baking soda, cinnamon and salt in a bowl and mix well. Beat the butter, brown sugar and sugar in a mixing bowl until creamy, scraping the bowl occasionally. Add the eggs and vanilla and beat until blended. Add the oats mixture and beat until combined. Stir in the walnuts.

Drop by rounded tablespoonfuls onto an ungreased cookie sheet. Bake at 350 degrees for 10 to 12 minutes or until golden brown. Cool on the cookie sheet for 1 minute. Remove to a wire rack to cool completely.

For the glaze, combine the sugar, skim milk, vanilla and cinnamon in a bowl and stir until of a glaze consistency. Tint with food coloring. Drizzle the glaze over the cooled cookies. Let stand until set.

Makes 4 dozen cookies

Even at the end of winter, most Louisiana gardens will yield some suitable foliage for an arrangement. Cut green branches from ligustrums, camellia, and gardenia bushes and mix with a few flowers from the supermarket or florist if nothing else is in bloom. Instead of one large arrangement in the table's center, place small, individual arrangements at each place setting.

EASTER EGG HUNT AT NOON

After a winter of hearty meals and winter vegetables, the long-anticipated lighter foods of spring are finally here. People can hardly wait to get back outside again and celebrate another Louisiana springtime among the vibrant green foliage, blooming azaleas, and redbud trees.

Guests: 6 Adults and 12 Children

DEVILED EGGS

SMOKED SALMON ROULADES

STRAWBERRY SPINACH SALAD

ROASTED ROSEMARY PORK
WITH ASPARAGUS

NEW POTATO CASSEROLE

ORANGE BEETS

MANDARIN ORANGE CAKE

CARROT COOKIES

DECORATED EASTER COOKIES
(See Ghoulish Sugar Cookies, RRRIV page 172)

Optional Menu Item
BAKED PINEAPPLE HONEY HAM

DEVILED EGGS

No Easter party is complete without a plate of deviled eggs. This is a southern tradition that will never go out of style. Top with ham or smoked salmon for variety.

1 dozen eggs, hard-cooked
11 ounces cream cheese, softened
2 tablespoons mayonnaise
1 tablespoon prepared yellow mustard
2 teaspoons Dijon mustard
1 teaspoon Worcestershire sauce
1 teaspoon salt
1/2 teaspoon Tabasco sauce
1/2 teaspoon pepper
3 tablespoons dill or sweet pickle relish
Paprika to taste
Pimento-stuffed olives, thinly sliced

Cut the eggs horizontally into halves, reserving the yolks and whites. Combine the reserved egg yolks and cream cheese in a food processor and process until blended. Add the mayonnaise, yellow mustard, Dijon mustard, Worcestershire sauce, salt, Tabasco sauce and pepper to the cream cheese mixture and process until smooth. Fold in the relish with a wide-mouthed spoon. Using a teaspoon, mound the egg yolk mixture into the reserved egg whites. Sprinkle with paprika and top with olive slices.

For variety, divide the egg yolk mixture into 2 equal portions. Add dill pickle relish to 1 portion and sweet pickle relish to the remaining portion. Sprinkle paprika over the eggs stuffed with sweet relish and sprinkle dill weed over the eggs stuffed with dill relish. If preparing less than 1 dozen eggs, mix approximately 1 ounce of cream cheese per egg yolk.

Makes 1 dozen eggs

On Easter Sunday, in Cajun culture, dyed Easter eggs are often used for "pacqueing." Pacque is the French word for Easter, but in South Louisiana, the word has come to be used to refer to a popular pastime that involves two children hitting, or "pacqueing," two boiled Easter eggs together to see which one is the strongest. When someone cracks another person's egg, the winner gets to keep both eggs. Playing this game has evolved into an art form, with people using special boiling techniques to ensure that the eggs' shells will be strong enough for pacqueing and little children hunting for rocks shaped like eggs that can be used to cheat.

SMOKED SALMON ROULADES

Cream cheese and capers are spread on salmon that is rolled up, chilled, and sliced. These roulades may be served as a cold hors d'oeuvre or as an accompaniment to a meal.

8 ounces whipped cream cheese, at room temperature
1/4 cup chopped fresh chives
1 tablespoon drained capers
1/4 teaspoon salt
1/4 teaspoon lemon pepper
1 pound smoked salmon, thinly sliced
3 tablespoons chopped fresh dill weed

Place an 11 1/2×30-inch sheet of plastic wrap on a hard surface, positioning the shorter ends to the right and left. Beat the cream cheese, chives, capers, salt and lemon pepper in a mixing bowl until combined.

Carefully center 1 slice of the salmon on the plastic wrap 3 inches from the shorter left side. Continue to arrange the sliced salmon, overlapping by 1 inch, until all the salmon is used. The salmon layer should measure approximately 6×24 inches and should end approximately 3 inches from the right side of the plastic wrap.

Spread the cream cheese mixture over the salmon and sprinkle with the dill weed. Starting at the long end, roll up to enclose the filling and wrap in the plastic wrap, securing the ends. Chill for 1 hour or longer.

Discard the plastic wrap and cut the roll into 2 equal portions. Cut each roll into 1/2-inch slices. Arrange the slices on a serving platter. Serve with toast points.

Serves 12

Junior League cookbooks are big money-makers throughout the South, but the popularity and longevity of RRR are truly phenomenal. Why it became a runaway best-seller is partly attributable to the irresistible appeal of all those recipes for gumbos, court bouillons, and jambalayas and partly to the determined selling of the Junior Leaguers. "When the book came out," says Martha (Monkey) Bowlus, 1960 chairman, "every member was given ten copies to sell. Then they came back for another ten. When people wrote us that they couldn't find filé for the gumbo in their local stores, we mailed them a little pack of it. For years no member dared to go out of town, whether to New Orleans, New York, or Paris, without a copy of RRR in their suitcase. I have shown it to people in bookshops, department stores, supermarkets, and airplanes, and I still don't travel without it."

—Good Housekeeping *magazine*

Strawberry Spinach Salad

Wonderful Louisiana strawberries are so plentiful during the spring months that whole flats of them may be purchased at roadside stands at bargain prices or "for a song."

1 cup pecan halves
1 package fresh baby leaf spinach
Crumbled blue cheese
Purple onions, sliced and separated into rings
1 pint fresh strawberries, sliced
1 (12-ounce) bottle Brianna's Blush Wine Strawberry Vinaigrette

Spread the pecans in a single layer on a baking sheet. Toast at 300 degrees for 10 to 15 minutes or until fragrant and light brown, stirring occasionally. Toss the pecans, spinach, blue cheese, onions and strawberries in a salad bowl. Add the desired amount of vinaigrette and toss to coat.

Serves 6

Roasted Rosemary Pork with Asparagus

Roasting the asparagus along with the pork gives it a delicious flavor.

3 tablespoons olive oil
2 tablespoons Dijon mustard
2 tablespoons fresh lemon juice
3 large garlic cloves, minced
4 teaspoons chopped fresh rosemary
1/2 teaspoon salt

1/2 teaspoon freshly ground pepper
1 (5-pound) center-cut pork loin
   roast
2 pounds fresh thick asparagus
   spears, trimmed and blanched

Preheat the oven to 400 degrees. Mix the olive oil, mustard, lemon juice, garlic, rosemary, salt and pepper in a bowl. Reserve 1 tablespoon of the olive oil mixture. Spread the remaining olive oil mixture over the fat side of the pork and arrange on a wire rack in a roasting pan.

Place the pork in the oven and reduce the oven temperature to 325 degrees. Roast for 2 hours. Toss the asparagus with the reserved olive oil mixture in a shallow dish. Arrange the asparagus around the pork and roast for 15 to 20 minutes longer or until a meat thermometer registers 160 degrees for medium or 170 degrees for well done. Slice the pork and serve immediately with the asparagus.

Serves 12

Blanching vegetables before roasting or grilling brings out their full flavor and ensures they cook through. Vegetables such as green beans, asparagus, carrots, or other root vegetables are easily blanched by placing them in rapidly boiling water. When the water returns to a full boil, drain the vegetables and immediately plunge into ice water to stop the cooking process. Drain and let stand for a few minutes, then roast or grill.

BAKED PINEAPPLE HONEY HAM

Delicious ham sandwiches are a delightful bonus the next day if you are lucky enough to have leftovers.

1 large ham, shank portion
1 (12-ounce) can Coca-Cola
1 (20-ounce) can crushed pineapple,
  drained
3 to 4 cups honey

1 cup packed brown sugar
1/4 cup yellow mustard
1 (20-ounce) can pineapple slices, drained
1 (4-ounce) jar maraschino cherries,
  drained

Trim the ham of the outer layer of fat and place the ham in a large stockpot. Add enough water to cover. Bring to a boil and boil for 15 minutes; drain. Add fresh water to cover again. Bring to a boil and boil for 15 minutes; drain. The boiling process takes away the salty flavor of the ham.

Place the ham on a sheet of foil large enough to enclose the ham. Transfer the foil and ham to a baking dish or large roasting pan. Pour the soda over the ham and seal the foil tightly. Marinate in the refrigerator for 2 to 10 hours.

Mix the crushed pineapple, honey, brown sugar and mustard in a bowl. Pour some of the pineapple mixture over the top of the ham and arrange the ham flat side down in the baking dish; seal the foil.

Bake at 275 degrees for 2 to 3 hours, basting with the pineapple mixture every 30 minutes. Arrange the pineapple slices 2 inches apart over the surface of the ham and secure with wooden picks 30 minutes before the end of the baking process. Place a cherry at the top of each wooden pick. Baste with the remaining pineapple mixture and bake for 30 minutes longer. Let stand until cool and slice as desired.

Serves 8 to 12

NEW POTATO CASSEROLE

New potatoes are creamier and less grainy than regular baking potatoes. This dish may be prepared in advance. Serve with any type of meat.

2 pounds new potatoes
Salt and pepper to taste
1 cup milk
1/2 cup sour cream

1/2 cup mayonnaise
1 envelope ranch salad dressing mix
4 slices bacon, crisp-cooked and crumbled

Parboil the potatoes in boiling water in a saucepan; drain. Cut the potatoes into quarters and place in a bowl. Season with salt and pepper. Add the milk, sour cream, mayonnaise and dressing mix to the potatoes and mix gently.

Spoon the potato mixture into a shallow baking dish. Bake at 350 degrees for 15 minutes. Sprinkle with the bacon.

Serves 6 to 8

ORANGE BEETS

These beets are simmered in orange juice and served at room temperature as a side dish. Alternatively, the beet mixture may be chopped and served as a relish with beef, pork, or game.

1 pound small beets
2 tablespoons cornstarch
1¼ tablespoons light brown sugar
1 (6-ounce) can frozen orange juice
  concentrate

3/4 cup cider vinegar
3/4 cup water
1 small onion, chopped
1 tablespoon butter

Cook the beets in boiling water in a saucepan for 7 minutes or until tender; drain. Peel and slice the beets. Combine the cornstarch and brown sugar in a saucepan and mix well. Stir in the orange juice concentrate, vinegar and water. Bring to a boil, stirring constantly. Cook until thickened, stirring constantly; reduce the heat to low. Cook for 5 minutes longer, stirring occasionally.

Sauté the onion in the butter in a skillet until tender. Add the beets to the sautéed onion and mix gently. Stir in the orange sauce. Simmer just until heated through, stirring constantly. Serve hot or at room temperature. You may prepare 1 day in advance and store, covered, in the refrigerator. Reheat before serving.

Serves 6

MANDARIN ORANGE CAKE

A package of cake mix and a tub of whipped topping makes this light and refreshing cake a snap to prepare. Perfect for an outdoor party on a warm day.

Cake
1 (2-layer) package yellow cake mix
1 cup water
2 tablespoons vegetable oil
6 egg whites

Orange Frosting
1 (15-ounce) can juice-pack crushed
  pineapple
1 (11-ounce) can mandarin oranges
2 small packages sugar-free vanilla instant
  pudding mix
9 ounces light whipped topping

For the cake, grease 3 cake pans and line the bottoms with baking parchment. Grease and flour the baking parchment. Combine the cake mix, water, oil and egg whites in a mixing bowl. Beat at medium speed for 2 minutes. Pour the batter evenly into the prepared pans and bake at 350 degrees for 20 to 25 minutes or until the layers test done. Cool in the pans for 10 minutes. Remove to a wire rack to cool completely.

For the frosting, combine the undrained pineapple, undrained mandarin oranges and pudding mix in a bowl and mix well. Add the whipped topping and mix until combined. Spread the frosting between the layers and over the top and side of the cake.

Serves 12

CARROT COOKIES

Carrot cake fans will love these crunchy carrot and oatmeal drop cookies. Great for an after-school snack.

> 1 cup unbleached flour
> 1/4 teaspoon baking powder
> 1/4 teaspoon baking soda
> 1/2 cup (1 stick) butter or margarine
> 1/2 cup sugar
> 1/2 cup packed light brown sugar
> 1/2 teaspoon vanilla
> 1 egg
> 1 cup quick-cooking oats
> 3/4 cup medium-fine chopped walnuts
> 1/2 cup flaked coconut
> 1/2 cup finely grated carrots

Stir the flour with a fork to aerate before measuring. Mix the flour, baking powder and baking soda together. Beat the butter, sugar, brown sugar and vanilla in a mixing bowl until creamy. Add the egg and beat until blended. Stir in the flour mixture, oats, walnuts, coconut and carrots.

Drop by rounded teaspoonfuls 2 inches apart onto a buttered cookie sheet. Bake at 350 degrees for 12 to 15 minutes or until light brown. Cool on the cookie sheet for 2 minutes. Remove to a wire rack to cool completely.

Makes 4 dozen cookies

FATHER'S DAY OUTDOOR GRILL

*With so much emphasis put on Mother's Day, dad's special day
does not always get the attention it deserves. Father's Day is mid-summer,
a time when social calendars are usually empty and markets
are filled with a bounty of vegetables and fruit. Round up the family,
fire up the grill, and declare dad the guest of honor.*

12 Guests

TOMATO TAPENADE

RICE PRIMAVERA SALAD

MIXED GREENS WITH
LEMON-BUTTERMILK DRESSING

PRIME RIB ON A PIT WITH
HORSERADISH-CHIVE SAUCE

ROASTED CORN ON THE COB WITH
SUN-DRIED TOMATO BUTTER

SUMMER COBBLER

AMARETTO CHEESECAKE

TOMATO TAPENADE

Serve pita bread, bagel chips, or another type of sturdy cracker with this alternative to the usual salsa. Toss any leftovers with mixed greens to make an outstanding salad.

> 1 pint grape tomatoes, cut into quarters
> 1/2 cup (2 ounces) crumbled feta cheese
> 4 to 5 tablespoons olive oil
> 1/4 cup chopped green onions
> 1/4 cup drained capers
> 1 1/2 to 2 ounces chopped black olives (optional)
> 2 tablespoons Italian seasoning
> Salt and pepper to taste

Mix the tomatoes, cheese, olive oil, green onions, capers, olives, Italian seasoning, salt and pepper in a bowl. Spoon the tomato mixture into a shallow baking dish. Bake at 350 degrees for 20 minutes. Serve warm with water crackers or French bread. If using fresh feta cheese, decrease the amount added due to the strong flavor.

Serves 12

I am so proud to have been a part of the first River Road Recipes *cookbook from its beginning. Even though our financial advisors did not think it was a good idea for the league, we continued to collect, edit, and select the best recipes during taste-testing parties. We presented the layout of the cookbook to the board for permission to present it to the membership to adopt it as a money-making project. It still gives me a fright when I think how close we came to being voted down.*

—*Emily Robinson, Chairman 1959*

RICE PRIMAVERA SALAD

2 zucchini
2 yellow squash
5 cups cooked long grain rice
1 large red bell pepper, chopped
1 purple onion, chopped
$3/4$ cup mayonnaise

$1/3$ cup buttermilk
2 tablespoons Dijon mustard
2 tablespoons white vinegar
$1^1/2$ teaspoons salt
$1/2$ teaspoon pepper

Cut the zucchini and yellow squash lengthwise into halves and slice the halves. Combine the zucchini, yellow squash, rice, bell pepper and onion in a bowl and mix well. Stir in the mayonnaise, buttermilk, mustard, vinegar, salt and pepper. Chill, covered, for 8 hours.

Makes 8 cups

MIXED GREENS WITH LEMON-BUTTERMILK DRESSING

This tangy and creamy salad dressing makes a great dip for raw vegetables.

Lemon-Buttermilk Dressing
$2/3$ cup buttermilk
$2/3$ cup mayonnaise
$1^1/2$ tablespoons fresh lemon juice
1 garlic clove, minced
$1/4$ teaspoon salt
$1/4$ teaspoon pepper
$1/2$ cup minced green onions (white and green parts)
Grated zest of 1 lemon

Salad
3 to 4 cups mixed salad greens

For the dressing, combine the buttermilk, mayonnaise, lemon juice, garlic, salt and pepper in a bowl and mix well. Stir in the green onions and lemon zest. Chill, covered, in the refrigerator for up to 1 week.
For the salad, toss the salad greens with the desired amount of dressing in a bowl. Serve immediately.

Serves 4 to 6

PRIME RIB ON A PIT

Smoky and rich, cut the rib-eye into thick slices like a steak, or slice thinly and serve on buns. Remember when cooking on a grill that the vent should be used to regulate the temperature. For high heat, keep the bottom vent by the coals open, but for lower cooking temperatures, keep the top vent open.

> 1 (8- to 10-pound) whole beef rib-eye, bone in
> Worcestershire sauce to taste
> Salt and pepper to taste
> Garlic powder to taste

Prepare the barbecue grill. Bring the rib-eye to room temperature; rinse and pat dry. Season with Worcestershire sauce, salt, pepper and garlic powder and arrange on the grill rack. Sear on all sides over hot coals. Lower the fire pan, if you have that feature on your pit, and grill over direct heat for about 2 hours or indirect heat, if desired, until a meat thermometer registers 145 degrees for medium-rare or to the desired degree of doneness. Slice as desired and serve with Horseradish-Chive Sauce.

Serves 8 to 10

HORSERADISH-CHIVE SAUCE

Homemade horseradish sauce complements beef so well, and the chives add a little color to the white sauce.

> 1 cup mayonnaise
> 1 cup sour cream
> 1/3 cup chopped green onions or chives
> 1/4 cup prepared horseradish
> 2 tablespoons Worcestershire sauce
> Freshly ground pepper to taste

Combine the mayonnaise, sour cream, green onions, horseradish and Worcestershire sauce in a bowl and mix well. Season with pepper. Chill, covered, until serving time. You may prepare 1 day in advance and store, covered, in the refrigerator.

Serves 8

ROASTED CORN ON THE COB WITH SUN-DRIED TOMATO BUTTER

Louisiana crawfish farmers often flood their fields in the off-season and plant corn, making it a plentiful staple in the summertime.

1 cup (2 sticks) unsalted butter, softened	2 garlic cloves, minced
3 large oil-pack sun-dried tomatoes, drained and finely chopped	1/16 teaspoon kosher salt
	Freshly ground pepper to taste
2 tablespoons finely chopped green onions	Fresh corn on the cob

Combine the butter, sun-dried tomatoes, green onions, garlic, salt and pepper in a food processor and process until blended. Spoon the butter into a crock or roll into a log. Chill, covered, for 2 hours or longer.

Wrap unshucked corn in foil. Arrange the foil-wrapped corn directly on the oven rack. Roast at 375 degrees for 45 minutes. Serve with the butter.

Variable servings

SUMMER COBBLER

The flavors of blueberries and peaches go so well together, and their arrival at the same time of the year makes them a convenient combination.

3 cups flour	8 to 10 ripe peaches, peeled and thickly sliced
1/3 cup sugar	
1 teaspoon cinnamon	1/2 cup fresh blueberries
3/4 cup (11/2 sticks) unsalted butter, chilled	1 to 11/2 cups sugar (depends on the sweetness of the peaches)
1/2 cup shortening, frozen	1/4 cup (1/2 stick) butter, cut into small pieces
10 tablespoons ice water	

Process the flour, 1/3 cup sugar and cinnamon in a food processor until blended. Add 3/4 cup butter and shortening and process until crumbly. Add the ice water and process until the mixture begins to form a ball. Roll the dough into a 12×16-inch rectangle on a lightly floured surface and fit into a 9×13-inch pan, allowing the excess dough to hang over the sides.

Combine the peaches, blueberries and 1 to 11/2 cups sugar in a bowl and mix gently. Spoon the peach mixture into the prepared pan and dot with 1/4 cup butter. Bring the excess dough over the top of the fruit filling. Bake at 425 degrees for 45 to 60 minutes or until brown and bubbly.

Serves 10 to 12

One of the most popular and simplest ways to cook fresh corn in Louisiana is simply toss the corn into the crawfish pot along with the potatoes. Listed below are other ways for preparing **Corn on the Cob.**

Boil by bringing a stockpot of lightly salted water to a boil, then adding the shucked corn. Return to a boil, reduce the heat to a simmer, and cook, covered, for three minutes.

Microwave by placing unshucked ears directly on the floor of the micro-wave. Microwave on High for two minutes. Turn the ears and microwave for two minutes longer. Let stand for three minutes, then shuck.

Grill by wrapping unshucked corn in foil and placing along the side of the grill rack, away from the direct heat. Grill for forty-five minutes, turning every fifteen minutes. The silk steam to the husks, so when the foil is removed, the corn will slip right out. For a skirt effect, pull the husk all the way down and trim it. Serve with infused butter.

Try this recipe for **Homemade Amaretto**. Dissolve 3 1/2 cups sugar in 2 cups boiling water in a heatproof container. Add 1 tablespoon instant coffee granules and stir until dissolved. Stir in 2 tablespoons almond extract, 5 teaspoons vanilla extract, 5 dashes Peychaud's bitters and 1 fifth vodka. Store in an airtight bottle. New Orleans pharmacist Antoine Peychaud developed Peychaud's bitters in the 1930s as a liquid tonic added to Cognac to cure ailments. The popularity of this cure-all toddy, which later became known as a Sazerac Cocktail, became enormous, and it was soon being served in coffeehouses all over the French Quarter.

AMARETTO CHEESECAKE

Delicious and easy to prepare with a crust made from shortbread cookies.

Shortbread Crust
1 (10-ounce) package shortbread cookies, finely ground
1/4 cup flour
1/4 cup sugar
5 tablespoons unsalted butter, softened
1 egg yolk, lightly beaten
2 tablespoons amaretto
1/2 cup slivered almonds, chopped

Filling
32 ounces cream cheese, softened
1 1/2 cups sugar
1/4 cup flour
3 eggs
1 egg white
1/3 cup amaretto
1 cup whipped cream

For the crust, mix the cookie crumbs, flour and sugar in a bowl. Add the butter to the crumb mixture and mix well. Stir in the egg yolk and liqueur. Reserve 1/3 of the crumb mixture. Add the almonds to the remaining crumb mixture and mix well.

Press the almond crumb mixture over the bottom of a greased 9-inch springform pan. Wrap the pan with foil or place the pan on a baking sheet to prevent spillage onto the oven floor. Bake at 350 degrees for 12 to 15 minutes or until light brown. Maintain the oven temperature. Freeze the crust until cool. Grease the side of the cooled pan and pat the reserved crumb mixture to the top of the pan.

For the filling, place the cream cheese in a mixing bowl. Add the sugar 1/2 cup at a time, beating until smooth after each addition. Add the flour and beat until blended. Add the eggs and egg white 1 at a time, beating well after each addition. Blend in the liqueur. Whisk in the whipped cream until smooth.

Spoon the filling into the prepared pan and place the pan on the center oven rack. Place a small pan of water on the lower oven rack. Bake for 10 minutes. Reduce the oven temperature to 250 degrees and bake for 35 minutes longer. Turn off the oven. Let stand in the oven with the door closed for at least 4 hours or up to overnight; do not peek. Chill until serving time. The flavor of the cheesecake is enhanced if baked 1 day in advance and stored, covered, in the refrigerator until serving time.

Serves 12

TROPICAL POOL PARTY

*A warm Louisiana summer evening combined with the lush beauty of
our native vegetation sets a romantic tone for a couple's shower
to honor a future bride and groom. Set up tables and chairs around the pool,
string lights on the trees, and place candles everywhere.*

6 to 8 Guests

SPIRIT MUSIC COCKTAIL

MARINATED CRAB CLAWS

CHICKEN SATÉ WITH PEANUT DIPPING SAUCE

SESAME-CRUSTED AHI TUNA WITH
THAI GINGER DIPPING SAUCE

SWEET POTATO TURNOVERS

TROPICAL FRUIT PLATTER

Optional Menu Items
MARINATED CRAWFISH

SWEET-AND-SOUR CHICKEN

SPIRIT MUSIC COCKTAIL

Originally called muzik di zumbi, which is Caribbean for "spirit music." This drink is inspired by the music of the islands.

2 cups cubed fresh mangoes	$1/2$ cup superfine sugar
3 cups water	Juice of 4 limes
$1/2$ cup white rum	$2/3$ cup grenadine
$1/2$ cup curaçao	$2/3$ cup superfine sugar

Process the mangoes and water in a blender until puréed. Strain the purée into a pitcher, discarding the solids. Add the rum, liqueur, $1/2$ cup sugar and lime juice to the purée and stir until the sugar dissolves.

Pour the grenadine and $2/3$ cup sugar into separate shallow bowls. Dip the rims of glasses in the grenadine and then rotate gently in the sugar to cover evenly. Fill the sugar-rimmed glasses with crushed ice and add the mango mixture. Serve immediately.

Serves 12

MARINATED CRAWFISH

$1^1/4$ cups olive oil	$1/2$ teaspoon pepper
$3/4$ cup cider or wine vinegar	Tabasco sauce to taste
$2^1/2$ tablespoons capers	3 pounds Louisiana crawfish tails
1 to 2 tablespoons chopped fresh parsley	3 or 4 green onions, chopped
	1 small red onion, thinly sliced
$2^1/2$ teaspoons celery seeds	Thinly sliced lemons
$1^1/2$ teaspoons salt	

Whisk the olive oil, vinegar, undrained capers, parsley, celery seeds, salt, pepper and Tabasco sauce in a large bowl. Add the crawfish tails, green onions, red onion slices and sliced lemons and mix well. Marinate, covered, in the refrigerator for 1 to 10 hours, stirring occasionally.

Serve as an appetizer with wooden picks, or spoon the crawfish mixture over a bed of shredded lettuce and serve as a salad. Great recipe for leftover crawfish.

Serves 6 to 8

MARINATED CRAB CLAWS

Always a favorite, no one can pass up sweet crab claws on a cocktail table.

1 cup fresh orange juice
1 cup fresh Ruby Red grapefruit juice
1 cup olive oil
1/2 cup raspberry vinegar

1/4 cup chopped fresh parsley
Salt and pepper to taste
2 pounds steamed jumbo crab claws

Whisk the orange juice, grapefruit juice, olive oil, vinegar, parsley, salt and pepper in a bowl. Pour the orange juice mixture over the crab claws in a shallow dish, turning to coat. Marinate, covered, in the refrigerator for 45 minutes, turning occasionally. Drain before serving.

Serves 6 to 8

CHICKEN SATÉ WITH PEANUT DIPPING SAUCE

Peanut Dipping Sauce
1/4 cup creamy peanut butter
Juice of 1 lime
2 teaspoons white wine vinegar
3 tablespoons brown sugar
1/2 cup finely chopped onion
1 tablespoon minced garlic
1/4 cup peanut oil
1/4 cup each coconut milk and water
2 tablespoons curry powder
1/2 teaspoon red pepper flakes

Chicken Saté
2/3 cup chile oil
1/2 cup rice wine vinegar
1/2 cup soy sauce
1/4 cup packed brown sugar
2 tablespoons hot Chinese mustard
2 teaspoons grated fresh gingerroot
2 pounds chicken tenders

For the sauce, whisk the peanut butter, lime juice, vinegar and brown sugar in a bowl until blended. Sauté the onion and garlic in the peanut oil in a large skillet for 5 minutes or until the onion is tender. Add the coconut milk, water, curry powder and red pepper to the onion mixture and mix well. Bring to a boil, stirring occasionally. Stir in the peanut butter mixture. Simmer until thickened, stirring frequently.

For the saté, mix the chile oil, vinegar, soy sauce, brown sugar, mustard and gingerroot in a bowl. Reserve 1/2 cup of the marinade. Pour the remaining marinade over the chicken in a shallow dish and turn to coat. Marinate, covered, in the refrigerator for 1 hour or longer, turning occasionally; drain.

Thread the chicken on water-soaked bamboo skewers. Grill for 3 to 5 minutes per side or until cooked through, basting with the reserved marinade frequently. Serve with the dipping sauce. Add grilled vegetables for a main entrée.

Serves 6 to 8

Sesame-Crusted Ahi Tuna with Thai Ginger Dipping Sauce

Sesame seeds give this Asian-inspired dish a nutty flavor.

Thai Ginger Dipping Sauce
1/4 cup soy sauce
1/4 cup rice wine vinegar
1 tablespoon minced fresh gingerroot
1 1/2 tablespoons wasabi paste

Ahi Tuna
3/4 cup olive oil
1/2 cup orange juice
1/2 cup soy sauce
3 tablespoons brown sugar
3 tablespoons hoisin sauce
3 tablespoons honey
1 teaspoon red pepper flakes
2 pounds fresh ahi tuna fillets
1 1/2 cups sesame seeds, toasted
1/4 cup olive oil

For the sauce, mix the soy sauce, vinegar and gingerroot in a bowl. Add the wasabi paste and stir until dissolved.

For the tuna, whisk 3/4 cup olive oil, orange juice, soy sauce, brown sugar, hoisin sauce, honey and red pepper flakes in a bowl. Pour over the tuna in a shallow dish, turning to coat. Marinate, covered, in the refrigerator for 30 minutes; drain. Coat the tuna with the sesame seeds.

Heat 1/4 cup olive oil in a large nonstick skillet over high heat. Sear the tuna in the hot oil for about 1 minute per side. Cut into bite-size pieces and thread on skewers. Serve with the sauce.

Serves 6 to 8

Sweet-and-Sour Chicken

1 (20-ounce) can juice-pack pineapple
   chunks
4 to 6 boneless skinless chicken breasts
Salt and pepper to taste
1 (8-ounce) can tomato sauce
1/2 (16-ounce) package brown sugar
1/3 cup apple cider vinegar
1 red bell pepper, cut into 1-inch squares
1 green bell pepper, cut into 1-inch
   squares
1 onion, coarsely chopped

Drain the pineapple, reserving the pineapple and juice. Season the chicken with salt and pepper. Grill the chicken over hot coals or sauté in a skillet sprayed with nonstick cooking spray until cooked through. Cool slightly and cut the chicken into bite-size pieces.

Combine the reserved pineapple juice, tomato sauce, brown sugar and vinegar in a skillet and mix well. Simmer for 15 minutes, stirring occasionally. Stir in the reserved pineapple, chicken, bell peppers and onion. Chill, covered, in the refrigerator until serving time. Reheat and serve in a chafing dish. The flavor is enhanced if prepared 1 day in advance.

Serves 4 to 6

Sweet Potato Turnovers

Mashed sweet potatoes in a flaky pastry filling.

3 large sweet potatoes, peeled and cut into
   quarters
1/8 teaspoon salt
1 1/4 cups sugar
1 teaspoon cinnamon
1 teaspoon vanilla extract
2 eggs, lightly beaten, or an equivalent
   amount of egg substitute
1 1/2 cups shortening
6 cups self-rising flour
1 cup (about) water

Combine the sweet potatoes and salt with enough water to cover in a large saucepan. Bring to a boil and boil until tender; drain. Mash the sweet potatoes in a bowl and stir in the sugar, cinnamon, vanilla and eggs.

Cut the shortening into the self-rising flour in a bowl until crumbly. Add the water 1 tablespoon at a time, stirring with a fork until the mixture forms a ball. Roll 1/8 inch thick on a lightly floured surface and cut into 4-inch rounds. Spoon some of the sweet potato mixture on 1/2 of each round and fold over to enclose the filling. Press the edge of the turnovers with a fork dipped in flour to seal and cut 3 vents in each.

Arrange the turnovers on a baking sheet sprayed with nonstick cooking spray. Bake at 400 degrees for 20 to 25 minutes or until brown. Remove to a wire rack to cool. Serve at room temperature or sauté in butter in a skillet just until heated through. You may freeze for future use. Reheat before serving.

Makes 1 1/2 dozen turnovers, or 3 dozen appetizer turnovers

TROPICAL FRUIT PLATTER

1 pineapple
2 mangoes
2 papayas
3 kiwifruit
2 Asian pears
2 banana leaves
1 small bunch finger bananas

Cut the green top off the pineapple and reserve. Cut the bottom off the pineapple. With the pineapple standing vertically, shave the outer skin off and discard. Cut down the center through the core. Cut each side through the core into halves. Remove the core and slice the remaining pineapple into 4 portions.

To prepare the mangoes, look at the fruit. They should look like slightly squashed footballs. There is a large flat pit in the center of each mango, and by looking, you can imagine how the pits sit. Using a long knife, cut on each side of the pits. Peel the mangoes and slice.

To prepare the papayas, cut into halves and discard the seeds. Peel and cut into wedges. Peel and slice the kiwifruit. Slice and core the pears; do not peel.

To serve, arrange the banana leaves on a large wooden platter. Place the reserved pineapple top and banana bunch in the center of the platter and surround with the prepared fruit.

Serves 6 to 8

LOUISIANA CRAWFISH BOIL

"They look like tiny lobsters," is the usual assessment when a visitor is introduced to Louisiana crawfish, and there is some truth to the idea. Like lobster meat, crawfish meat is white and sweet. Like lobsters, crawfish are brown when alive and turn red when boiled. But unlike lobsters, crawfish come from lakes and rivers, not the ocean, and are usually only three inches long. Most outsiders call them "crayfish," but call them that in Louisiana, and everyone will know you're not a native!

6 to 8 Guests

CRAWFISH

RED POTATOES

CORN ON THE COB

The difference between Creole and Cajun cooking has been the subject of many debates. Both types have their roots in French cuisine. However, it is generally acknowledged that Creole cooking is found more often in the more urban areas of Louisiana and tends to be more elaborate in the style of Grande Cuisine, consisting of delicate blends, subtle combinations of flavors, and complex sauces. Most of the earliest recipes were brought over from Europe by many of the sophisticated French and Spanish Creoles who settled in Louisiana. After the Louisiana Purchase in 1803, there were large immigrations of Germans, Italians, and Hungarians, including an influx of slaves from Africa, all of which has resulted in a strong ethnic influence being brought to the Creole cooking style.

"TINY LITTLE LOBSTERS"

The short period from March to May is the peak of the crawfish harvest, a season that is much anticipated in Louisiana. During the harvest period, crawfish are at their best in quality and quantity, and the prices are the lowest of the year. Louisianans build many springtime social occasions around the cooking and eating of crawfish. However they are to be prepared, from the simplest crawfish boil to the most elegant crawfish bisque, the local appetite for them is insatiable.

Peeling and eating crawfish is a skill most locals learn as children, but can easily be mastered by any outsider who does not fret about getting a little messy. Never wear white to a crawfish boil, as it is impossible to keep from being squirted by the crawfish juice, which leaves a tough stain. Review these steps before proceeding to a crawfish boil.

1. Hold the crawfish in both hands and twist off the tail.

2. At the open end of the tail, peel off two to three sections of the shell to expose about one-fourth of the meat.

3. To completely remove the meat, pinch the end of the tail with one hand and gently pull on the exposed tail meat with the other hand until the meat slides out of the shell. Removing the black vein is optional.

4. It is a fun challenge to try and get the meat out of the claws by cracking the larger claws with your teeth and sucking out the meat. The smaller claws usually are not worth bothering with.

5. "Sucking the heads" is also a tradition where everyone is encouraged to suck out the delicious juices from the broken-off end of the crawfish head. This can be messy, but it is also fun.

LOUISIANA CRAWFISH BOIL

Live crawfish are generally sold in onion sacks that hold about twenty-five to thirty pounds. A good rule of thumb is to allow five pounds of crawfish per person. Crawfish spoil quickly, so keep them alive and cold until time to boil. If you won't be boiling immediately, hose down the sacks of crawfish every thirty minutes or so until the boiling water is ready. Crawfish boiling pots are available for purchase in most Louisiana hardware stores or may be purchased by mail order. Do not try to boil crawfish in the kitchen! When choosing the brand of crab boil you will be using, read the directions on the package carefully since all seasonings are different. If you use a brand that contains additional salt, you may want to add less salt during the process. This recipe uses unsalted crab boil and salt is added.

20 gallons water	6 small yellow onions, cut into
40 pounds live crawfish	quarters
2 boxes salt	8 frozen ears of corn
Salt-free crab boil, per directions	4 lemons, cut into halves
5 pounds small red potatoes	1 bag ice
8 heads garlic, cut into halves	

Fill a large crawfish pot fitted with a boiling basket with 20 gallons water and place on an outdoor propane heater. Bring to a boil.

Place the crawfish in an aluminum tub, sprinkle with 1 box of the salt and fill with water. Let the crawfish rinse and purge in the salt water for 2 to 3 minutes. Drain and rinse the crawfish with fresh water. Discard any floating crawfish.

Add the remaining box of salt and crab boil to the boiling water. Add the potatoes and garlic to the boiling basket and return to a boil. Add the crawfish, onions, corn and lemons.

Bring to a boil; this will take approximately 10 minutes. Turn off the heat and let stand for 10 minutes. Add the bag of ice to force the seasonings to the bottom of the pot. Let stand for 10 minutes longer.

Remove the boiling basket with the crawfish and vegetables and drain. Spread the drained contents on tables covered with newspapers. For variety, add artichokes, oranges, mushrooms and/or sausage to the crawfish pot.

Serves 6 to 8

Leftover crawfish may be frozen for later use in gumbo, étouffée, or other dishes. Peel crawfish and rinse the tails in cold water to remove the fat, which can cause tails to take on an unpleasant flavor when frozen. Drain and pack the crawfish in resealable plastic freezer bags or freezer containers. Add just enough cold water to cover the tails, leaving a one-half-inch headspace. Freeze for up to nine months. Frozen crawfish should not be boiled again, as it causes a loss of texture and flavor. When ready to use, simply add the thawed tails to the recipe and prepare as directed.

Around the Town

$\mathscr{B}$aton Rouge finds many occasions and many places to celebrate with food, whether a family reunion at the camp or a picnic on the levee of the Mississippi River. People here know how to make a fine portable feast, and there are so many places to go with it.

Because social life in Louisiana is food-centered, we enjoy frequent shared celebrations of faith, family, and friendship. A loving gift of food welcomes a new baby, nurses an illness, or mourns a death.

With some of the most beloved Louisiana dishes, the cooking is part of the entertainment. The crawfish pot or the cochon du lait pit is a gathering place and center of activity. Everyone contributes to the shared meal, with a casserole side dish, an extra bag of oysters, or some fresh deer sausage.

Because Louisianans love to linger, the feast is likely to stretch on and on. So when a crowd gathers, plentiful food and long visits are the order of the day.

AFTER THE HUNT

For good reason, Louisiana is known as "The Sportsman's Paradise." Hunting and fishing are a ritual, and hunting camps can be as primitive as a tent or old trailer or as elaborate as a marsh lodge with fine furnishings. Louisianians grow up hunting, fishing, and cooking with old hands at "the camp." Each hunter has a specialty, so whatever is on the menu is likely freshly prepared by the resident expert.

6 Guests

OLD-FASHIONED COCKTAIL

BACON-WRAPPED DOVE BREASTS

GRILLED BARBECUED OYSTERS

GRILLED QUAIL AND POMEGRANATE SALAD

ROASTED GARLIC-GLAZED DUCK BREASTS

HEARTY GRITS CASSEROLE

SWEET POTATO BISCUITS

BREAD PUDDING WITH HARD SAUCE

OLD-FASHIONED COCKTAIL

Southern men who hunt and fish traditionally mix up a batch of old-fashioned cocktails to bring to the camp. In the evening, all that is left to do is pour over ice and drink.

Simple Syrup
1 cup sugar
1 cup water

Old-Fashioned Cocktail
3 cups bourbon
10 ounces club soda
1 tablespoon bitters

For the syrup, combine the sugar and water in a saucepan. Heat until the sugar dissolves, stirring occasionally. Bring to a boil and boil for 1 minute. Let stand until cool and store, covered, in the refrigerator.

For the cocktail, mix 1 cup of the syrup, bourbon, club soda and bitters in a pitcher. Pour over crushed ice in glasses. Garnish with orange slices and maraschino cherries.

Serves 8

BACON-WRAPPED DOVE BREASTS

This is a delicious and different appetizer. Be sure to remove any buck shot from the dove before grilling.

12 dove breasts, deboned
Salt and pepper to taste
1/2 jar jalapeño chiles, drained, sliced and rinsed
8 ounces thinly sliced bacon

Season the dove with salt and pepper. Wrap each dove breast around 1 jalapeño chile slice. Encircle each with a slice of bacon and secure with wooden skewers. Grill over hot coals until the dove is cooked through and the bacon is crisp, turning occasionally. Serve immediately.

Serves 6 to 8

Anyone can be taught to cook oysters, but opening takes a little practice. The equipment you will need includes an oyster knife and heavy rubber gloves. The oyster's shell is very rough and in some places sharp enough to cause a bad cut if protective gloves are not worn. Place the oyster on a flat surface with the rounded side down. Insert the tip of the oyster knife into the hinge between the top and bottom shells. Carefully pry the two shells slightly apart, then slide the knife between the oyster meat and the top shell and sever the muscle that connects them. Carefully remove the top shell while trying to avoid loosing the oyster juice. Finally, slide the knife under the oyster and sever the muscle connected to the bottom shell.

After removing the oyster, discard the top shells, but retain the bottom shells. Dishes such as Oysters Rockefeller and Oysters Bienville are traditionally served in the empty half shells. Before using them for this purpose, scrub with a stiff brush and wash in the dishwasher.

GRILLED BARBECUED OYSTERS

Bring a sack of oysters to throw on the grill along with the Bacon-Wrapped Dove Breasts on page 217. Rinse them thoroughly, then arrange on a grill rack. Oysters are much easier to shuck when they are grilled first.

> 2 dozen unshucked oysters, scrubbed and rinsed
> 1¹/2 cups barbecue sauce
> 2/3 cup chopped green onions
> 1/3 cup chopped fresh cilantro
> 2 lemons, cut into wedges
> Cracked pepper to taste

Arrange the unshucked oysters flat side down on a preheated grill rack. Grill, with the lid down, for 2 minutes. The top shell should pop slightly open. Refer to the sidebar for the technique for opening the oyster shells. Spoon the barbecue sauce over the tops of the oysters and sprinkle with the green onions and cilantro.

Return the bottom shells to the grill rack. Grill, with the lid down, for 1 minute longer. Arrange the oysters on rock salt on a serving platter. Serve with lemon wedges and cracked pepper.

Serves 6

Grilled Quail and Pomegranate Salad

The crunchy whole seeds of a pomegranate are edible and are great in salads.

1/2 cup balsamic vinegar
2 tablespoons olive oil
1 tablespoon garlic powder
Salt and pepper to taste
6 frozen quails, split
2 bags baby greens salad mix
Seeds and juice of 1/2 pomegranate
1/2 cup green piñons or pumpkin seeds, toasted or fried
1/2 cup (2 ounces) shredded Parmesan cheese
Juice of 1 lime
1/4 cup extra-virgin olive oil
1/2 loaf French bread, sliced and toasted

Whisk the vinegar, 2 tablespoons olive oil, garlic powder, salt and pepper in a bowl. Add the quail halves and toss to coat. Marinate at room temperature for 15 to 20 minutes, turning occasionally; drain.

Arrange the quail skin side down on a grill rack over hot coals. Grill for 5 minutes; turn. Grill, with the lid down, for 5 minutes longer. Remove to a platter.

Toss the greens, pomegranate seeds and juice, piñons and cheese in a salad bowl. Drizzle with the lime juice, 1/4 cup olive oil and any collected pan juices from the quail and toss to coat. Divide the greens mixture evenly among 4 salad plates. Top each with 3 quail halves and drizzle with additional olive oil. Serve with the French bread toasts.

Serves 4

To remove pomegranate seeds, cut the fruit horizontally into halves and hold each half over a bowl, cut side down. Use a wooden spoon to tap firmly on the pomegranate, and most of the seeds will fall right out. Use your fingers or a spoon to loosen any remaining seeds and to pick out any white membrane. Red, luscious, and exotic-looking, pomegranates are also fun to use for decorating. Use them in centerpieces, floral arrangements, holiday wreaths, or gift baskets.

Decorate using the fruits of nature that can be found in your own backyard. Dried hydrangeas and branches of nandina or holly heavily laden with berries, added to magnolia leaves and aspidistra, give the table a woodsy feel. When combined with feathers and a bird's nest complete with eggs, the look is stunning. Pewter, brass, wooden trays, or dough bowls are ideal to hold these rustic arrangements. Citrus fruits such as kumquats and satsumas are plentiful in Louisiana throughout the fall and winter and make simple, natural-looking garnishes.

ROASTED GARLIC-GLAZED DUCK BREASTS

Frozen domestic boneless duck breasts may be purchased year-round in Louisiana and seasonally in other areas. The Roasted-Garlic Glaze is also delicious served over a pork loin or chicken.

Roasted Garlic Glaze
1 head garlic
1 small onion, cut into quarters and caramelized
1/3 cup olive oil
1 jar apricot preserves

Duck
6 boneless duck breasts
Salt and pepper to taste

For the glaze, cut the top off the garlic and discard. Place the remaining garlic head and onion on a sheet of foil large enough to enclose. Drizzle with the olive oil and seal the foil tightly. Roast at 375 degrees for 30 to 40 minutes or until the garlic is tender. Let stand until cool.

Squeeze the roasted garlic purée into a saucepan and add the onion and preserves. Simmer for 10 minutes, stirring occasionally. Let stand until cool.

For the duck, season the duck with salt and pepper. Arrange the duck on a rack in a roasting pan. Bake at 400 degrees for 45 to 55 minutes or until brown and the juices run clear. Brush the duck with the glaze and bake for 5 minutes longer. Serve immediately.

Serves 6

HEARTY GRITS CASSEROLE

Grits are not just for breakfast or brunch. Serve as an alternative for the usual potatoes or rice. This casserole is hearty enough to make a meal or can be prepared as a side dish for a crowd.

2¹/4 cups water	2 tablespoons grated Parmesan cheese
1¹/2 cups skim milk	1 pickled jalapeño chile, minced
1 teaspoon salt	2 cups skim milk
1¹/4 cups quick-cooking grits	2 eggs
4 ounces cooked ham, chopped (3/4 cup)	3 egg whites
3/4 cup (3 ounces) shredded reduced-fat Monterey Jack cheese	

Bring the water, 1¹/2 cups skim milk and salt to a boil in a heavy 3-quart saucepan over medium-high heat. Add the grits gradually, whisking constantly. Simmer, covered, over low heat for 5 minutes, stirring occasionally. Remove from the heat. Stir in the ham, Monterey Jack cheese, Parmesan cheese and jalapeño chile.

Whisk 2 cups skim milk, eggs and egg whites in a bowl until blended. Add the grits mixture to the egg mixture gradually, stirring constantly; the mixture will be lumpy. Spoon the grits mixture into a greased shallow 2-quart baking dish. Bake at 325 degrees for 45 to 50 minutes or until the top is set and the edges are light brown. Let stand for 10 minutes before serving.

Makes 6 entrée servings

SWEET POTATO BISCUITS

The convenience of using an all-purpose baking mix and canned sweet potatoes means that even inexperienced bakers can whip up these biscuits in no time.

1 (15-ounce) can yams	1/2 cup milk
4 cups baking mix	1/4 cup (1/2 stick) butter, melted
1/2 teaspoon cinnamon	

Drain the yams, reserving 1/2 cup of the liquid. Mash the yams in a bowl and stir in the baking mix and cinnamon. Whisk the milk and reserved liquid in a bowl and stir into the yam mixture until blended.

Roll 1 inch thick on a lightly floured surface and cut with a 2¹/2-inch cutter. Arrange the rounds on a baking parchment-lined baking sheet. Bake at 450 degrees for 10 minutes. Remove from the oven and brush with some of the butter.

Return the biscuits to the oven. Bake for 3 to 5 minutes longer or until golden brown. Remove from the oven and brush with the remaining butter. Serve immediately.

Makes 2 dozen biscuits

BREAD PUDDING WITH HARD SAUCE

While it is true that different types of bread will change the consistency of the pudding, the end result is always good, so use whichever type of bread you prefer. Dry bread works best since it soaks up the custard well and is also excellent for French toast. This hearty dessert is the perfect finale to an "end of the season" hunter's feast and can be prepared in advance.

Bread Pudding
1 1/2 cups sugar
1/2 cup (1 stick) butter
3 eggs
1 (12-ounce) can evaporated milk
1 1/2 cups warm water
1 tablespoon vanilla extract
1/8 teaspoon salt
1 loaf dry French bread, torn into
   1-inch cubes
1/2 cup raisins
1 to 2 teaspoons cinnamon

Hard Sauce
2 cups whole milk
3/4 cup sugar
2 tablespoons cornstarch
2 eggs
1/2 cup rum, brandy or whiskey
2 teaspoons butter
2 teaspoons vanilla extract

For the pudding, beat the sugar and butter in a deep 2-quart baking dish. Add the eggs 1 at a time, beating well after each addition. Beat in the evaporated milk, warm water, vanilla and salt. Immerse the bread into the egg mixture until coated. Fold in the raisins and cinnamon. Bake at 350 degrees for 45 minutes.

For the sauce, scald the milk in a saucepan. Whisk the sugar, cornstarch and eggs in a bowl until blended and stir into the milk. Cook over medium heat until thickened, stirring frequently. Remove from the heat. Stir in the rum, butter and vanilla and spoon the warm sauce over the warm pudding.

Serves 6 to 8

BUNDLE OF JOY

A nutritious, delicious meal is the best gift for a family with a new baby, particularly if it's the second or third child. When deciding what to prepare, consider the tastes of the whole family, and remember that nursing mothers usually avoid spicy food. Choose an entrée that freezes well, in case the family is blessed with more food than it can immediately eat.

8 Guests

CRAWFISH TURNOVERS

MIXED SALAD GREENS WITH TOMATO BASIL VINAIGRETTE

CHICKEN TORTELLINI

CRÈME DE MENTHE BROWNIES

Optional Menu Item
CHICKEN AND WILD RICE

CRAWFISH TURNOVERS

These little triangle-shaped turnovers are easy to make using a bag of frozen crawfish tails and frozen phyllo pastry.

1 1/2 cups chopped onions
1 cup chopped bell pepper
1 cup chopped celery
1 cup sliced mushrooms
1/2 cup chopped green onions
1 garlic clove, minced
1 (10-ounce) can reduced-sodium
    reduced-fat cream of
    mushroom soup

1 pound peeled cleaned crawfish
    tails
2 teaspoons parsley flakes
1 1/2 teaspoons basil
1 teaspoon oregano
1/2 teaspoon cayenne pepper
1/4 teaspoon thyme
16 sheets frozen phyllo pastry,
    thawed

Heat a large nonstick skillet sprayed with butter-flavor nonstick cooking spray over medium-high heat until hot. Sauté the onions, bell pepper, celery, mushrooms, green onions and garlic in the hot skillet until the vegetables are tender. Reduce the heat to low. Stir in the soup, crawfish, parsley flakes, basil, oregano, cayenne pepper and thyme. Simmer for 5 to 10 minutes, stirring occasionally.

Arrange 1 sheet of the pastry on a damp tea towel, keeping the remaining pastry covered with a damp tea towel or paper towel. Lightly spray the sheet with butter-flavor nonstick cooking spray. Layer with another sheet of the pastry and spray with butter-flavor nonstick cooking spray. Cut the stack crosswise into 4 strips with scissors or a sharp knife. Working with 1 strip at a time and keeping the remaining strips covered with a damp tea towel, spoon approximately 2 teaspoons of the crawfish mixture at the base of the strip. Fold the right bottom corner over to form a triangle and continue folding the triangle back and forth to the end of the strip. Arrange the turnover seam side down on a baking sheet sprayed with butter-flavor nonstick cooking spray. Repeat the procedure with the remaining pastry sheets, butter-flavor nonstick cooking spray and remaining crawfish mixture.

Spray the tops of the turnovers with butter-flavor nonstick cooking spray and bake at 350 degrees for 35 minutes or until golden brown. Remove to a serving platter and garnish as desired. Serve warm.

Makes 32 turnovers

Mixed Salad Greens with Tomato Basil Vinaigrette

Instead of making a fussy vegetable side dish, purchase a bag of mixed salad greens from the grocery store and prepare a recipe of this vinaigrette that can be served immediately or a few days later.

1 cup extra-virgin olive oil
1/2 cup chopped fresh basil
1/2 cup red wine vinegar
1 tablespoon Dijon mustard
1 tablespoon sugar

1 pint cherry tomatoes, cut into quarters
1/2 cup (2 ounces) crumbled feta cheese
Salt and pepper to taste
Mixed salad greens

Whisk the olive oil, basil, vinegar, mustard and sugar in a bowl. Stir in the tomatoes and feta cheese and season with salt and pepper. Let stand for 10 minutes. Store in the refrigerator in a jar with a tight-fitting lid.

Toss the salad greens with the desired amount of vinaigrette in a salad bowl. Serve immediately.

Serves 8

Chicken Tortellini

The use of reduced-fat cheese and light sour cream will lower the fat grams and calories without sacrificing the flavor.

1 (8-ounce) package fresh cheese tortellini
4 ounces Monterey Jack cheese, sliced
4 boneless skinless chicken breasts, cut into bite-size pieces
Flour
1/3 stick margarine
1 onion, chopped
1 (10- to 14-ounce) can chicken broth

1 (4-ounce) can mushrooms, drained
2 chicken bouillon cubes
1 teaspoon sugar
4 ounces Monterey Jack cheese, shredded or cubed
1/2 cup sour cream

Place the tortellini in a 9×11-inch baking dish sprayed with nonstick cooking spray. Layer with the sliced cheese. Coat the chicken on all sides with flour. Sauté the chicken in the margarine in a skillet until light brown. Spoon the chicken over the prepared layers using a slotted spoon, reserving the pan drippings.

Sauté the onion in the reserved pan drippings until tender. Add the broth, mushrooms, bouillon cubes and sugar. Bring to a boil and boil for 5 minutes, stirring occasionally. Add the shredded cheese and stir until melted. Stir in the sour cream. Pour the mushroom mixture over the prepared layers. Bake, covered with foil, at 275 degrees for 45 minutes. You may prepare up to 2 days in advance and store, covered, in the refrigerator. Bake at 300 degrees for 45 minutes.

Serves 6

CHICKEN AND WILD RICE

1 (3-pound) chicken, cut up
2 (6-ounce) packages quick-cooking long
   grain and wild rice
1 small onion, chopped
1/2 cup (1 stick) butter
1/4 cup flour
11/2 cups heavy cream

1 (6-ounce) can sliced water chestnuts,
   drained and chopped
1 (4-ounce) jar sliced mushrooms, drained
1 tablespoon chopped fresh parsley
1 teaspoon salt
1/2 teaspoon pepper
1 (2-ounce) package sliced almonds

Combine the chicken with enough water to cover in a stockpot. Bring to a boil over high heat; reduce the heat to medium. Cook until the chicken is tender. Drain, reserving 11/2 cups of the broth. Chop the chicken into bite-size pieces, discarding the skin and bones. Cook the rice using the package directions.

Sauté the onion in the butter in a heavy saucepan until tender. Stir in the flour. Cook for 1 to 2 minutes or until thick and bubbly, stirring constantly. Stir in the chicken, reserved broth, rice, heavy cream, water chestnuts, mushrooms, parsley, salt and pepper. Spoon the chicken mixture into a lightly greased 7×11-inch baking dish and sprinkle with the almonds. Bake at 350 degrees for 20 minutes or until brown and bubbly.

Serves 8

CRÈME DE MENTHE BROWNIES

For a quick homemade dessert, bake a batch of brownies from a package mix and top with Crème de Menthe Icing. This mint and chocolate icing makes ordinary brownies or cakes extra special.

1 (22-ounce) package brownie mix
2 cups sifted confectioners' sugar
1/4 cup (1/2 stick) butter, softened
2 tablespoons crème de menthe, amaretto or coffee
2 ounces unsweetened chocolate
2 tablespoons butter

Prepare and bake the brownie mix using the package directions for a 9×13-inch baking pan sprayed with nonstick cooking spray. Cool in the pan on a wire rack.

Combine the confectioners' sugar, 1/4 cup butter and crème de menthe in a mixing bowl and beat until blended. Spread over the top of the brownies and let stand until set. Heat the chocolate and 2 tablespoons butter in a double boiler until blended, stirring frequently. Spread the chocolate mixture over the prepared layers. Let stand until cool and cut into squares or bars.

Makes 2 dozen brownies

FIREWORKS ON THE LEVEE

Watching Fourth of July fireworks from the banks of the Mississippi River is a Baton Rouge tradition. People arrive downtown early in the morning to stake out a great viewing spot and enjoy all-day festivities.

8 Guests

Fried Chicken Tenders with Honey Mustard Sauce

Corn and Black Bean Salad

BLT Wraps with Herbed Mayonnaise

Red, White and Blue Sugar Cookies

FRIED CHICKEN TENDERS WITH HONEY MUSTARD SAUCE

On the way to the fireworks show, pick up an order of chicken tenders. They taste good at room temperature and are a delicious, mess-free finger food. Serve with your homemade Honey Mustard Sauce.

1 cup mayonnaise	3 sprigs of parsley, chopped
1/4 cup prepared mustard	1/2 teaspoon sugar
1/4 cup vinegar	1/16 teaspoon salt
1/4 cup honey	1 cup vegetable oil
1/4 onion, finely chopped	Chicken tenders

Combine the mayonnaise, prepared mustard, vinegar, honey, onion, parsley, sugar and salt in a bowl and mix well. Add the oil gradually, whisking constantly until incorporated. Chill, covered, until serving time. Serve with chicken tenders. You may store, covered, in the refrigerator for several weeks.

Serves 8

In 1988, the movie Blaze *was being filmed in Baton Rouge, and the wardrobe area for the actors was set up in rented office space that happened to be right across from the Junior League office. For many months, we would see famous actors strolling in and out.*

One day, League president Alice Greer spotted actor Paul Newman leaving and said, "Quick, Debbie! Get some River Road Recipes *cookbooks!" So, I swiftly fished some copies out of the closet and returned, presuming that SHE was going to run after him. Wrong!*

Alice securely placed the books under her arm, grabbed mine, and out we went, two determined women quickly advancing on an equally determined movie star and his driver, who obviously didn't relish autograph seekers. As soon as they spotted us, they picked up their pace. Alice, completely undaunted, increased ours.

Mr. Newman reached his car and quickly eased himself into the front seat, obviously relieved to escape us. However, when he tried to close his door, it wouldn't budge. Looking up in speechless disbelief, he saw Alice, holding onto the handle. Alice sweetly smiled and said, "Mr. Newman, we are from the Junior League, an organization of committed volunteers, not a young baseball club as you all think, and we would be honored if you would accept copies of our nationally recognized cookbooks."

His demeanor quickly transformed from irritation to delight as he graciously accepted the books with a smile. Then, just as quickly, the car moved and the door closed in unison, leaving Alice and me standing alone.

Reflecting back on this great memory, I realize that those people who seek to seize the day are what make our cookbooks the great success they are today.

Debbie Terrell, Chairman 1988

Corn and Black Bean Salad

This cool, multi-color salad is better if prepared one day in advance.

Spicy Cilantro Dressing

$1/2$ cup corn oil
$1/4$ cup red wine vinegar
3 tablespoons chopped fresh cilantro
2 tablespoons fresh lemon or lime juice
1 teaspoon hot pepper sauce
1 teaspoon chili powder

Salad

2 (15-ounce) cans black beans, drained and rinsed
2 (12-ounce) cans whole kernel corn, drained
2 tomatoes, chopped
$1^{1/2}$ red bell peppers, finely chopped
1 cup diagonally sliced green onions
1 cup chopped red onion
2 jalapeño chiles, seeded and finely chopped (optional)
2 garlic cloves, minced

For the dressing, combine the corn oil, vinegar, cilantro, lemon juice, hot pepper sauce and chili powder in a jar with a tight-fitting lid and seal tightly. Shake to mix.

For the salad, combine the beans, corn, tomatoes, bell peppers, green onions, onion, jalapeño chiles and garlic in a bowl and mix gently. Add the dressing and toss to coat. Chill, covered, for 6 to 10 hours. Spoon into a salad bowl and garnish with sprigs of cilantro and/or red onion wedges.

Serves 8

Insulate hot and cold dishes with newspapers. After wrapping the dish in foil, wrap and tape multiple layers of newspaper around the dish. The dish will stay hot or cold for hours, and any leakage that might occur is not a problem since the newspaper will be discarded.

BLT Wraps

Roll these BLT Wraps in foil, baking parchment, or waxed paper and cut into halves just before serving. The wrapper can be peeled down as the sandwich is eaten, making a good holder. Just remember to pack a knife.

>   1 package pecan-smoked bacon or any type bacon
>   1 cup Herbed Mayonnaise (below)
>   8 (10-inch) flour tortillas
>   1 head baby romaine, coarsely shredded
>   3 tomatoes, thinly chopped
>   2 avocados, sliced

Arrange the bacon in a single layer on a baking sheet. Bake at 350 degrees for 10 minutes or until brown and crisp; drain on paper towels.

Spread the mayonnaise over 1 side of each tortilla. Layer each with shredded lettuce, chopped tomato, 3 slices of the bacon and sliced avocado and roll to enclose the filling. Wrap each roll individually in baking parchment, twisting the ends to seal. Slice diagonally into halves just before serving.

Makes 8 wraps

Herbed Mayonnaise

>   2 cups mayonnaise
>   1/4 cup chopped green onions
>   1/4 cup chopped fresh parsley
>   1 tablespoon chopped fresh basil
>   1 teaspoon chopped fresh thyme
>   1 teaspoon lemon juice

Combine the mayonnaise, green onions, parsley, basil, thyme and lemon juice in a bowl and mix well. Store, covered, in the refrigerator. Dried herbs may be substituted for the fresh herbs, but fresh is preferred.

Makes 2 cups

Red, White and Blue Sugar Cookies

To make patriotic sugar cookies, use food coloring to tint two cans of ready-made white frosting red and blue. Leave another can of frosting plain white. Cut out cookies into stars or flag shapes and frost with red, white, and blue frosting, using white sprinkles for stars.

3 cups flour
1/2 teaspoon baking powder
1/2 teaspoon baking soda
1/2 teaspoon salt
1 cup (2 sticks) butter or margarine
1 cup sugar
1 egg
2 tablespoons milk
1 teaspoon vanilla extract
3 (16-ounce) cans white frosting
Red and blue food coloring
White sprinkles

Sift the flour, baking powder, baking soda and salt together. Cream the butter and sugar in a bowl with a fork. Add the egg to the creamed mixture and stir until blended. Stir in the milk and vanilla. Add the flour mixture and mix until smooth.

Roll the dough on a lightly floured surface and cut into rectangular shapes to resemble a flag or into stars. Arrange on an ungreased cookie sheet. Bake at 400 degrees for 5 to 7 minutes or until light brown. Cool on the cookie sheet for 2 minutes. Remove to a wire rack to cool completely.

Tint 2 cans of the frosting separately with red and blue food coloring. Decorate the cookies to resemble American flags, using the sprinkles for stars.

Makes 2 to 3 dozen cookies

Insulated cookie sheets are good for preventing burning, but they do not conduct heat as quickly as regular aluminum cookie sheets, so baking time may be longer. Dark metal cookie sheets are excellent heat conductors, but there is a greater risk of burning. Remember to always use a timer with every batch, as cookies bake quickly, so every minute counts.

HARVEST MOON HAYRIDE

Summer is long in Louisiana, and fall is gratefully welcomed.
For Baton Rougeans, it's time to dig out those few warm sweaters and plan
an outing in the crisp autumn air. It's perfect weather for taking
the Scout troop to the corn maze or the children to the pumpkin patch.

8 Guests

ROASTED RED BELL PEPPER DIP

BAKED POTATO SOUP

SUNNY VEGETABLE SALAD

BAKED HAM SANDWICHES
(RRRIV page 194)

FOOL'S TOFFEE

CHOCOLATE CHIP PEANUT BUTTER COOKIES

Optional Menu Item
BLACK BEAN SOUP

ROASTED RED BELL PEPPER DIP

This dip can be prepared in no time using a jar of roasted bell peppers or pimentos. However, if you have a garden full of fresh peppers, roasting them yourself is very easy and rewarding.

1 teaspoon olive oil
1 small red onion, cut into quarters
1 (7-ounce) jar roasted red bell peppers, drained
12 fresh basil leaves, crushed, or 1/2 teaspoon dried basil
12 ounces cream cheese, softened

Bagel chips
Chilled blanched fresh asparagus spears
Cherry tomatoes
Red, green, orange and/or yellow bell pepper strips
Fresh mushrooms

Drizzle the olive oil over the onion in a small baking dish. Bake at 400 degrees for 45 minutes or until tender. Let stand until cool. Process the onion, roasted peppers and basil in a food processor until puréed. Add the cream cheese and pulse until combined. Chill, covered, for 3 hours or longer.

To serve, mound the cream cheese mixture in the center of a serving platter. Surround with bagel chips, asparagus spears, cherry tomatoes, bell pepper strips and mushrooms.

Makes 2 1/2 cups

BAKED POTATO SOUP

Think about a loaded baked potato and bring along all of the extras normally found on a baked potato bar to top off this soup. Pack containers of cheese, sour cream, scallions, bacon bits, and/or sliced jalapeño chiles and let everyone pick and choose their favorite toppings.

4 to 6 large potatoes, peeled and cut into quarters
Salt to taste
1/2 cup flour
1/2 cup (1 stick) butter
4 cups chicken stock

2 cups milk
Pepper to taste
1 pound Cheddar cheese, shredded
1 pound bacon, crisp-cooked and crumbled
1 bunch green onions, finely chopped

Combine the potatoes and salt with enough water to cover in a large saucepan. Bring to a boil over high heat; reduce the heat. Cook until the potatoes are tender; drain. Cut into large chunks.

Combine the flour and butter in a large saucepan and cook over medium heat for 1 minute or until thickened and bubbly. Stir in the stock and milk. Cook until thickened, stirring frequently. Season with salt and pepper and stir in the potatoes.

Cook until only a few chunks of potatoes remain, stirring occasionally. Add the cheese, bacon and green onions and mix well. Cook just until the cheese melts, stirring frequently. Pour into a thermos to keep warm. Serve with the desired toppings. Substitute half-and-half for the milk for a thicker consistency.

Serves 8 to 10

BLACK BEAN SOUP

1 onion, chopped
1 carrot, grated
2 tablespoons vegetable oil
3 (15-ounce) cans black beans
3 to 4 cups chicken broth
1 cup salsa
1/2 cup sherry
1 (11-ounce) can tomatoes with green chiles
1 tablespoon cumin
1 tablespoon chili powder
Juice of 1 lime
Chopped fresh cilantro to taste

Sauté the onion and carrot in the oil in a large saucepan for 10 to 15 minutes or until tender. Process 1 can of the undrained beans with 1 cup of the broth in a blender until puréed. Add the purée to the onion mixture and mix well. Process another can of undrained beans and another cup of the broth in the blender until puréed and add to the onion mixture.

Stir the remaining can of undrained beans, remaining broth, salsa, sherry, undrained tomatoes, cumin and chili powder into the bean purée. Bring to a boil; reduce the heat. Simmer for 20 minutes, stirring occasionally. Stir in the lime juice and cilantro. Ladle into soup bowls and garnish with sour cream and chopped green onion tops.

Serves 6 to 8

Anne Arbour remembers how the Monteleone Hotel gift shop began stocking River Road Recipes. *Anne, her sisters, and her mother spent the weekend there while in New Orleans and took turns going into the gift shop inquiring about a copy of* River Road Recipes. *Finally, the clerk said, "This is about the sixth request I've had in only two days for that book. Can you tell me how I can purchase some?" It was Anne, incidentally, who named the book.*

—*Ellen Jolly,* The Baton Rouge Enterprise, *1980*

Sunny Vegetable Salad

This salad incorporates a variety of fall and winter produce for a good mixture of colors, textures, and flavors that suit the season perfectly. It's also a good way to include vegetables in a menu of pick-up foods, making a nice change from the usual vegetable tray.

3 cups broccoli florets
3 cups cauliflower florets
1 cup (4 ounces) shredded Cheddar cheese
1/2 cup chopped onion
1/4 cup raisins
1/2 cup mayonnaise

1/4 cup sugar
1 tablespoon cider vinegar or red wine
   vinegar
4 slices bacon, crisp-cooked and crumbled
2 tablespoons sunflower seed kernels

Toss the broccoli, cauliflower, cheese, onion and raisins in a salad bowl. Combine the mayonnaise, sugar and vinegar in a bowl and mix well. Add the mayonnaise mixture to the broccoli mixture and mix until coated. Chill, covered, for 1 hour. Sprinkle with the bacon and sunflower kernels just before serving.

Serves 8

Fool's Toffee

Saltine crackers may seem like an unusual ingredient to use in a toffee recipe, but do not be "fooled" into thinking this is a mistake. This secret ingredient makes the toffee much lighter and crispier than using graham crackers. Teenagers love to make this candy. Makes a great gift for teachers, coaches, or friends.

36 to 40 saltine crackers (1 sleeve)
1 cup (2 sticks) butter
1 cup packed dark brown sugar
2 cups (12 ounces) milk chocolate chips
1/2 to 1 cup chopped pecans

Line a 10×17-inch baking pan with foil and coat the foil with butter. Arrange the crackers in a single layer with sides touching in the prepared pan. Combine 1 cup butter and brown sugar in a saucepan. Bring to a boil over medium heat, stirring constantly. Boil for 4 minutes, stirring constantly.

Pour the butter mixture over the crackers. Using a wooden spoon, spread the mixture evenly over the crackers. Bake at 350 degrees for 5 minutes. Sprinkle with the chocolate chips and let stand for 2 minutes or until the chocolate chips soften. Spread the chocolate evenly over the prepared layers using a knife or metal cake spatula. Sprinkle with the pecans and press lightly. Chill for 30 minutes or until set. Break into pieces and store in a covered container in the refrigerator.

Serves 8 to 12

CHOCOLATE CHIP PEANUT BUTTER COOKIES

These thick cookies are loaded with chunks of peanuts and chocolate chips.

2 cups flour
1/2 teaspoon baking powder
1/2 teaspoon baking soda
1/2 teaspoon salt
3/4 cup creamy peanut butter
1/2 cup (1 stick) unsalted butter, softened
1/2 cup sugar
1/2 cup packed brown sugar
2 eggs
1 teaspoon vanilla extract
2 cups (12 ounces) semisweet chocolate chips
1/2 cup (3 ounces) peanut butter chips
1/2 cup dry-roasted peanuts

Mix the flour, baking powder, baking soda and salt together. Beat the peanut butter, butter, sugar and brown sugar in a mixing bowl until smooth and creamy, scraping the bowl occasionally. Add the eggs and vanilla and beat until blended. Add the flour mixture and beat at low speed until smooth. Stir in the chocolate chips, peanut butter chips and peanuts.

Shape the dough by teaspoonfuls into balls and arrange 2 inches apart on a lightly buttered cookie sheet. Flatten the balls with the heel of your hand or with a fork. Bake on the middle oven rack at 350 degrees for 10 minutes or until firm to the touch and light brown. Cool on the cookie sheet for 3 minutes. Remove to a wire rack to cool completely. Store in an airtight container.

Makes 4 dozen cookies

I LOVE A PARADE

St. Patrick's Day, Mardi Gras, Earth Day, LSU or SU Homecoming...
almost any festive occasion is reason enough for a parade in Louisiana.
During Mardi Gras, you can attend two parades a day in South Louisiana,
more if your timing is just right. The parade party host is usually
the person who lives nearest the parade route. Friends and family gather for
hours before and after the parade to eat, drink, and compare beads.
The atmosphere is laid-back and unstructured, and invitations are usually
just a casual word or phone call bidding guests to drop by.
Just before the parade rolls past, kids and ice chests are packed into
wagons for the migration down the street to watch the spectacle.

Serves a Crowd

GRAPE SALSA

HERB CHEESE BALL

WHITE BEAN CHILI

OVERNIGHT BRISKET

SHOE PEG CORN SALAD

NO-BAKE CANDY BARS

On parade day, guests come and go all day. Choose a menu that can be made entirely ahead of time, and feature foods that can remain safe to eat after several hours at room temperature.

Grape Salsa

This colorful salsa is a tasty combination of sweet and spicy flavors and makes a beautiful presentation.

> 1 bunch seedless green grapes, cut into halves
> 1 bunch seedless red grapes, cut into halves
> 1 pint grape tomatoes
> 1/2 to 1 purple onion, chopped
> 1/2 green bell pepper, chopped
> 1/2 red, yellow or orange bell pepper, chopped
> 1 bunch cilantro, stems removed and chopped
> 3 garlic cloves, finely chopped
> 1 jalapeño chile, seeded and chopped
> Juice of 3 limes
> Olive oil to taste

Combine the grapes, tomatoes, onion, bell peppers, cilantro, garlic and jalapeño chile in a bowl and mix well. Add the lime juice and olive oil and toss to coat. Let stand at room temperature for 1 hour. Serve as an appetizer with corn chips or as a side salad.

Serves a crowd

Herb Cheese Ball

12 ounces cream cheese, softened
1/4 cup (1/2 stick) butter, softened
1 garlic clove, minced
1 tablespoon chives
11/2 teaspoons basil

11/2 teaspoons tarragon
1 teaspoon parsley flakes
1/2 teaspoon thyme
1/4 teaspoon white pepper

Combine the cream cheese, butter, garlic, chives, basil, tarragon, parsley flakes, thyme and white pepper in a bowl and mix until combined. Shape the cream cheese mixture into a ball and wrap in plastic wrap. Chill in the refrigerator for up to 3 days. Serve with Triscuits.

Serves a crowd

White Bean Chili

This chili, made with chicken and white beans, is creamier and lighter than the traditional chili, very much like a cassoulet. Substitute Great Northern, cannellini, or lima beans for the white beans if desired.

1 pound dried white beans
4 cups chicken broth
1 onion, chopped
1 garlic clove, minced
4 cups chopped cooked chicken
1 (4-ounce) can chopped
    green chiles

1 tablespoon chopped fresh parsley
1 teaspoon (scant) oregano
1/8 teaspoon cayenne pepper
3 cups (12 ounces) shredded
    Pepper Jack cheese
1 cup chopped green onions

Sort and rinse the beans. Combine the beans with enough water to generously cover in a bowl. Let stand for 8 to 10 hours; drain. Combine the beans, broth, onion and garlic in a large heavy saucepan. Bring to a boil over high heat; reduce the heat.

Simmer for 2 to 3 hours or until the beans are tender, stirring occasionally. Stir in the chicken, green chiles, parsley, oregano and cayenne pepper.

Simmer for 1 hour longer, stirring occasionally. Ladle into chili bowls. Sprinkle with the cheese and green onions.

Serves 10 to 12

To shape a dip or spread, line a bowl or container that is the desired shape with plastic wrap. Fill with the dip or spread and chill until firm. Invert onto a serving platter and carefully remove the plastic wrap. Garnish with fresh herbs.

Overnight Brisket

Brisket is great for a crowd since it goes a long way and can sit out for several hours. Serve on buns, French bread, or pistolettes along with horseradish, purple onions, and plenty of extra barbecue sauce.

> 1 (10-pound or larger) beef brisket with fat
> Salt and pepper to taste
> 2 cups dark sweet-and-sour sauce
> 1 bottle liquid smoke
> 1 onion, chopped or sliced

Arrange the brisket fat side up on a sheet of heavy-duty foil large enough to enclose the brisket. Place the foil and brisket in a roasting pan. Season the brisket with salt and pepper and rub 1 cup of the sauce over the surface. Pour the liquid smoke over the top and sprinkle with the onion. Seal the foil to enclose the brisket.

Pour 1 to 2 cups of water in the roasting pan. Bake at 250 degrees for 8 hours. Drain the pan drippings from the foil packet and remove all visible fat from the brisket. Rub the remaining 1 cup sauce over the surface of the brisket. Seal the foil and bake for 1 hour longer. Slice as desired.

Serves a crowd

Shoe Peg Corn Salad

Widely grown in the south, Shoe Peg corn is also known as sweet corn or country gentleman. Using a canned or frozen product makes cooking for a crowd much easier. Always rinse canned corn before using.

> 4 (11-ounce) cans Shoe Peg corn, drained and rinsed
> 2 (2-ounce) jars pimento, drained
> 1 cup chopped green bell pepper
> 1 cup chopped onion
> 1 cup chopped celery
> 1 cup vinegar
> 1 cup vegetable oil
> 2/3 cup sugar
> 2 teaspoons salt
> 1 teaspoon pepper

Combine the corn, pimento, bell pepper, onion and celery in a bowl and mix well. Whisk the vinegar, oil, sugar, salt and pepper in a bowl until combined. Add the vinegar mixture to the corn mixture and toss gently to coat. Chill, covered, for 8 to 10 hours. Drain before serving.

Serves a crowd

NO-BAKE CANDY BARS

Instead of cutting this dessert into bars, try using cookie cutters to cut out seasonal shapes like four-leaf clovers for a St. Pat's Day party or fleur-de-lis for Mardi Gras.

    1¹/2 cups creamy peanut butter
    1¹/4 cups sugar
    1 cup white corn syrup
    5 cups Special-K, coarsely crushed
    2 cups (12 ounces) milk chocolate or semisweet chocolate chips

Combine the peanut butter, sugar and syrup in a microwave-safe bowl. Microwave until blended; stir. Pour the peanut butter mixture over the cereal in a bowl and stir to coat. Spread the cereal mixture in a 9×13-inch dish sprayed with nonstick cooking spray.

    Place the chocolate chips in the same bowl that contained the peanut butter mixture and microwave until melted; stir. Spread the melted chocolate over the prepared layer and chill for 1 hour or until firm. Cut into bars. Store in the refrigerator or freeze for future use.

Makes 5 dozen bars

Spinach Madeline, one of the most famous recipes to come out of River Road Recipes, *was named as one of the Century's Best Recipes in an article that appeared in the* Houston Chronicle *in December 1999. The original appears in RRRI, and a light version is featured in RRRIII: A Healthy Collection. The recipe's creator, Madeline Nevill Reymond, created this legendary recipe by accident. She was a young and inexperienced cook when she decided to use up a jalapeño cheese roll that she had in her refrigerator by adding it to a spinach dish she was preparing for a ladies' luncheon. The result was a dish that became one of the most popular special-occasion vegetable dishes in Louisiana. This is evidenced every year by the empty freezers in the grocery stores at Christmas time after all the frozen spinach packages have been snatched up. When Kraft Foods decided to discontinue making the jalapeño cheese roll called for in the recipe, hundreds of distraught cooks called Kraft Foods to protest. The powers-that-be at Kraft were amused by Louisiana's devotion to their jalapeño cheese roll, but discontinued the product anyway. Fortunately, the RRR committee developed a new version of Spinach Madeleine in 2000 so that cooks can still serve this outstanding dish. After all, many Baton Rougeans consider Spinach Madeleine to be as important as the turkey or ham during the holiday season!*

TAKE ME OUT TO THE TAILGATE

In Baton Rouge, football, baseball, and basketball seasons are celebrated with near manic enthusiasm. True fans dress from head to toe in the team colors and pack up tables, chairs, tablecloths, and enough food and drinks to feed themselves and anyone else who happens to wander by. Candles and lanterns allow the party to continue long after the game is over. This menu is perfect for a fall or spring day spent on campus socializing and people-watching.

12 Guests

SPICY CURRY DIP

FESTIVE ORZO SALAD

MEATLESS MUFFALETTA

STROMBOLI SANDWICHES

CRAWFISH ROLL SANDWICHES

CARROT CUPCAKES WITH CREAM CHEESE ICING

HOME RUN BARS

Spicy Curry Dip

Serve with fresh vegetables or chips.

1 cup mayonnaise
2 tablespoons Durkee sauce
1 tablespoon (heaping) horseradish
1 teaspoon celery seeds
1 teaspoon (scant) curry powder

$1/2$ teaspoon Worcestershire sauce
$1/8$ teaspoon pepper
$1/8$ teaspoon Tabasco sauce
$1/4$ garlic clove, minced

Combine the mayonnaise, Durkee sauce, horseradish, celery seeds, curry powder, Worcestershire sauce, pepper, Tabasco sauce and garlic in a bowl and mix well. Serve with cauliflower florets, radishes, bell pepper strips, grape tomatoes, sliced avocados, celery sticks and green onions. Store, covered, in the refrigerator.

Makes 1 1/4 cups

Festive Orzo Salad

Orzo cooks quickly. Add chopped grilled chicken breasts or steamed shrimp for a hearty entrée salad.

Balsamic Vinaigrette
$3/4$ cup light olive oil
$1/4$ cup red balsamic vinegar
1 tablespoon yellow mustard
$3/4$ teaspoon sugar

Salad
1 bunch asparagus spears
16 ounces orzo
1 (14-ounce) can artichoke hearts, drained
  and chopped
1 (2-ounce) can sliced black olives, drained
1 small red bell pepper, coarsely chopped
1 small yellow bell pepper, coarsely
  chopped
$1/4$ to $1/2$ purple onion, chopped
$1/2$ (8-ounce) jar sun-dried tomatoes,
  drained and chopped
8 ounces feta cheese, crumbled
10 fresh basil leaves, coarsely chopped

For the vinaigrette, combine the olive oil, vinegar, mustard and sugar in a jar with a tight-fitting lid and seal tightly. Shake to blend.

For the salad, snap off the woody ends of the asparagus spears. Steam until tender-crisp; drain. Cut each spear into 4 or 5 portions. Cook the pasta using the package directions; drain.

Combine the pasta, artichokes, olives, bell peppers, onion and sun-dried tomatoes in a bowl and mix well. Add the vinaigrette and toss to coat. Add the asparagus, cheese and basil and mix gently. Marinate, covered, in the refrigerator for 2 to 10 hours, stirring occasionally. Let stand at room temperature for 30 minutes before serving.

Serves 10 to 12

MEATLESS MUFFALETTA

There are as many different spellings for this Italian sandwich as there are varieties. Delicious no matter which spelling you choose.

1/4 cup balsamic vinegar
1/4 cup olive oil
1 garlic clove, minced
1 tablespoon chopped fresh basil
1 tablespoon chopped fresh oregano
1 (9-ounce) jar olive salad
1 cup thinly sliced zucchini
1 cup thinly sliced yellow squash
1 (6-ounce) jar marinated artichoke hearts
1/2 cup drained pickled cherry peppers, chopped
1/2 cup drained banana pepper rings
1 round loaf sourdough bread
12 ounces smoked mozzarella cheese, sliced

Whisk the vinegar, olive oil, garlic, basil and oregano in a bowl until incorporated. Mix the undrained olive salad, zucchini, yellow squash, undrained artichoke hearts, cherry peppers and banana pepper rings in a bowl. Add the vinegar mixture and toss to coat. Marinate at room temperature for 30 minutes.

Cut the bread loaf horizontally into halves using a serrated knife. Remove the centers of each half carefully, leaving a 1-inch shell. Spoon 2/3 of the olive salad mixture into the bottom half of the loaf. Layer with the mozzarella cheese and remaining olive salad mixture. Top with the remaining bread half and press lightly to compact. Slice as desired.

Serves 6 to 8

STROMBOLI SANDWICHES

Men love this big, hearty sandwich, which is similar to a calzone on a bun. The sweet fennel seeds in the Italian sausage combine with other herbs to provide a great flavor.

2 pounds Italian sausage, casings removed	2 (12-ounce) jars sliced mushrooms,
2 pounds ground beef	drained
2 large onions, finely chopped	1/2 cup (2 ounces) grated Parmesan cheese
1 cup chopped bell pepper	1/2 teaspoon rosemary, crushed
2 large garlic cloves, crushed	1/2 teaspoon oregano
2 (8-ounce) cans tomato sauce	2 loaves French bread
2 (6-ounce) cans tomato paste	8 ounces low-moisture mozzarella cheese,
1/2 cup water	shredded

Brown the sausage and ground beef in a heavy saucepan, stirring until crumbly; drain. Add the onions, bell pepper and garlic and mix well. Cook for 5 minutes, stirring frequently. Stir in the tomato sauce, tomato paste and water and cook for 5 minutes, stirring occasionally. Add the mushrooms, Parmesan cheese, rosemary and oregano and simmer for 10 minutes, stirring occasionally.

Slice the bread loaves horizontally into halves and fill the bottom halves with the hot sausage mixture. Top with the mozzarella cheese and replace the top halves; wrap securely in foil. Bake at 400 degrees for 6 to 8 minutes or until the cheese melts. Cut each loaf into 6 sandwiches.

Serves 12

CRAWFISH ROLL SANDWICHES

Crawfish are substituted in this sandwich, which is similar to a New England lobster roll. Assemble these sandwiches at the last minute, and make sure they are packed to stay cold.

4 (12-ounce) packages crawfish tails,	2 cups mayonnaise
rinsed and coarsely chopped	2 tablespoons Dijon mustard
1 cup chopped celery	Juice of 2 lemons
1 cup chopped green onions	2 French bread baguettes, split
1 cup chopped red bell pepper	Curly leaf lettuce leaves
2 teaspoons garlic powder	3 tomatoes, sliced
1 teaspoon salt	

Combine the crawfish, celery, green onions, bell pepper, garlic powder and salt in a bowl. Stir in the mayonnaise, mustard and lemon juice. Chill, covered, for 30 minutes.

To serve, mound 1 1/2 cups of the crawfish filling on each bread bottom. Dress with lettuce and the tomatoes and top with the remaining bread halves. Cut each sandwich into halves.

Serves 4

CARROT CUPCAKES WITH CREAM CHEESE ICING

Using baby food carrots in this recipe eliminates the time and mess of grating and cooking fresh carrots. Adding carrots or zucchini to a cake or bread batter guarantees a moist product.

Carrot Cupcakes

2 cups flour
2 cups sugar
2 teaspoons baking soda
1 teaspoon salt
1 teaspoon cinnamon
1 1/2 cups canola oil
4 medium eggs
4 (4-ounce) jars puréed baby food carrots (Heinz or Gerber Stage 2)
1 cup chopped pecans

Cream Cheese Icing

8 ounces cream cheese, softened
1/2 cup (1 stick) butter or margarine, softened
1 1/2 teaspoons vanilla extract
1 (16-ounce) package confectioners' sugar
1 cup chopped pecans

For the cupcakes, mix the flour, sugar, baking soda, salt and cinnamon in a bowl. Whisk the canola oil and eggs in a bowl until blended. Stir in the carrots. Add the flour mixture to the carrot mixture 1/3 at a time, blending well after each addition. Stir in the pecans.

Spoon the batter evenly into 24 paper-lined muffin cups. Bake at 350 degrees for 30 to 35 minutes or until a wooden pick inserted in the center comes out clean. Cool in the pan for 10 minutes. Remove to a wire rack to cool completely.

For the icing, beat the cream cheese and butter in a mixing bowl until light and fluffy, scraping the bowl occasionally. Blend in the vanilla. Add the confectioners' sugar gradually, beating well after each addition. Continue to beat until the icing is light and fluffy, adding additional confectioners' sugar or vanilla for the desired consistency. Fold in the pecans. Spread the icing over the tops of the cupcakes.

Makes 2 dozen cupcakes

HOME RUN BARS

These decadent, chewy, gooey bars are an updated version of that old favorite, Rice Krispy Treats.

4 cups toasted oat cereal
4 cups crisp rice cereal
5 (2-ounce) chocolate-covered peanut crunch bars, coarsely chopped
1 1/2 cups honey
1/2 cup sugar
1/2 cup packed brown sugar
1 3/4 cups peanut butter
2 teaspoons vanilla extract
1 cup (6 ounces) semisweet chocolate chips, melted
1/2 cup cocktail peanuts

Combine the cereals and 1/2 of the candy bars in a bowl and mix well. Combine the honey, sugar and brown sugar in a saucepan. Cook over medium heat until the sugar dissolves, stirring frequently. Remove from the heat. Stir in the peanut butter and vanilla. Pour the warm peanut butter mixture over the cereal mixture and toss to coat.

Press the cereal mixture into a 9×13-inch pan sprayed with nonstick cooking spray. Bake at 325 degrees for 12 minutes. Cool for 5 minutes. Drizzle the melted chocolate over the top of the baked layer and sprinkle with the remaining chopped candy bars and peanuts. Let stand at room temperature until cool. Cut into bars.

Makes 2 to 3 dozen bars

*R*iver Road Recipes III: A Healthy Collection *was introduced in 1995 as a logical response to growing lifestyle trends calling for healthier, lighter eating. The book features many time-honored favorites from the previous* River Road Recipes *cookbooks, modified as lighter versions. It also includes newer recipes that busy cooks can use to feed hungry families in thirty minutes or less. Linda Vannoy, a registered dietitian and nutritionist, provided a nutritional analysis for each recipe along with tips for healthy substitutions or cooking methods where appropriate. Linda points out, "What people find in this book is a balance. They can create meals that are healthier and still taste good."*

FEAST OF ST. JOSEPH

*Many Italian Catholic families in South Louisiana follow the tradition
of preparing a tavola di San Giuseppe, a table of St. Joseph, to honor his feast
day. A table groaning with plenty is a major component of the feast.
Typical dishes include fish, pasta, vegetables (especially artichokes), and breads
that have been formed in symbolic shapes such as crosses, chalices, and wreaths.*

12 Guests

STUFFED ARTICHOKES

SENSATION SALAD
(RRRI page 24)

MUDICA

SUNDAY SPAGHETTI
WITH MEATBALLS AND EGGS

GARLIC FRENCH BREAD

SEED COOKIES

ITALIAN FIG COOKIES

BISCOTTI

Optional Menu Item
VEAL RAVIOLI

STUFFED ARTICHOKES

8 to 12 artichokes
4 cups Italian-style bread crumbs
1 cup (4 ounces) grated Parmesan cheese
1 cup chopped celery leaves
1/2 cup chopped fresh parsley
1/2 cup chopped green onions
5 garlic cloves, crushed
Salt and pepper to taste
1/4 cup olive oil

Discard the tough outer leaves of the artichokes and cut the stems to form flat bases. Trim the prickly tips of the leaves. Combine the bread crumbs, cheese, celery leaves, parsley, green onions, garlic, salt and pepper in a bowl and mix well. Stuff the bread crumb mixture between the leaves.

Arrange the stuffed artichokes in a large Dutch oven and drizzle with the olive oil. Add enough water to the pan to measure 1 inch. Steam, covered, for 1 hour.

Serves 8 to 12

MUDICA

These slightly sweet-tasting bread crumbs are commonly sprinkled over spaghetti and meatballs or any Italian dish. It is also traditionally sprinkled on the table to represent the sawdust from St. Joseph's workshop.

3 tablespoons extra-virgin olive oil
3 cups coarse fresh bread crumbs
2 tablespoons sugar

Heat the olive oil in a large sauté pan or cast-iron skillet over medium heat. Add the bread crumbs and stir with a wooden spoon to coat. Cook until golden brown, stirring occasionally. Remove the crumbs to a bowl and stir in the sugar. Use as a substitute for Parmesan cheese.

Makes 3 cups

A St. Joseph's altar is made up of three tiers of tables symbolizing the Holy Trinity. The tables are covered with white cloths and usually decorated with lilies, a statue of the saint, and symbols of his craft, such as hammers, saws, and other woodworking tools. The food is offered as a gift to St. Joseph, and is not eaten. Guests who visit a St. Joseph's table are usually gifted with fava beans, in remembrance of the food that saved the Sicilians from starvation.

SUNDAY SPAGHETTI WITH MEATBALLS AND EGGS

Adding hard-cooked eggs to braised dishes such as spaghetti is very typical of Spanish or Mexican cuisine.

Italian Tomato Sauce

1/2 cup olive oil
1 cup chopped celery
1 cup chopped onion
1/2 cup chopped green bell pepper
2 (28-ounce) cans whole tomatoes, chopped
2 (11-ounce) cans tomatoes with green chiles
2 (8-ounce) cans tomato sauce
3 tablespoons sugar
2 teaspoons celery seeds
2 teaspoons parsley flakes
2 teaspoons basil
3 garlic cloves, minced
3 bay leaves
1 teaspoon salt
1 teaspoon black pepper
1/8 teaspoon red pepper

Meatballs and Assembly

2 slices white bread, toasted
2 pounds ground chuck
1 cup seasoned bread crumbs
1 cup chopped onion
1 cup chopped celery
1/2 cup chopped green bell pepper
1/2 cup (2 ounces) grated Parmesan cheese
3 eggs, lightly beaten
1 teaspoon salt
1 teaspoon pepper
1 teaspoon basil
1 teaspoon oregano
1/4 cup olive oil
1 dozen eggs, hard-cooked and peeled
2 pounds vermicelli, cooked and drained

For the sauce, heat the olive oil in a 12-quart stockpot over medium heat. Sauté the celery, onion and bell pepper in the hot oil until tender. Stir in the undrained tomatoes, tomato sauce, sugar, celery seeds, parsley flakes, basil, garlic, bay leaves, salt, black pepper and red pepper. Simmer, covered, for 1 hour, stirring occasionally. Discard the bay leaves.

For the meatballs, moisten the toasted bread with water and tear. Combine the bread, ground chuck, seasoned bread crumbs, onion, celery, bell pepper, cheese, 3 beaten eggs, salt, pepper, basil and oregano in a bowl and mix well. Shape the ground chuck mixture into 2-inch balls. Brown the meatballs in the olive oil in a skillet. Add the meatballs to the sauce and mix well.

Simmer for 11/2 hours, stirring occasionally. Add the hard-cooked eggs to the sauce and simmer for 30 minutes longer, stirring occasionally. Spoon the sauce over the hot pasta on dinner plates.

Serves 12

VEAL RAVIOLI

Red Sauce
3 garlic cloves, chopped
1/3 cup olive oil
2 pounds ripe tomatoes, peeled, seeded and coarsely chopped, or
    1 (28-ounce) can chopped stewed tomatoes
1 1/4 teaspoons crushed red pepper
Salt to taste

Ravioli
3 tablespoons finely chopped shallots
3 tablespoons olive oil
1 pound ground veal
1/4 cup dry white wine
1 garlic clove, minced
2 tablespoons chopped fresh flat-leaf parsley
1 teaspoon freshly ground nutmeg
3/4 teaspoon salt
1/4 teaspoon freshly ground pepper
1/2 cup (2 ounces) freshly grated Parmesan cheese
2 dozen ravioli wrappers or won ton wrappers
8 quarts water
Salt to taste

For the sauce, sauté the garlic in the olive oil in a large skillet for 1 minute. Stir in the tomatoes; reduce the heat. Simmer for 3 minutes, stirring frequently. Add the red pepper and salt and cook for 5 minutes, stirring occasionally.

For the ravioli, sauté the shallots in the olive oil in a skillet for 2 minutes. Add the veal and cook until the veal is brown and crumbly, stirring constantly; drain. Stir in the wine, garlic, parsley, nutmeg, salt and pepper. Remove from the heat. Let stand until cool. Stir in the cheese. You may prepare up to this point and store, covered, in the refrigerator for up to 2 days.

Mound 1 teaspoon of the veal mixture on each ravioli wrapper. Dip fingers in water and run around the filling. Fold over to enclose the filling and seal the edges.

Bring the water and salt to taste to a boil in a stockpot over high heat. Add the ravioli; reduce the heat. Simmer until the ravioli float to the top; drain. Toss the ravioli with the warm sauce in a bowl. Serve immediately.

Serves 4 to 6

St. Joseph is credited for saving the Sicilian farmers in the Middle Ages from a severe drought that had left them with only fava beans for nourishment. Legend says that the farmers prayed to St. Joseph, who was known as the patron of fathers and carpenters, and shortly thereafter, rain came and ended the drought.

GARLIC FRENCH BREAD

 1 loaf French bread
 1/2 cup (1 stick) butter
 2 or 3 garlic cloves, crushed
 3 to 4 teaspoons chopped fresh parsley

Cut the loaf horizontally into halves. Combine the butter and garlic in a microwave-safe dish. Microwave until the butter melts and stir.

Brush the butter mixture over the cut sides of the bread halves and sprinkle with the parsley. Place the cut sides together to form a loaf and arrange on a baking sheet. Bake at 350 degrees for 10 minutes or until crisp. Slice as desired.

Serves 12

SEED COOKIES

These small, rectangular cookies covered with crunchy sesame seeds are truly worth the effort.

 4 cups flour
 2 teaspoons baking powder
 1 1/2 cups shortening
 1 cup sugar
 2 eggs, slightly beaten
 1 teaspoon vanilla extract
 3/4 cup milk
 1 cup sesame seeds

Sift the flour and baking powder together. Beat the shortening and sugar in a mixing bowl until creamy. Add the eggs and vanilla and beat until smooth. Blend in the flour mixture. Add just enough of the milk 1 tablespoon at a time until the dough adheres, mixing constantly.

Divide the dough into 6 equal portions. Roll each portion into a log the size of your index finger; the thinner the log, the crisper the cookies. Cut each log into 2- to 3-inch sections.

Pour the remaining milk into a shallow dish. Dip each section in the milk and coat with the sesame seeds. Arrange on a greased cookie sheet. Bake at 350 degrees for 10 to 12 minutes or until light brown. Cool on the cookie sheet for 2 minutes. Remove to a wire rack to cool completely. Store in an airtight container.

Makes 2 1/2 to 3 dozen cookies

ITALIAN FIG COOKIES

A traditional Southern Italian holiday cookie. Fig trees are abundant in Louisiana, but in order to get some, you have to harvest them fast enough to beat the birds.

Fig Filling
5 pounds fresh figs, ground
2 (16-ounce) packages raisins, ground
1¹/2 pounds pecans, ground
1 orange, ground
¹/2 (2-ounce) bottle vanilla extract
2 teaspoons cinnamon
1 teaspoon allspice
1 teaspoon ground cloves
1¹/2 cups sugar
1 cup water
Olive oil to moisten hands

Pastry
4 pounds all-purpose flour
2 pounds cake flour
1¹/2 teaspoons salt
1³/4 pounds shortening
1 cup (2 sticks) margarine
3 cups sugar
4 cups warm water

Confectioners' Sugar Icing
1 (1-pound) package confectioners' sugar
1 (12-ounce) can evaporated milk
1 small bottle lemon juice
Food coloring
Candy sprinkles

For the filling, combine the figs, raisins, pecans, orange and vanilla in a bowl and mix well. Stir in the cinnamon, allspice and cloves. Dissolve the sugar in the water and stir into the fig mixture. Shape the fig mixture into a ball. Pinch off small portions of the ball with olive oil-coated hands and roll into approximately 84 long narrow logs. Set aside.

For the pastry, mix the all-purpose flour, cake flour and salt in a large bowl. Cut in the shortening and margarine until crumbly. Dissolve the sugar in the warm water and gradually add to the flour mixture, mixing constantly. Knead until an easily managed dough forms. Divide the dough into 4 equal portions. Working with 1 portion at a time, cut off small sections of the dough and roll on a lightly floured surface until the desired thickness; the thinner the dough, the thinner the finished cookie. Cut into 1×6-inch rectangles. Arrange 1 of the fig logs lengthwise in the center of each rectangle. Wrap the sides of the dough around the fig rolls and seal the edges. Arrange seam side down and cut into individual cookies approximately 1¹/2 inches long.

Arrange the cookies seam side down on a greased cookie sheet. Cut slits in the top of each. Bake at 350 degrees for 20 minutes or until light brown on the bottom. Cool on the cookie sheet for 2 minutes. Remove to a wire rack to cool completely.

For the icing, mix the confectioners' sugar with just enough of the evaporated milk and lemon juice in a bowl until of a glaze consistency. Tint with pastel colors. Drizzle the cookies with the icing and top with the sprinkles. Let stand until set.

Makes 7 dozen cookies

PROGRESSIVE DINNER PARTY

One old neighborhood tradition in Baton Rouge is the progressive dinner party. Everyone has a hand in the process as guests travel from house to house for each course. A great idea for a supper club, this party takes the pressure off one person, as each person shares in the cooking. It's also a good plan for keeping prom-bound teens occupied and supervised for an evening before heading to the dance.

8 Guests

Cocktail Hour
LOUISIANA MARTINI

SUGAR AND SPICE PECANS

CRAWFISH CHEESECAKE

MUSHROOM PÂTÉ

SAVORY BRIE

Dinner
BABY BLUE SALAD

SEAFOOD-STUFFED PORK TENDERLOIN

BAKED TOMATOES

ZUCCHINI CASSEROLE

Dessert and Coffee
LEMON CREAM PIE

TOASTED NUT PIE

WHITE CHOCOLATE RASPBERRY PIE

COFFEE

Louisiana Martini

Finish it in southern style by garnishing with pickled okra or pickled green beans instead of the usual olive.

2 cups vodka
12 dashes dry vermouth
2 teaspoons olive juice
Ice
6 spicy pickled green beans
6 garlic-stuffed green olives
6 lemon twists
6 pickled okra

Combine the vodka, vermouth, olive juice and ice in a cocktail shaker and shake vigorously. Strain into a chilled pitcher, discarding the ice. Thread 6 skewers with equal amounts of the green beans, olives, lemon twists and okra. Pour into martini glasses and garnish each with 1 skewer.

Serves 6

Sugar and Spice Pecans

Roast these spicy pecans in your oven for an addictive cocktail snack.

1 pound pecan halves
1/4 cup (1/2 stick) butter, melted
2 tablespoons sugar
2 tablespoons (heaping) brown sugar
1 teaspoon Morton Nature's Seasons Seasoning Blend
1 teaspoon curry powder

Toss the pecans with the butter in a bowl. Add a mixture of the sugar, brown sugar, seasoning blend and curry powder to the pecan mixture and mix well.

Spread the pecans in a single layer on a baking sheet. Toast at 275 degrees for 45 minutes, stirring at 15-minute intervals. Remove the pecans to a plate and let stand until cool. Store in an airtight container.

Makes 4 cups

Even though Cajun cooking is generally regarded as more homey and rustic while Creole cooking is usually perceived as being more cultured, there are many similarities between the two. Both types are known for using rich sauces, homemade stocks, prolonged cooking times, and, of course, copious amounts of spices. Many of the ingredients used are interchangeable between the two styles. Rice, for example, is used in great quantities in both types of cooking and is grown on a major scale in Louisiana. Many Creole and Cajun dishes also start with a roux, a mixture of flour and oil that serves as a base for building many recipes. The combination of chopped onion, celery, and bell peppers, known as the "Holy Trinity," is used in countless Creole and Cajun recipes. Louisiana's waterways tie both types of cooking together in the abundance of food that is harvested from bayous, lakes, rivers, and the Gulf of Mexico. Shellfish, such as crab, shrimp, oysters, and crawfish, fresh and salt water fish, and, to some degree, ducks, frogs, and turtles are all found in kitchens across the state.

CRAWFISH CHEESECAKE

A savory and delicious crawfish treat.

Crawfish Topping	**Cheesecake**
2 tablespoons olive oil	1 cup bread crumbs
1 tablespoon fresh lemon juice	$1/2$ cup (1 stick) butter, melted
1 teaspoon lemon pepper	1 pound crawfish tails
1 teaspoon Creole seasoning	2 tablespoons olive oil
1 pound crawfish tails	Salt and white pepper to taste
1 (14-ounce) can artichoke hearts,	Creole seasoning to taste
drained and chopped	24 ounces cream cheese, softened
$1/2$ cup drained capers	3 eggs
$1/2$ cup Creole mustard	2 egg yolks
$1/4$ cup ketchup	1 tablespoon fresh lemon juice
3 tablespoons prepared horseradish	1 tablespoon chopped fresh parsley
2 tablespoons chopped fresh parsley	1 teaspoon chopped garlic

For the topping, heat the olive oil, lemon juice, lemon pepper and Creole seasoning in a skillet. Sauté the crawfish in the hot oil mixture; drain. Chill, covered, in the refrigerator. Add the artichokes, capers, mustard, ketchup, horseradish and parsley to the sautéed crawfish just before spreading on the top of the cheesecake.

For the cheesecake, toss the bread crumbs and butter in a bowl until coated. Press the crumb mixture over the bottom of a 10-inch springform pan sprayed with nonstick cooking spray. Sauté the crawfish in the olive oil in a skillet for 1 to 2 minutes. Season with salt, white pepper and Creole seasoning. Let stand until cool and coarsely chop.

Process the cream cheese, eggs, egg yolks, lemon juice, parsley, garlic, Creole seasoning, salt and white pepper in a food processor until blended. Fold in the crawfish mixture. Spoon the crawfish mixture into the prepared pan. Bake at 300 degrees for $1^{1}/4$ hours or until set. Spread with the topping. Serve at room temperature or chilled with assorted party crackers.

Serves 12 to 15

MUSHROOM PÂTÉ

Garnish with sprigs of fresh parsley and serve with water crackers or melba rounds.

1 pound fresh mushrooms, chopped
2 tablespoons butter
8 ounces cream cheese, softened

1 teaspoon seasoned salt
1/2 teaspoon garlic salt
Pepper to taste

Sauté the mushrooms in the butter in a skillet over medium-high heat until the liquid evaporates. Cool to room temperature. Process the sautéed mushrooms, cream cheese, seasoned salt, garlic salt and pepper in a food processor until smooth. Spoon the mushroom mixture into a lightly greased mold. Chill, covered, until serving time. Serve with assorted party crackers.

Serves 12

SAVORY BRIE

Most of the ingredients for this sophisticated appetizer are probably already in your pantry.

1 head garlic, top removed
1/4 cup extra-virgin olive oil
1 (8-ounce) round Brie cheese
1/4 cup chopped olives

1/4 cup chopped sun-dried tomatoes
2 tablespoons chopped pecans
2 tablespoons chopped fresh parsley
2 tablespoons chopped fresh basil

Place the garlic in a small baking dish and drizzle with the olive oil. Roast, covered with foil, at 325 degrees for approximately 35 minutes. Let stand until cool.

Cut the rind from the top of the Brie and arrange the round on an ovenproof platter. Squeeze the roasted garlic over the top of the Brie and spread evenly to cover. Sprinkle with the olives, sun-dried tomatoes and pecans. Bake at 400 degrees for 12 minutes or until the Brie is soft. Sprinkle with the parsley and basil and serve with assorted party crackers.

Serves 12

BABY BLUE SALAD

A nice blend of fruit and cheese. Sliced cherry tomatoes may be used if strawberries are not in season. Tomato basil feta may also be substituted for the blue cheese.

Balsamic Dijon Vinaigrette
1 cup olive oil
1/2 cup balsamic vinegar
3 tablespoons Dijon mustard
3 tablespoons honey
2 garlic cloves, crushed
1/4 teaspoon salt
1/4 teaspoon pepper

Salad
1/4 cup sugar
1 cup water
1 cup walnut halves or pieces
2 tablespoons sugar
1 tablespoon chili powder
1/4 teaspoon red pepper
12 ounces mixed salad greens (romaine and baby spinach)
2 (11-ounce) cans mandarin oranges, drained
2 pints fresh strawberries, sliced
4 ounces blue cheese, crumbled

For the vinaigrette, whisk the olive oil, vinegar, mustard, honey, garlic, salt and pepper in a bowl until incorporated.

For the salad, dissolve 1/4 cup sugar in the water in a bowl. Add the walnuts to the sugar mixture and mix well. Let stand for 10 minutes; drain. Mix 2 tablespoons sugar, chili powder and red pepper in a small bowl. Add the walnuts and toss to coat. Spread the walnuts on a baking sheet lined with foil. Toast at 350 degrees for 5 minutes; stir. Toast for 5 minutes longer. Remove to a plate to cool.

Toss the salad greens, mandarin oranges, strawberries and cheese in a large salad bowl. Add the desired amount of vinaigrette and mix until coated. Sprinkle with the walnuts. Serve immediately.

Serves 8

RIVER ROAD RECIPES

Janice Couvillion, chairman of the marketing committee for the River Road Recipes *cookbook, believes there is a simple reason for the book's success.*

"Not only are the recipes easy to follow and make, they're just downright good," she says. Couvillion credits that to area residents' love of food. "Everything we do in South Louisiana is based on food. People can't stand to see you not eating. Whether it's a funeral or a football party, people will have food," she says. "I have pretty much traveled around the world, and I haven't eaten better food than what we have here. People love to eat, and it shows in their cooking."

—Karen Haram, Express-News, *1997, San Antonio, Texas*

SEAFOOD-STUFFED PORK TENDERLOIN

Make this dish ahead of time so that when guests arrive at your house for the main course, all that is needed is a quick reheating.

Pork Tenderloin
1 (3- to 4-pound) pork tenderloin,
    butterflied
Salt and black pepper to taste
Red pepper to taste
1/2 cup chopped green onions
1/4 cup chopped fresh parsley
1 tablespoon minced garlic
1/4 teaspoon oregano
6 tablespoons butter
12 ounces crawfish tails

Basting Sauce
1/4 cup (1/2 stick) butter
1/4 cup water
2 tablespoons Worcestershire sauce
1 tablespoon honey

Shrimp Sauce
1/4 cup (1/2 stick) butter
1/2 cup chopped green onions
1/4 cup chopped fresh parsley
1 tablespoon chopped onion
1 pound (30 to 40 count) shrimp, peeled
    and deveined
4 ounces crawfish tails
1 teaspoon salt
1/2 teaspoon oregano
1/2 teaspoon thyme
1/2 teaspoon white pepper
1/4 teaspoon Worcestershire sauce
1/8 teaspoon Tabasco sauce
1 cup heavy cream

For the tenderloin, season the pork with salt, black pepper and red pepper. Sauté the green onions, parsley, garlic and oregano in the butter in a saucepan for 5 minutes. Stir in the crawfish. Sauté for 5 minutes longer. Place the pork flat on a sheet of foil and spread the crawfish stuffing down the center. Secure with kitchen twine to enclose the filling. Bring the sides of the foil up to form an edge. Arrange on a grill rack. Add 2 handfuls of wet mesquite chips to the hot coals. Grill, with the lid down, for 45 minutes or to the desired degree of doneness.

For the basting sauce, combine the butter, water, Worcestershire sauce and honey in a saucepan. Simmer just until heated through, stirring occasionally. Baste the pork at 10-minute intervals after the pork begins to brown.

For the shrimp sauce, melt the butter in a saucepan. Sauté the green onions, parsley and onion in the butter for 5 minutes. Stir in the shrimp, crawfish, salt, oregano, thyme, white pepper, Worcestershire sauce and Tabasco sauce. Sauté for 5 minutes. Add the heavy cream and mix well. Sauté for 3 minutes longer.

To serve, cut the pork into 1-inch slices. Drizzle each serving with some of the Shrimp Sauce.

Serves 12

BAKED TOMATOES

Try to use Creole or Roma tomatoes in this recipe. If neither is available, use the freshest, ripest tomatoes you can find in your area.

6 Creole or Roma tomatoes	2 tablespoons chopped fresh basil
Salt to taste	1 tablespoon chopped fresh parsley
2 cups fresh bread crumbs	Pepper to taste
1 cup (4 ounces) freshly grated Parmesan cheese	1/4 cup (1/2 stick) butter

Cut the tomatoes into halves and squeeze the halves to remove the seeds. Sprinkle with salt. Arrange cut side up in a single layer in a 9×13-inch baking dish. Chill in the refrigerator.

Mix the bread crumbs, cheese, basil, parsley, salt and pepper in a bowl and sprinkle the crumb mixture over the cut sides of the tomatoes; do not pack too tightly. Dot with the butter. Add a small amount of water to the baking dish and bake at 300 degrees for 20 to 30 minutes or until the tomatoes are tender and the crumb topping is brown.

Serves 6 to 12

ZUCCHINI CASSEROLE

This recipe is a real boon to gardeners looking for new ways to prepare all those fresh summer vegetables. Substitute yellow squash for the zucchini, or use a combination of both.

10 to 12 zucchini, sliced	2 cups (8 ounces) shredded Cheddar cheese
1 onion, chopped	
1/4 cup (1/2 stick) butter	3/4 cup bread crumbs
Salt and pepper to taste	1/4 cup (1/2 stick) butter
1 cup sour cream	

Steam the zucchini just until tender. Drain and pat dry with paper towels. Sauté the onion in 1/4 cup butter in a skillet until tender.

Layer the zucchini, sautéed onion, salt, pepper, sour cream and cheese 1/3 at a time in a greased 2-quart baking dish. Sprinkle with the bread crumbs and dot with 1/4 cup butter. Bake at 350 degrees for 30 minutes.

Serves 8

LEMON CREAM PIE

When entertaining a large crowd, offer a variety of desserts as well as the chocolate favorites. A good mix includes something lemony and something nutty as well as something to please the chocolate addicts.

1 cup sugar
3¹/2 tablespoons cornstarch
1 tablespoon grated lemon zest
1 cup milk
¹/2 cup lemon juice
3 egg yolks, lightly beaten

¹/4 cup (¹/2 stick) margarine, melted
1 cup sour cream
1 baked (9-inch) pie shell
1 cup whipping cream, whipped
4 lemons, thinly sliced and twisted

Combine the sugar, cornstarch and lemon zest in a saucepan and mix well. Stir in the milk, lemon juice and egg yolks. Cook over medium heat until thickened, stirring constantly. Stir in the margarine until blended. Let stand until room temperature.

Add the sour cream to the lemon mixture and mix well. Spoon into the pie shell and spread with the whipped cream, sealing to the edge. Top with the lemon twists. Store, covered, in the refrigerator.

Serves 6 to 8

TOASTED NUT PIE

A variation on traditional pecan pie, this one uses an assortment of mixed nuts for an attractive look and a wonderful texture.

1 cup dark corn syrup
1 cup sugar
3 eggs, beaten
1 teaspoon vanilla extract
¹/4 teaspoon cinnamon
1¹/2 cups mixed nuts
1 unbaked (9-inch) pie shell

Combine the corn syrup, sugar, eggs, vanilla and cinnamon in a bowl and mix well. Stir in the mixed nuts. Spoon the nut mixture into the pie shell. Bake at 325 degrees for 1 hour.

Serves 6 to 8

The tempting smell of coffee brewing on a cold day is the perfect aroma for a winter gathering. Coffee takes the edge off the cold and is homey and welcoming. A surge in popularity has brought a bewildering array of coffee types and brands to store shelves. Choosing a coffee can be almost as complex as choosing a good wine. Stick with a good quality, basic type in a trusted brand and guests will be satisfied. Refer to page 262 for handy tips on setting up a Coffee Bar.

A Coffee Bar lets guests serve themselves, freeing the host to enjoy the party or tend to other matters. Here are some tips for setting up a well-stocked, self-serve coffee bar that will ensure great-tasting and plentiful coffee for everyone.

Use freshly purchased beans or ground coffee and fresh cold water.

Resist the temptation to use a silver coffee service. Instead, use two thermal carafes—one for caffeinated and one for decaffeinated. These will keep coffee hot for several hours.

Measure carefully when brewing the coffee. Use two tablespoons of coffee per six ounces of water.

Consider offering a variety of milks, creamers, and sugars. A big bowl of whipped cream is a delicious indulgence that's hard to resist. Shakers filled with cinnamon, nutmeg, and baking cocoa are a nice touch.

Remember to stock plenty of swizzle sticks and cocktail napkins. Use labels or tent cards to make sure ingredients are easily identifiable.

For a nice aroma, scatter coffee beans around the coffee bar.

White Chocolate Raspberry Pie

Instead of its usual place on top of the pie, the meringue is placed on the bottom to form a light and airy shell.

2 egg whites
$1/2$ teaspoon white vinegar
$1/2$ teaspoon vanilla extract
$1/4$ teaspoon salt
$1/2$ cup sugar
1 baked (9-inch) pie shell
1 cup (6 ounces) white chocolate morsels

$1/4$ cup water
2 egg yolks, lightly beaten
$1/2$ cup raspberry jam
1 cup whipping cream
$1/2$ teaspoon vanilla extract
$1/4$ cup sugar

Beat the egg whites, vinegar, $1/2$ teaspoon vanilla and salt in a mixing bowl until soft peaks form. Add $1/2$ cup sugar gradually, beating constantly until stiff peaks form. Spread the meringue over the bottom and up the side of the pie shell. Bake at 325 degrees for 15 to 20 minutes or until light brown. Let stand until cool.

Microwave the white chocolate in a microwave-safe dish or heat in a double boiler over simmering water until melted; stir. Add the water and egg yolks to the white chocolate and stir until smooth. Spread approximately $1/4$ cup of the chocolate mixture in the prepared pie shell. Let stand until set. Speed up the process by chilling in the refrigerator. Spread the jam over the prepared layers.

Beat the whipping cream in a mixing bowl until soft peaks form. Add $1/2$ teaspoon vanilla and $1/4$ cup sugar gradually and mix well. Fold the remaining chocolate mixture into the whipped cream and spread over the jam. Freeze until firm. Garnish with fresh or frozen raspberries and white chocolate curls. If you are concerned about using raw egg yolks, use eggs pasteurized in their shells, which are sold at some specialty food stores, or use an equivalent amount of pasteurized egg substitute.

Serves 8

SATURDAY ANTIQUING TRIP

*Just a short drive from Baton Rouge are the fine shopping towns of
New Orleans, St. Francisville, Natchez, and Denham Springs,
all favorite destinations for Baton Rouge ladies. Let this menu inspire
you to call your best friends, pack a cute lunch for everyone,
and hit the road. Your shopping excursion may become an annual event.*

4 Guests

CHICKEN FUSILLI SALAD

GARDEN QUICHE

POTATO CHIP COOKIES
(RRRII page 210)

MUD PIES

Optional Menu Item
ASIAN CHICKEN WRAPS

Chicken Fusilli Salad

For a fun, disposable container, purchase Chinese take-out cartons from a party store and fill each with individual servings of the pasta salad.

4 ounces fusilli
8 ounces boneless skinless chicken breasts, cut into bite-size pieces
3/4 cup julienned green bell pepper
3/4 cup julienned red bell pepper
2 green onions, chopped
2 tablespoons olive oil

1/3 cup pine nuts
2 teaspoons minced fresh gingerroot
1 garlic clove, minced
1 tablespoon soy sauce
1 tablespoon lemon or lime juice
Salt and pepper to taste

Cook the pasta using the package directions; drain. Sauté the chicken, bell peppers and green onions in the olive oil in a skillet over medium-high heat for 3 minutes. Stir in the pine nuts, gingerroot and garlic.

Sauté for 3 minutes longer or until the chicken is cooked through. Stir in the soy sauce, lemon juice, salt and pepper. Toss the chicken mixture with the pasta in a bowl. Serve immediately.

Serves 2

Garden Quiche

1 refrigerator pie pastry
2 carrots, shredded
1 squash, shredded
1/2 red bell pepper, chopped
1 tablespoon margarine
2 tablespoons apple juice
1 cup 2% milk

3 eggs
1/2 cup egg substitute
1/2 teaspoon Italian seasoning
1/2 teaspoon salt
1/4 teaspoon pepper
1 cup chopped fresh spinach
1 cup (4 ounces) shredded Swiss cheese

Roll the pie pastry 1/8 inch thick on a lightly floured surface and fit into a 9-inch pie plate. Fold the edge under and crimp. Bake at 400 degrees for 8 minutes. Let stand until cool.

Sauté the carrots, squash and bell pepper in the margarine in a large skillet over medium-high heat for 7 minutes or until tender. Stir in the apple juice. Cook until the juice is absorbed, stirring frequently.

Whisk the 2% milk, eggs, egg substitute, Italian seasoning, salt and pepper in a bowl until blended. Add the carrot mixture, spinach and cheese to the milk mixture and mix well. Pour into the baked pie shell and place on the lowest oven rack. Bake for 40 minutes or until set. Let stand for 10 minutes before serving. You may substitute 5 eggs for the 3 eggs and 1/2 cup egg substitute.

Serves 8

ASIAN CHICKEN WRAPS

Package these wraps in baking parchment or waxed paper, cut into halves, and pack in brown paper bags. Tuck in attractive paper napkins and plastic utensils.

Asian Dressing

1 cup canola oil
1/2 cup rice wine vinegar
2 tablespoons minced fresh gingerroot
1 tablespoon soy sauce
1 tablespoon minced garlic
1 tablespoon sugar
1/2 teaspoon cracked red pepper

Wraps

1 rotisserie chicken, or 4 to 6 grilled or poached
   chicken breasts
1 cup chopped cabbage
1 cup chow mein noodles
1/2 cup slivered almonds, toasted
1/2 cup chopped red bell pepper
1/4 cup chopped green bell pepper
4 green onions, chopped
2 tablespoons sesame seeds, toasted
4 to 6 large tortilla wraps

For the dressing, combine the canola oil, vinegar, gingerroot, soy sauce, garlic, sugar and red pepper in a bowl and whisk until the sugar dissolves.

For the wraps, chop the chicken into bite-size pieces, discarding the skin and bones. Combine the chicken, cabbage, noodles, almonds, bell peppers, green onions and sesame seeds in a bowl and mix well. Add the dressing to the cabbage mixture and toss to coat. Spread the cabbage mixture over the tortillas and roll to enclose the filling. Wrap each roll individually in baking parchment and secure with tape. Cut each wrap diagonally into halves.

Serves 4 to 6

MUD PIES

Cookies
2/3 cup flour
1/4 teaspoon baking powder
1/8 teaspoon salt
8 ounces semisweet chocolate
2 tablespoons butter
3/4 cup packed brown sugar
2 eggs
1 teaspoon vanilla extract

Chocolate Glaze
2 ounces semisweet chocolate
2 tablespoons butter
1 teaspoon light corn syrup
1/2 teaspoon vanilla extract

For the cookies, mix the flour, baking powder and salt in a bowl. Combine the chocolate and butter in a microwave-safe bowl. Microwave on High for 1 minute and stir until smooth. Beat the brown sugar and eggs in a mixing bowl at high speed for 3 minutes or until thickened. Add the chocolate mixture and vanilla to the egg mixture gradually, beating constantly until blended. Add the flour mixture gradually, beating at low speed until smooth.

Drop by rounded teaspoonfuls onto a greased cookie sheet. Bake at 350 degrees for 10 to 12 minutes or until crisp around the edges. Cool on the cookie sheet for 2 minutes. Remove to a wire rack to cool completely.

For the glaze, combine the chocolate and butter in a microwave-safe bowl. Microwave on High for 1 minute and stir until smooth. Stir in the corn syrup and vanilla. Spoon 1 teaspoon of the glaze over the center of each cookie. Let stand for 30 minutes or until set.

Makes 3 dozen cookies

FAMILY REUNION

Louisiana family reunions usually involve popular Creole and Cajun foods and can occur for just about any occasion, including visiting relatives or a holiday. A Lenten fish fry or cochon du lait are meant to last all day, with everyone contributing a little lagniappe, such as a side dish, beer, or a sack of crawfish, to the meal.

Serves a Crowd

MARINATED MUSHROOMS

MIXED GREENS WITH CANE SUGAR AND
CREOLE MUSTARD VINAIGRETTE

POTATO SALAD
(RRRI page 35)

JAMBALAYA

SOUTHERN-FRIED CATFISH WITH
TARTAR SAUCE

PECAN-CRUSTED OKRA

ALMOND JOY CAKE

CHOCOLATE PEANUT BUTTER PIE

Tossing a green salad takes just the right touch. The trick is to coat the leaves with dressing, yet keep them whole, crisp, and unbruised. A large salad bowl is the key—you will have plenty of elbow room. Drizzle the dressing around the upper inside of the bowl so that it runs down and coats the bowl. Use your hands to gently fold the greens so each leaf is lightly coated on each side. Add a taste of salt and pepper and serve immediately.

MARINATED MUSHROOMS

Measure the ingredients directly into a resealable plastic bag. When you arrive at your destination, simply transfer the mushrooms to a bowl and serve with wooden cocktail picks.

1/4 cup red wine vinegar
2 tablespoons chopped fresh basil
2 teaspoons salt
2 teaspoons chopped fresh parsley
1 teaspoon pepper

1 garlic clove, slivered
1/8 teaspoon Tabasco sauce
6 tablespoons olive oil
3 green onions, chopped
1 pound fresh mushrooms, trimmed

Combine the vinegar, basil, salt, parsley, pepper, garlic and Tabasco sauce in a large jar or container with a tight-fitting lid and seal tightly. Shake to mix. Add the olive oil and green onions and seal tightly. Shake to mix. Add the mushrooms and seal tightly. Shake to coat.

Let stand at room temperature for 4 to 5 hours. Continue marinating in the refrigerator for 2 more hours, shaking occasionally.

Serves 6 to 8

MIXED GREENS WITH CANE SUGAR AND CREOLE MUSTARD VINAIGRETTE

Make things easy and pick up large bags of pre-washed mixed salad greens from the grocery store and toss in a big salad bowl with this delicious homemade vinaigrette.

1/2 cup chopped onion
1 tablespoon minced garlic
1/2 cup vegetable oil
1/2 cup red wine vinegar
1 1/2 tablespoons cane syrup

1 tablespoon Creole mustard
Juice of 1 lemon
Salt and pepper to taste
Mixed salad greens

Sauté the onion and garlic in the oil in a saucepan until the onion is tender. Stir in the vinegar. Remove from the heat. Add the syrup and mustard and mix well. Stir in the lemon juice, salt and pepper. Let stand until cool. Store in the refrigerator.

Toss the salad greens with the desired amount of vinaigrette in a salad bowl. Add chopped apples and chopped pears for variety.

Variable servings

JAMBALAYA

At just about any big party in Louisiana, you will find Jambalaya. It is inexpensive to prepare, feeds a crowd, and everyone loves it. At large festivals, it is not unusual to see men making Jambalaya for hundreds of people in gigantic sugar kettles.

2 pounds pork, cubed	3/4 cup chopped green onions
Salt and black pepper to taste	2 or 3 garlic cloves, minced
1 cup canola oil	2 pounds long grain rice
1 1/2 pounds chicken, poached, skinned, boned and coarsely chopped	6 1/2 cups water
	3 tablespoons hot sauce
	2 teaspoons salt
1 1/2 pounds sausage, sliced	2 teaspoons red pepper
1 pound onions, chopped	6 beef bouillon cubes
1 bell pepper, chopped	3 tablespoons Kitchen Bouquet

Season the pork with salt and black pepper. Fry the pork in the canola oil in a heavy cast-iron pan or Dutch oven until cooked through, turning frequently; reduce the heat. Cook over low heat for 30 minutes, stirring occasionally. Add the chicken and sausage and mix well. Cook for 10 minutes, stirring frequently. Remove the pork mixture to a bowl using a slotted spoon, reserving the pan drippings.

Sauté the onions, bell pepper, green onions and garlic in the reserved pan drippings until the onions are tender. Return the pork mixture to the pan and mix well. Add the rice, water, hot sauce, salt, red pepper, bouillon cubes and Kitchen Bouquet and mix well. Bring to a boil; reduce the heat.

Simmer for 5 minutes, stirring occasionally. Bake, covered, at 300 degrees for 45 minutes; do not peek. Remove the cover and bake for 20 minutes longer or until the rice is tender.

Serves a crowd

The combination of chopped onion, green bell pepper, and celery is referred to as "The Trinity" in South Louisiana. Many traditional Cajun and Creole recipes start with these ingredients. To save preparation time, keep resealable plastic bags of each in the freezer, chopped and ready to use. Then just open the freezer and scoop out a handful of these essential ingredients.

269

Cornmeal-crusted, deep-fried catfish is an old Southern favorite. Louisiana's waterways are full of this white-fleshed fish, which explains why catfish is so common in the state's cuisine. Catfish devotees can tell you it is simple to prepare and very versatile, coming to the table in so many delicious ways. Frying is the most popular, but catfish can also be grilled, baked, sautéed, or broiled. Remove the catfish skin before cooking. Catfish is fully cooked when the color has changed from translucent to white. Do not cook until it flakes... this signals overcooking.

Southern-Fried Catfish with Tartar Sauce

A Friday fish fry is a tradition in many Louisiana families, especially during Lent. Everyone in the family brings something extra to add to the meatless meal of catfish, hush puppies, and French fries, resulting in a tremendous feast that takes all day to consume.

Tartar Sauce
2 cups mayonnaise
1/2 cup minced green onions
1/2 cup dill pickle relish
1/2 cup minced fresh parsley
1/4 cup drained capers, chopped
1/4 cup minced fresh chives

Catfish
5 pounds catfish fillets
2 cups buttermilk
2 cups yellow cornmeal
1 cup flour
1 tablespoon paprika
Salt and pepper to taste
Peanut oil for frying
1 red onion, sliced
1 lemon, cut into wedges

For the sauce, combine the mayonnaise, green onions, pickle relish, parsley, capers and chives in a bowl and mix well. You may store, covered, in the refrigerator for several weeks.

For the catfish, cut the fillets into 1-inch-thick strips. Soak the catfish in the buttermilk in a shallow dish in the refrigerator for 20 minutes. Mix the cornmeal, flour, paprika, salt and pepper in a shallow dish. Add enough peanut oil to a large skillet to measure 4 inches and heat to 350 degrees.

Drain the catfish and coat with the cornmeal mixture. Fry in the hot oil for 4 minutes or until brown and crisp; drain. Arrange the catfish on a serving platter with the onion and lemon wedges. Serve with the sauce.

Serves 8

PECAN-CRUSTED OKRA

The pecans add an extra crunch to this Louisiana specialty.

1/2 cup flour
1/2 cup cornmeal
1/2 cup finely chopped toasted pecans
1 teaspoon salt

1/4 teaspoon red pepper
1 pound fresh okra, cut into 1/4-inch slices
Peanut oil for frying

Combine the flour, cornmeal, pecans, salt and red pepper in a shallow dish and mix well. Add the okra to the flour mixture and toss lightly to coat.

Add enough peanut oil to a skillet to measure 2 inches and heat to 375 degrees. Fry the okra in batches in the hot oil for 4 minutes or until golden brown; drain. Serve immediately.

Serves 4

ALMOND JOY CAKE

Chocolate, coconut, and almonds combine for a cake with a flavor similar to a well-loved candy bar. For neat slices, chill for several hours before cutting.

1 (2-layer) butter chocolate cake mix
1 cup milk
1 cup sugar
24 marshmallows
1 (14-ounce) package shredded coconut
1 1/2 cups sugar

1 cup evaporated milk
1/2 cup (1 stick) butter
2 cups (12 ounces) semisweet chocolate
  chips
Whole almonds, lightly toasted (optional)

Bake the cake using package directions for a 9×13-inch cake pan. Bring the milk and 1 cup sugar to a boil in a saucepan. Boil for 1 minute; reduce the heat. Stir in the marshmallows and cook until blended, stirring constantly. Stir in the coconut and pour over the hot cake.

Bring 1 1/2 cups sugar, the evaporated milk and butter to a boil in a saucepan; reduce the heat to low. Add the chocolate chips and mix well. Cook until blended, stirring frequently. Fold in the almonds. Pour the chocolate mixture over the warm layers. Let stand until set and cut into squares. You may freeze for future use.

Makes 1 to 2 dozen squares

CHOCOLATE PEANUT BUTTER PIE

A chocolate cookie crust and a little bit of coffee give this pie a chocolate café flavor.

2 cups creamy peanut butter
16 ounces cream cheese, softened
2 cups sugar
2 teaspoons vanilla extract
1¹/2 cups whipping cream
2 (9-inch) chocolate cookie pie shells
1 cup (6 ounces) semisweet chocolate chips
7 tablespoons hot coffee

Beat the peanut butter and cream cheese in a mixing bowl until creamy, scraping the bowl occasionally. Add the sugar and beat until fluffy. Blend in the vanilla.

Beat the whipping cream in a chilled bowl until soft peaks form. Fold the whipped cream into the peanut butter mixture and spoon evenly into the pie shells. Freeze for 30 minutes or longer.

Mix the chocolate chips and hot coffee in a bowl until smooth. Spread the chocolate mixture over the tops of the frozen pies. Freeze until serving time.

Serves 12 to 16

I had just completed a year as the Assistant Chair for River Road Recipes *when I attended my first national self-publishers' seminar in Nashville, Tennessee. Naturally, I was well aware of* River Road Recipes' *national number-one status, but I guess I did not truly appreciate the magnitude of its success until I got to the very first event, an evening cocktail party. I filled out a name tag that said I was from* River Road Recipes *in Baton Rouge, Louisiana, stuck it on, and started to mingle. Within minutes, other self-publishers demanding to know in five minutes or less how to sell a million cookbooks surrounded me. I was not prepared to receive so much attention and wished I had worn something cuter to the party instead of coming straight from the airport. From that point on, people followed me around for two days, asking me for advice, telling me about their individual publishing problems in great detail, and asking me how to solve them. This went on even when I ducked into the bathroom! I have to admit, it was very flattering even though I didn't deserve to be turned into a cookbook celebrity. That honor goes to all the hard-working ladies who came before me, who made* River Road Recipes *the success that it is today.*

—Tanja Van Hook Foil, Chairman 2002-2003

RELAXING AT THE CAMP

Because Baton Rouge is near lakes, hunting spots, and the beach, many residents own or borrow camps or beach houses for weekend getaways and entertaining. If invited, friends and family jump at the chance for a spell by the water.

12 Guests

FRIED SOFT-SHELL CRABS

BLACK BEAN SALAD

CABBAGE SALAD

LOUISIANA SEAFOOD BOIL

TARTAR SAUCE AND COCKTAIL SAUCE

FROSTED BROWNIES

POPSICLES

When entertaining away from your primary residence, a little advance preparation will keep you out of the kitchen and on the boat or the beach with your company. Before the trip, make a list of the menus for each meal and the ingredients or special equipment that will be required. Choose recipes that can be assembled in advance and frozen. When it is time to go, wrap the frozen dishes in newspapers and pack into ice chests. The frozen food will help to keep the other items in the ice chest cold and will be ready to cook or chill when you get to your destination.

Fried Soft-Shell Crabs

2 cups all-purpose flour
Salt and pepper to taste
Creole seasoning to taste
2 cups milk
6 eggs
18 cocktail-size soft-shell crabs (approximately 3 inches long)
3 cups corn flour
3/4 cup olive oil
6 tablespoons butter

Mix the all-purpose flour, salt, pepper and Creole seasoning in a shallow dish. Whisk the milk and eggs in a bowl until blended. Coat the crabs with the seasoned flour mixture, dip in the milk mixture and coat with the corn flour.

Heat 1/4 cup of the olive oil and 2 tablespoons of the butter in a sauté pan over medium heat. Fry 6 of the crabs in the hot butter mixture for 2 to 3 minutes per side or until golden brown; drain. Repeat the process with the remaining olive oil, remaining butter and remaining crabs. Serve immediately.

Serves 6

Black Bean Salad

1 (12-ounce) can Shoe Peg corn, drained and rinsed
1 (15-ounce) can black beans, drained and rinsed
1 (11-ounce) can tomatoes with green chiles, drained
3 green onions, chopped
1 tablespoon red wine vinegar
1 tablespoon olive oil

Combine the corn, beans, tomatoes, green onions, vinegar and olive oil in a salad bowl and mix well. Serve at room temperature or chilled.

Serves 6

CABBAGE SALAD

Lemon Dressing
1/4 cup extra-virgin olive oil
3 tablespoons fresh lemon juice
1 teaspoon grated lemon zest
1 garlic clove, crushed
1/2 teaspoon salt
Freshly ground pepper to taste

Salad
1 (16-ounce) package thinly sliced cabbage
2 or 3 green onions, diagonally sliced
1 small carrot, coarsely shredded
1 tablespoon chopped fresh flat-leaf parsley

For the dressing, whisk the olive oil, lemon juice, lemon zest, garlic, salt and pepper in a bowl until incorporated.

For the salad, toss the cabbage, green onions, carrot and parsley in a salad bowl. Add the dressing and mix until coated. Chill, covered, until serving time.

Serves 4

"*THIS is real!...As a chef of the Cajun cuisine, I give kudos, high praises, and maybe even a Lord's prayer or two for how authentic the recipes are in this cookbook. . .We are talking down home, Momma done come out da kitchen and slapped some vittles on the table that'll make love to your nose, hug your heart, and stuff that belly! This is for people who want to make Cajun food at home for themselves without having to figure out what endive is used for. In conclusion, if you want some Cajun 'Good Lovin,' you'll find it right here in these books. Buy them and cook yourself up a whole mess of happiness.*"

—Comments posted about River Road Recipes *cookbooks on a well-known cookbook review website in 2002. The anonymous author gave RRR a five-star rating.*

LOUISIANA SEAFOOD BOIL

Most locals probably could not tell you who taught them how to boil seafood; they have just always known. While it may look easy, there is more to it than just boiling water, especially if you want to ensure a perfectly cooked product every time. While those who frequently cook boiled seafood usually do not bother with written instructions, the right seasonings, proper preparation, and exact cooking times all play an important part in the finished product.

1 bag shrimp and crab boil seasoning	5 pounds small new potatoes
2 heads garlic	3 pounds small onions
2 lemons, cut into halves	1 dozen frozen ears of corn
2 dozen live crabs, rinsed	1 pound sausage, sliced
	12 pounds fresh shrimp, rinsed

Fill a large seafood stockpot fitted with a wire basket halfway with water and bring to a boil. Add the shrimp and crab boil seasoning, garlic and lemons and bring to a boil. Add the crabs. Boil, covered, for 2 minutes. Add the potatoes, onions, corn and sausage. Return to a boil; this process takes about 10 minutes.

Add the shrimp to the stockpot and return to a boil. Turn off the heat. Let stand, covered, for 10 to 15 minutes. The longer the standing time, the spicier the product. Remove the basket from the stockpot and drain. Spread the contents on a table covered with newspapers, discarding the seasoning bag, lemons and garlic.

Serves 12 to 16

FROSTED BROWNIES

Brownies
3/4 cup flour
2 teaspoons baking cocoa
1/8 teaspoon salt (optional)
1 1/2 cups (3 sticks) butter or margarine
1 cup sugar
2 eggs, beaten
1 tablespoon boiling water
1/2 cup chopped pecans
1 teaspoon vanilla extract

Chocolate Frosting
1/2 (16-ounce) package confectioners' sugar
1 (5-ounce) can evaporated milk
2 tablespoons butter or margarine
1 1/2 teaspoons baking cocoa
1/2 teaspoon vanilla extract
Pecan halves (optional)

For the brownies, sift the flour, baking cocoa and salt together. Beat the butter in a mixing bowl until creamy. Add the sugar, eggs and boiling water gradually, beating constantly until blended. Blend in the flour mixture. Stir in the pecans and vanilla.

Spoon the batter into a greased and lightly floured 9×9-inch baking pan. Bake at 350 degrees for 20 minutes. Cool in the pan on a wire rack. You may double the recipe and bake in an 11×15-inch baking pan. Increase the baking time to 25 minutes.

For the frosting, beat the confectioners' sugar, evaporated milk, butter, baking cocoa and vanilla in a mixing bowl to a spreading consistency, scraping the bowl occasionally. Spread the frosting over the top of the brownies. Top with pecan halves. Let stand until set and cut into bars.

Makes 2 to 3 dozen brownies

Crabs should always be alive when dropped into boiling water, as cooking a dead crab is dangerous and can result in food poisoning. Boil the crabs for twenty-four to thirty minutes. Follow these guidelines when opening crabs:

Remove the two large claw legs and use the handle of a knife or mallet to crack the claw shells. Use your fingers or a knife to remove the claw meat.

Snap off the remaining smaller walking legs by twisting and pulling each one off. Bits of meat may be found at each joint.

Turn the crab over and use fingers or a knife to pry up and snap off the long apron. Pry open and lift the hinged shell top up and break off, similar to opening a jewelry box. Discard the empty top shell.

Use a knife to scrape off and discard the white fingers. Use your hands to crack the shell in half down the center, and then break each piece in half again to expose the chambers. Break into the fanned-out leg cavities to find the crab meat. If necessary, use knives or picks.

HISTORY OF THE JUNIOR LEAGUE OF BATON ROUGE

In 1932, twenty-five young women determined to serve their community formed the Baton Rouge Junior Service League. The organization was admitted as a member of the Association of the Junior Leagues of America in 1956. Today, the Association of Junior Leagues International has 296 member organizations in four countries and more than 193,000 individual members.

As one of the eighteenth largest in the Association of Junior Leagues International, the Baton Rouge Junior League boasts as many members as some of the community's largest employers. Junior League volunteers have embraced the challenge of founding new organizations, raising seed money, and providing much-needed volunteers. Emerging nonprofits have benefited from Junior League training on critical organizational skills, volunteer management, fund development, and leadership. Such a transfer of knowledge has helped these organizations grow into major forces in the community. Junior League members have become integral leaders within many nonprofits by serving as executive directors, developmental directors, board members, and volunteers.

Since the beginning, the Junior League has trained hundreds of outstanding leaders to address community issues with enthusiasm, knowledge, and compassion. During the Great Depression, members provided milk and flour to feed hungry families. Junior League volunteers also provided medical services through financial donations and personal involvement with the East Baton Rouge Health Unit and local Red Cross. During World War II, members made bandages, staffed the USO, and sold defense bonds to support home-front efforts.

In the late 1940s, Junior League volunteers supported enrichment programs for children such as children's theater and story hour projects. Programs to assist the disabled were created in the late 1950s on through the 1970s.

The volunteer and fund-raising efforts of the Junior League formed the Baton Rouge Speech and Hearing Foundation. In the 1960s, the creation of the Louisiana Arts and Science Center (LASC) further enhanced the Junior League's focus on education. Education initiatives such as Adopt-a-School, LASC Discovery Depot, and Growing Pains were major projects for members in the 1980s. In an effort to encourage community voluntarism, the Junior League collaborated with the United Way to create Volunteer Baton Rouge.

In the late 1980s, the Junior League focused efforts on the special needs of middle school children. It enhanced the community through projects such as Symphony at Twilight, Arts in Education, Greater Baton Rouge Food Bank, Habitat for Humanity, and Young Leaders Academy School. During the late 1990s, the Junior League focused on school readiness for children ages zero to six for five years in an effort to ensure that all Baton Rouge children enter school physically, socially, and intellectually ready to learn.

In 2003, the Junior League clarified and redefined its vision, which states: The Junior League of Baton Rouge, Inc., will enhance the quality of life in the Baton Rouge community in the areas of physical health, education, and cultural development. New endeavors aimed at achieving this vision include Kid's Café, an after-school nutritional education and etiquette program for at-risk youth; Kaleidoscope, a computer lab for homeless youth; and Teachers Matter, a program to help retain public school teachers.

For over seven decades, the Junior League of Baton Rouge has developed the potential of women to serve as caring and dynamic leaders in the community. Each year, members participate in training on leadership skills, personal development, community awareness, and contemporary social issues. This training gives members the ability to strengthen the community with their skills, understanding, and commitment.

ACKNOWLEDGMENTS

Special thanks to the following:

PHOTOGRAPHY
David Humphreys
Wes Kroninger, assistant

FOREWORDS
Tommy C. Simmons
Mary Ann Sternberg

MAP
Kevin Harris,
Kevin Harris Architect LLC

SERVICES
Floral Design,
Lance Hayes Designs
Food Styling,
Margo E. Bouanchaud, Inc.

PROPS
Ambrosia Bakery
Custom Linens
Mary and George Karam
Victoria's Toy Station

HOMES
Megan and Phillip Foco
Margo and Lance Hayes
Miriam and Ty McMains
Linda and Gene Ohmstede
Suzette and Douglas Say
Katherine and Paul Spaht

RECIPE CONTRIBUTORS

Mary Aycock
Leigh Barbato
Betty Brown Berry
Ronnie Bodin
Dovie Brady
Kate Brady
Mary Mullen Brinson
Aimee Broussard
Kema Bueche
Michelle Cambias
Melisse Campbell
Sheryl Campbell
Ursula Carmena
Amy Wood Carmouche
Ashley Casey
Laurie Chapple
Ann Lynn Colvin
Jean W. Comeaux
Kathy Cook
Nancy Crawford
Katherine Crosby
Anne Davis
Randi Deaton
Karen Brannon Deumite
Emily DiStefano
Yolanda Dixon
Anne Eaton
Mary Eddy
Rachel Ehricht
Tammy Smith Fabre
Shannon Farho
Marylea Fears
Kim Feltner
Judy Foil
Tanja Foil
Jennifer P. Frederick
Greta Fry
Julie K. Fuller
Maggie Genius
Vicki Giamalva
Margaret Lee Goodwin

Alice Greer
Jan Purdin Groves
Charlene Delaune Guarisco
Liz Harris
Cupid Hart-James
Margo Bouanchaud Hayes
Tara Leigh Hayes
Kathleen I. Howell
Pamela Hubbell
Barbara Hughes
Louise Jeter
Vickie Bernard Johnson
Tereza Kean
Molly D'Aquin Kimble
Tracey Koch
Edy Landreneau Koonce
Kristen Landry
Merri Lee
Lucile Lieux
Linda Limbocker
Amy Groves Lowe
Susan Mathews
Jena H. Maughan
Anne McCanless
Karen McCullen
Nancy McDonald
Lynn McKnight
Britt Melton
Camille C. Michelli
Connie Miller
Suzanne Willoughby Miller
Nancy Mills
Lisa Mitchell
Sybil Monday
Mary Ann Monsour
Patience Moreno
Kim Morgan
Kim Musgrove
Dianna Odom
Beth O'Quinn
Pam Parker

Jamie Pellegrin
Julie Perrault
Jennifer A. Poche'
Mary Fitzpatrick Pollard
Judy Judice Powers
Blair Purgerson
Jan Querbes
Lisa Ann Moore Quinlan
Katherine Ragland
Michelle Reimsnyder
Lee Reeves
Emily Roberts Robinson
Martha Rome
Mary Fischer Rothermel
Elise Routier
Heidi Rowley
Ellen Salmon
Lynn Goodwin Savoie
Suzette Say
Allison Sceroler
Ashley Schonberg Roussel
Denise Powers Sellers
Michele Shaffer
Martha Singer
Martha Singletary
Ann C. Solanas
Kristen Spring
Peggy Strange
Jennifer Strasner
Gina Tarajano
Doreen Atchison Taravella
Dorothy Wilkinson Townsend
Heather Truax
Julie Hiatt Vascocu
Anne Claire Waguespack
Lynda Waguespack
Tracie Way
Lissa Weston
Kelly Patrick Williams
Jeannine Woodward
Patty Young

RECIPE TESTERS

Mary Aycock
Carol Anne Blitzer
Jackie Boudinot
Nancy Breitenbach
Ashley Casey
Joan W. Chastain
Audra Collett
Kathy Cook
Colette Dean
Emily DiStefano
Brigid Durel
Shannon Farho
Tanja Foil
Jennifer P. Frederick
Greta Fry
Laurie Gagnet

Vickie Giamalva
Liz Harris
Margo Bouanchaud Hayes
Patti Hiller
Mary Frances Hopkins
Vickie Bernard Johnson
Tereza Kean
Trudy Kiggans
Tracey Koch
Edy Koonce
Kristen Landry
Susan Landry
Melanie LaPorte
Linda Limbocker
Traci May
Anne McCanless
Susanna McCarthy
Mary McGinnis
Dianna Odom
Jamie Pellegrin
Julie Perrault
Cindy Rice
Jenny Ridge
Estelle Rome
Martha Rome
Mary Fischer Rothermel
Robbie Rubin
Marcia Sanchez
Suzette Say
Allison Sceroler
Barbara Schwartzenburg

Katherine Sessions
Martha Singletary
Margo Spielman
Jennifer Strasner
Gina Tharp
Kristen Thompson
Krista Valluzzo
Mary Kate Valluzzo
Linda Vannoy
Anne Claire Waguespack
Dana C. Watkins
Teri Watson
Lissa Weston
Susan White
Kelly Patrick Williams
Patty Young

INDEX

For additional copies of *River Road Recipes IV,* or for order
information on *River Road Recipes* series cookbooks, please contact:

Junior League of Baton Rouge

800-204-1726

www.juniorleaguebr.com